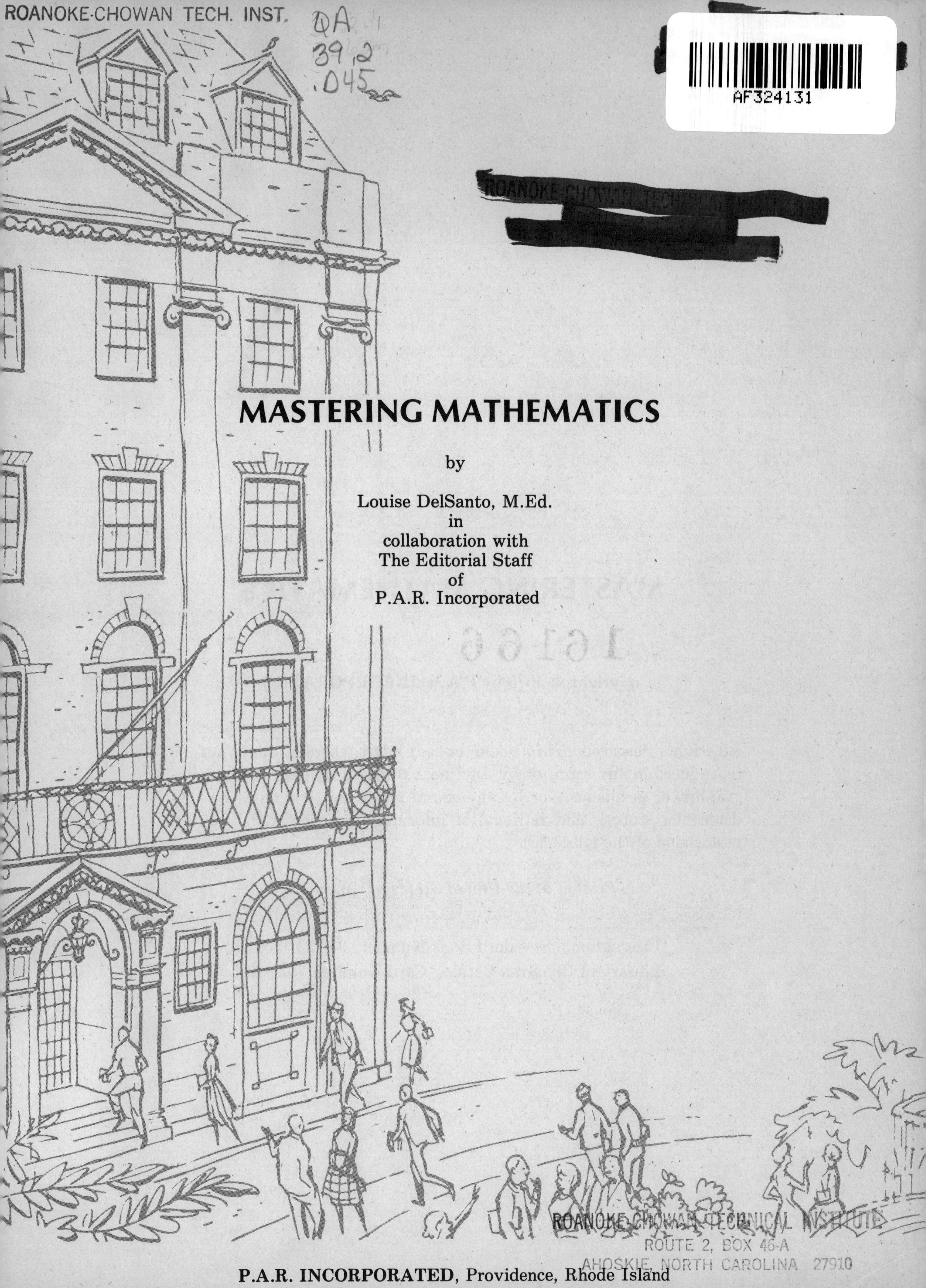

# MASTERING MATHEMATICS

by

Louise DelSanto, M.Ed.
in
collaboration with
The Editorial Staff
of
P.A.R. Incorporated



**P.A.R. INCORPORATED**, Providence, Rhode Island

# MASTERING MATHEMATICS

## 16166

Copyright © 1975 by P.A.R. INCORPORATED



*Printed in the United States of America*

International Standard Book Number: 0-913310-38-7
Library of Congress Catalog Card Number: 75-2049

# CONTENTS

## GENERAL MATHEMATICS

**CONTENTS** (Continued)      **Page**

iv

**CONTENTS** (Continued)            **Page**

v

CONTENTS (Continued)

Page



ALGEBRA

**CONTENTS** (Continued)  **Page**

**PLANE GEOMETRY**

vii

**CONTENTS** (Continued)

# GENERAL MATHEMATICS

# GENERAL MATHEMATICS

## READING AND WRITING NUMBERS

### Arabic System—Integers and Decimals

Our number system was invented by the Arabs. The value of each numeral depends upon its *place*. For example:

4 is read as four
40 is read as forty
400 is read as four hundred.

In the first position the numeral 4 represents four units. In the second position, 4 represents 4 x 10 units. In the third position, 4 represents 4 x 100 units. In order to facilitate the reading of numbers, we group them in units of three and usually separate the groups by commas:

60,458,907,657

In each group the first numeral on the right is units; the second, tens; the third, hundreds. The above number is read as "sixty billion, four hundred fifty-eight million, nine hundred seven thousand, six hundred fifty-seven." In reading integers do not use "and." Read numbers the shortest possible way. 1,406 is read "fourteen hundred six," not "one thousand four hundred six."

### Exercise 1

Read the following figures:

| | | | | | |
|---|---|---|---|---|---|
| (a) | 55,646,808 | (d) | 10,000,458,975 | (g) | 465,672,408 |
| (b) | 4,900,009 | (e) | 808,009,606 | (h) | 80,763,029 |
| (c) | 106,456,837 | (f ) | 77,050,731,310 | (i ) | 5,679,005,050 |

Write the following figures:

(a) Eighty million, seven hundred sixty-three thousand, twenty-nine.
(b) Ten billion, four hundred fifty-eight thousand, nine hundred seventy-five.
(c) Four million, nine hundred thousand, nine.
(d) Fifty-five million, six hundred forty-six thousand, eight hundred eight.

## DECIMALS

In the Arabic system, the value of the numeral is multiplied by ten as we move from right to left. To express values less than 1, we use the decimal point. The value of the numeral is divided by 10 as we move from the decimal point to the right:

$$.4444$$

The above decimal is read as "Four thousand four hundred forty-four ten thousandths."

Read the following figures thus:

.4—four tenths
.04—four hundredths
.004—four thousandths
.0004—four ten thousandths

*Exercise 3*

Read the following figures:

(a)  55,055.5
(b)  6,967.67
(c)  100,006.676
(d)  14,580.8856
(e)  703,703.703
(f)  1,505.069

| (g) | 2,960.0008 | (j) | 5,000.005 | (m) | 729.0086 |
| (h) | 22,022.0022 | (k) | 9,009.009 | (n) | 7,007.7007 |
| (i) | 4,678.009 | (l) | 40,004.0004 | (o) | 3,033.033 |

## *Exercise 4*

Write the following as decimals:

(a) Six hundred and six hundredths.

(b) Twelve hundred twelve and twelve thousandths.

(c) Fifty thousand and fifty thousandths.

(d) One million, six hundred thousand, fifty-four and fifty-four thousandths.

(e) Fourteen hundred four and fourteen hundred four ten thousandths.

# FUNDAMENTAL OPERATIONS, PROOFS, AND SHORT CUTS

### ADDITION

To develop accuracy and speed in addition, we suggest the following practices:

1. When adding a column of figures, name or think of results only. For example, in adding 3, 7, 8, 4, we say "10, 18, 22." This is shorter than "three and seven are ten; ten and eight are eighteen"; etc.

2. Whenever possible, group the numbers; that is, combine two or more numbers at sight into a single number, just as you group the letters s-p-e-e-d in reading the word. Practice alone can develop this skill. Notice the grouping indicated in the following column of figures:

$$\left.\begin{matrix} 3 \\ 4 \\ 2 \end{matrix}\right\} 9 \qquad \text{The first group is read as } 9$$

$$\left.\begin{matrix} 6 \\ 2 \\ 2 \end{matrix}\right\} 19 \qquad \text{The second group is read as } 10$$

$$\left.\begin{matrix} 4 \\ 2 \end{matrix}\right\} 25 \qquad \text{The third group is read as } 6$$

$$\left.\begin{matrix} 9 \\ 3 \end{matrix}\right\} 37 \qquad \text{The fourth group is read as } 12$$

The results in succession are 9, 19, 25, 37.

The long way would give eight sub-totals and the final answer. The time saving feature is obvious.

3. It is advisable to memorize those combinations which occur frequently so that the response becomes mechanical. Practice saying $7+8=15$, $7+5=12$, $8+5=13$, etc.

4. Develop the habit of proving the answer. Good business practice demands that all computations should be checked for accuracy.

PROOFS FOR ADDITION

(a) Add the columns the opposite way. If you started at the top and added down, reverse the process to prove the result.

(b) Cashier's Method: Add each column of figures separately, but do not carry from one column to the next. Arrange the totals as follows:

| | | |
|---|---|---:|
| 6,408 | | |
| 3,394 | The first column totals | 25 |
| 6,786 | The second column totals | 29 |
| 735 | The third column totals | 21 |
| 8,092 | The fourth column totals | 23 |
| ——— | | ——— |
| 25,415 | | 25,415 |

*Exercise 5 (Oral)*

The purpose of this drill is to develop speed. Read at sight the sum of each combination. Continue until you can complete the exercise in twenty seconds:

| 7 | 5 | 4 | 9 | 4 | 4 | 6 | 3 | 8 | 6 | 8 | 3 | 9 | 1 | 8 | 5 |
|---|---|---|---|---|---|---|---|---|---|---|---|---|---|---|---|
| 2 | 3 | 6 | 1 | 5 | 2 | 6 | 9 | 2 | 3 | 8 | 2 | 2 | 7 | 3 | 2 |
| — | — | — | — | — | — | — | — | — | — | — | — | — | — | — | — |

| 3 | 1 | 4 | 2 | 4 | 1 | 6 | 1 | 2 | 6 | 3 | 5 | 8 | 5 | 7 | 9 |
|---|---|---|---|---|---|---|---|---|---|---|---|---|---|---|---|
| 7 | 1 | 3 | 1 | 4 | 8 | 2 | 4 | 2 | 1 | 3 | 5 | 4 | 9 | 6 | 6 |
| — | — | — | — | — | — | — | — | — | — | — | — | — | — | — | — |

| 5 | 7 | 3 | 9 | 6 | 8 | 7 | 8 | 6 | 9 | 8 | 7 | 4 |
|---|---|---|---|---|---|---|---|---|---|---|---|---|
| 1 | 5 | 1 | 9 | 8 | 7 | 4 | 9 | 5 | 7 | 5 | 7 | 9 |
| — | — | — | — | — | — | — | — | — | — | — | — | — |

*Exercise 6 (Oral)*

*Drill in grouping.* Make groups of two figures each, as you add. Name the results only. Thus in problem "a," starting at the top, by adding in groups of two numbers the results are: 13, 23, 31, 41, 52, 63.

4

| (a) | (b) | (c) | (d) | (e) | (f) | (g) | (h) | (i) | (j) |
|-----|-----|-----|-----|-----|-----|-----|-----|-----|-----|
| 4 | 5 | 8 | 7 | 8 | 6 | 4 | 7 | 9 | 9 |
| 9 | 7 | 5 | 7 | 4 | 6 | 7 | 8 | 8 | 3 |
| 3 | 4 | 7 | 4 | 6 | 4 | 5 | 6 | 5 | 7 |
| 7 | 6 | 2 | 8 | 3 | 4 | 1 | 2 | 6 | 8 |
| 6 | 2 | 4 | 5 | 3 | 2 | 2 | 6 | 3 | 6 |
| 2 | 7 | 6 | 7 | 4 | 8 | 7 | 4 | 3 | 9 |
| 8 | 6 | 9 | 6 | 2 | 5 | 4 | 7 | 6 | 5 |
| 2 | 1 | 1 | 1 | 9 | 6 | 5 | 4 | 2 | 5 |
| 5 | 4 | 2 | 3 | 4 | 2 | 3 | 5 | 3 | 4 |
| 6 | 4 | 7 | 4 | 5 | 4 | 7 | 3 | 7 | 5 |
| 4 | 5 | 4 | 5 | 2 | 4 | 4 | 1 | 2 | 6 |
| 7 | 5 | 3 | 6 | 8 | 3 | 2 | 5 | 9 | 2 |
| — | — | — | — | — | — | — | — | — | — |
| Totals .. | .. | .. | .. | .. | .. | .. | .. | .. | .. |

## Exercise 7

Find the annual total sales for each department and the monthly total for all departments:

a.

REPORT ON SALES

| Month | Millinery | Clothing | Shoes | Hand Bags | Totals |
|-------|-----------|----------|-------|-----------|--------|
| January | 2,945.67 | 9,805.37 | 1,468.35 | 943.70 | ............ |
| February | 2,060.50 | 7,468.90 | 948.30 | 784.36 | ............ |
| March | 4,673.00 | 12,229.40 | 2,960.25 | 1,549.39 | ............ |
| April | 4,039.20 | 13,770.35 | 2,472.78 | 2,046.37 | ............ |
| May | 1,846.39 | 9,456.40 | 2,006.37 | 1,273.44 | ............ |
| June | 2,635.30 | 8,895.70 | 3,785.79 | 946.30 | ............ |
| July | 1,846.35 | 6,907.00 | 1,862.57 | 683.47 | ............ |
| August | 1,536.70 | 7,780.50 | 1,740.63 | 749.37 | ............ |
| September | 5,638.42 | 11,436.70 | 3,246.73 | 1,936.22 | ............ |
| October | 3,075.09 | 13,738.25 | 2,872.94 | 1,039.79 | ............ |
| November | 2,482.25 | 11,640.40 | 3,050.70 | 946.37 | ............ |
| December | 2,009.45 | 9,720.65 | 1,986.37 | 1,830.95 | ............ |
| Totals ........ | ........ | ........ | ........ | ........ | ............ |

Prove by checking the final totals of the vertical columns against the final totals of the horizontal columns.

b.   Add and prove the results.

| 1)  4,605 | 2)  56,307 | 3)  4,680.55 |
|---|---|---|
| 26,817 | 649,607 | 549.8609 |
| 4,983 | 70,546 | 72.004 |
| 95,735 | 423 | 3,663.32 |
| | 37,634 | 987.6984 |

c.   Add horizontally and prove the results.

1)   721 + 83 + 904 + 621 + 405 + 75

2)   8.5 + 2.73 + .26 + .09 + 3.805

3)   $561.25 + $671.54 + $1,312.06 + $674.51


SUBTRACTION

The usual method of "making change" is to add from the amount of the sale to the next higher money unit. If the amount of the sale is 47¢ and the clerk is giving change of $1.00, he gives the customer 3¢ and says 50¢, then he gives 50¢ and counts $1.00. He subtracts by adding to 47¢ an amount that brings it up to $1.00. We apply this method to subtraction.

(a) Deduct 21.24 from 96.24

| 96.79 | 4+5=9 The difference is 5 |
|---|---|
| 21.24 | 2+5=7   "    "    " 5 |
| ——— | 1+5=6   "    "    " 5 |
| 75.55 | 2+7=9   "    "    " 7 |

(b) Deduct 94.17 from 635.25

635.25
94.17
———
541.08

We cannot deduct 7 from 5.

We therefore borrow one from the next higher unit, the ten column, and raise 5 to 15.

7+8=15

We used one of the "ten" units leaving 1 as a remainder.

1+0=1
4+1=5
9+4=13

Since we borrowed one unit from the hundreds column, we reduced the 6 to 5.

6

The *minuend* is the number which is to be reduced. The *subtrahend* is the number which is deducted from the minuend.

$$639 \text{ minuend}$$
$$-47 \text{ subtrahend}$$
$$592 \text{ remainder}$$

## Exercise 8 (Subtraction)

| a. | 9 | 8 | 6 | 7 | 8 | 9 | 8 | 7 | 9 |
|---|---|---|---|---|---|---|---|---|---|
|  | 3 | 2 | 2 | 4 | 3 | 5 | 1 | 2 | 4 |

| b. | 15 | 14 | 18 | 17 | 18 | 16 | 17 | 13 | 16 |
|---|---|---|---|---|---|---|---|---|---|
|  | 9 | 7 | 5 | 9 | 4 | 7 | 4 | 5 | 3 |

| c. | 24 | 27 | 22 | 21 | 26 | 28 | 23 | 20 | 25 |
|---|---|---|---|---|---|---|---|---|---|
|  | 17 | 16 | 13 | 15 | 19 | 14 | 12 | 11 | 18 |

| d. | 32 | 38 | 34 | 37 | 30 | 35 | 31 | 36 | 33 |
|---|---|---|---|---|---|---|---|---|---|
|  | 27 | 29 | 22 | 21 | 26 | 23 | 28 | 24 | 25 |

| e. | 46 | 53 | 67 | 80 | 44 | 92 | 39 | 71 | 63 |
|---|---|---|---|---|---|---|---|---|---|
|  | 38 | 45 | 59 | 72 | 36 | 88 | 24 | 64 | 59 |

| f. | 59 | 48 | 73 | 62 | 36 | 76 | 28 | 32 | 54 |
|---|---|---|---|---|---|---|---|---|---|
|  | 30 | 39 | 67 | 54 | 28 | 62 | 15 | 27 | 47 |

You should repeat this exercise until you can complete it in 60 seconds.

## Exercise 9

To find the new balance use the following procedure. Add to the old balance the amount of the deposit. From this total subtract the total amount of money made out in checks. The remainder is the new balance.

|  | Old Balance | Deposit | Checks | New Balance |
|---|---|---|---|---|
| a. | 654.39 | 145.70 | 269.35 | ? |
| b. | 329.36 | 285.63 | 347.60 | ? |
| c. | 840.09 | 248.27 | 193.38 | ? |
| d. | 1269.75 | 132.24 | 478.26 | ? |
| e. | 746.32 | 398.47 | 348.12 | ? |
| f. | 1927.36 | 408.35 | 976.33 | ? |

|      | Old Balance | Deposit | Checks | New Balance |
|------|-------------|---------|--------|-------------|
| g.   | 468.70      | 571.28  | 630.74 | ?           |
| h.   | 1055.48     | 94.62   | 587.37 | ?           |
| i.   | 361.05      | 281.35  | 118.32 | ?           |
| j.   | 941.83      | 483.79  | 589.73 | ?           |
| k.   | 736.27      | 632.28  | 730.56 | ?           |

To prove your results, add the old balance and deposit; then add the checks and new balance. The totals should agree.

## Exercise 10

Find the net amount for each invoice by subtracting the discount from the invoice amount. Then total all columns and prove your results.

|      | Invoice Amount | Discount | Net Amount |
|------|----------------|----------|------------|
| a.   | 236.47         | 4.73     | ........   |
| b.   | 93.32          | .93      | ........   |
| c.   | 781.28         | 23.44    | ........   |
| d.   | 967.90         | 19.36    | ........   |
| e.   | 343.83         | 10.31    | ........   |
| f.   | 563.76         | 5.64     | ........   |
| g.   | 834.45         | 16.64    | ........   |
| h.   | 175.53         | 5.26     | ........   |
| i.   | 62.27          | 1.24     | ........   |
| j.   | 129.00         | 2.58     | ........   |
| Totals | —            | —        | —          |

## MULTIPLICATION

In order that you may understand the subject matter presented in this section, it will be necessary to know the terms used.

*Multiplicand* is the unit or number which is to be multiplied.

*Multiplier* is the multiplying number.

*Product* is the result of multiplication.

The multiplicand and multiplier are called *factors:*

$$2\times3=6$$
$$15 \text{ yards} \times 4 = 60 \text{ yds.}$$

2 is the multiplicand; 3 is the multiplier; 6 is the product; 2 and 3 are factors.

When you speak of 15 yards of cloth, 20 machines, $500, 8 bushels, you
are using *concrete* numbers, but when you say 15, 20, 5, 8 you are using
*abstract* numbers. The multiplier is always an abstract number. If the
multiplicand is a concrete number, the product is expressed in terms of the
same unit. In the example given above, the answer is 60 *yards*.


*Exercise 11 (Oral)*

Multiply at sight, using as multipliers 2, 3, 4, 5, 6, 7, 8, 9. Repeat this
drill until you can do these problems at the rate of 120 a minute. 4, 7, 6,
9, 11, 3, 8, 2, 5, 12, 13.


PROVING MULTIPLICATION

1.  Interchange the multiplier and multiplicand

| *Illustration* 4,695 | *Proof* 347 |
|---|---|
| 347 | 4695 |
| 32865 | 1735 |
| 18780 | 3123 |
| 14085 | 2082 |
| 1629165 | 1388 |
| | 1629165 |

2.  Divide the product by either factor

$$4{,}695$$
$$347\overline{)1{,}629{,}165}$$
$$1388$$
$$2411$$
$$2082$$
$$3296$$
$$3123$$
$$1735$$
$$1735$$

9

a.  Find the total for each of the following:

| | | |
|---|---|---|
| 10 doz. shirts | @ $60.00 | $..... |
| 13 doz. ties | @ 24.00 | $..... |
| 11 doz. ties | @ 32.00 | $..... |
| 15 doz. gloves | @ 40.00 | $..... |
| 24 doz. prs. socks | @ 5.00 | $..... |
| 18 doz. prs. pajamas | @ $48.00 | $..... |

Total  $.....

b.  Find the total value:

| | | |
|---|---|---|
| 61 yd. | @ $.75 | $...... |
| 78 yd. | @ .49 | ...... |
| 35 yd. | @ 1.05 | ...... |
| 136 yd. | @ .64 | ...... |
| 78 yd. | @ .78 | ...... |
| 226 yd. | @ .99 | ...... |

Total  $......

c.  Find the total payroll:

| Employee | Hours | Rate | Wages |
|---|---|---|---|
| A | 43 | $1.40 | $..... |
| B | 36 | 1.36 | $..... |
| C | 45 | 2.05 | $..... |
| D | 23 | 1.95 | $..... |
| E | 32 | 2.10 | $..... |
| F | 21 | 2.75 | $..... |
| G | 44 | 1.85 | $..... |

Total Payroll  $.....

There are ways of shortening our calculations, thereby saving time and labor. We present a few practical short-cuts. Use them wherever possible to get results quickly and possibly avoid making mistakes.

1. To multiply an integer by 10, 100, 1000, etc.
   Add as many zeros to the multiplicand as there are zeros in the multiplier.

$$765 \times 10 = 7,650$$
$$765 \times 100 = 76,500$$
$$765 \times 1000 = 765,000$$

If the multiplicand has a decimal, move the point to the right, as many places as there are zeros in the multiplier.

$$14.05 \times 10 = 140.5$$
$$14.05 \times 100 = 1,405$$
$$14.05 \times 1000 = 14,050$$

2. To multiply a number by 11, 101, 1001, etc.
   *First step:* Multiply by 10, 100, 1000, etc.
   *Second step:* Add the multiplicand to the product.

| | | |
|---|---|---|
| $76 \times 10 = 760$ | $76 \times 100 = 7,600$ | $76 \times 1000 = 76,000$ |
| $76 \times 1 \quad 76$ | $76 \times 1 \quad 76$ | $76 \times 1 \quad 76$ |
| $76 \times 11 \quad 836$ | $76 \times 101 \quad 7,676$ | $76 \times 1001 \quad 76,076$ |

3. To multiply a number by 9, 99, 999, etc., multiply by 10, 100, 1000, etc.; then deduct the multiplicand.

| | | |
|---|---|---|
| $176 \times 10 = 1,760$ | $176 \times 100 = 17,600$ | $176 \times 1000 = 176,000$ |
| $176 \times 1 \quad 176$ | $176 \times 1 \quad 176$ | $176 \times 1 \quad 176$ |
| $176 \times 9 \quad 1,584$ | $176 \times 99 \quad 17,424$ | $176 \times 999 \quad 175,824$ |

4. To multiply a number by a fractional part of a hundred the fractional parts of a hundred are called *aliquot parts*. The ones frequently used are listed below. You should memorize them in order to use them effectively.

| *Halves* | *Quarters* | *Eighths* |
|---|---|---|
| $50 = \frac{1}{2}$ of 100 | $25 = \frac{1}{4}$ of 100 | $12\frac{1}{2} = \frac{1}{8}$ of 100 |
| | $75 = \frac{3}{4}$ of 100 | $37\frac{1}{2} = \frac{3}{8}$ of 100 |
| | | $62\frac{1}{2} = \frac{5}{8}$ of 100 |
| | | $87\frac{1}{2} = \frac{7}{8}$ of 100 |

| *Sixteenths* | *Thirds* | *Sixths* |
|---|---|---|
| 6 1/4 = 1/16 of 100 | 33 1/3 = 1/3 of 100 | 16 2/3 = 1/6 of 100 |
| | 66 2/3 = 2/3 of 100 | 83 1/3 = 5/6 of 100 |

To multiply a number by a fractional part of a hundred, first multiply by 100 and then multiply by the fractional part of a hundred.

*Illustration:* $\quad$ 762 × 33 1/3

*First step:* $\quad$ 762 × 100 = 76,200

*Second step:* $\quad$ 76,200 × 1/3 = 25,400

5. To multiply a number by aliquot parts of 1, 100, or 1000, study the following table. The fraction in the first column indicates the aliquot part of 1, 10, 100, 1000.

| | *1.* | *10.* | *100.* | *1000.* |
|---|---|---|---|---|
| ⅛ | .12½ | 1¼ | 12½ | 125 |
| ¼ | .25 | 2½ | 25 | 250 |
| ½ | .5 | 5 | 50 | 500 |
| ⅝ | .62½ | 6¼ | 62½ | 625 |
| ¾ | .75 | 7½ | 75 | 750 |
| ⅞ | .87½ | 8¾ | 87½ | 875 |

*Principle:* When the multiplier is an aliquot part of a number, use the latter as a multiplier and then multiply the answer by the fractional part of the number.

*Illustrations:* $\quad$ 24 × 8¾ $\qquad\qquad$ 8¾ = ⅞ of 10

*Short-cut:* $\quad$ 24 × 10 = 240 $\qquad$ 240 × ⅞ = 210

$\qquad\qquad$ 720 × 625 $\qquad\qquad$ 625 = ⅝ of 1,000

$\qquad\qquad$ 720 × 1000 = 720,000 $\qquad$ 720,000 × ⅝ = 450,000

Skill in using aliquot parts reduces the mechanics of computations to a minimum.

## *Exercise 13*

Make the following extensions mentally:

a) 60 hammers @ .33⅓ ....... $\qquad$ h) 48 trowels @ .25 .......

b) 56 saws @ .87½ ....... $\qquad$ i) 66 screens @ .66⅔ .......

c) 88 locks @ .62½ ....... $\qquad$ j) 74 knives @ .99 .......

d) 32 bolts @ .06¼ ....... $\qquad$ k) 96 batteries @ .06¼ .......

e) 42 brushes @ .83⅓ ....... $\qquad$ l) 101 hammers @ .49 .......

f) 72 pliers @ .37½ ....... $\qquad$ m) 99 saws @ .65 .......

g) 36 planes @ .50 ....... $\qquad$ n) 101 bulbs @ .13 .......

o) 76 bolts      @ .09      ........      s) 99 knives      @ .27      ........
p) 99 brushes    @ .84      ........      t) 64 funnels     @ .12½     ........
q) 78 pliers     @ .99      ........      u) 25 strainers   @ .16      ........
r) 24 planes     @ .75      ........      v) 24 sockets     @ .06¼     ........

## Exercise 14

Find the invoice amount:

| | | | |
|---|---|---|---|
| 46 ft. of 2 in. galvanized pipe | @ | .40 | ........ |
| 32 ½ in. valves | @ | .87½ | ........ |
| 6 wash basins | @ | 19.40 | ........ |
| 280 ft. 1 in. galvanized pipe | @ | .11 | ........ |
| 6 bathtubs | @ | 85.00 | ........ |
| 6 escutcheons | @ | .65 | ........ |
| 5 2-in. gate valves | @ | 4.25 | ........ |

## Exercise 15

a)  62½ is what part of 100? ....   j) 1¼ is what part of  10? ....
b)  2½     "      "     10? ....    k) 66⅔    "      "    100? ....
c)  .12½   "      "      1? ....    l)  6⅔    "      "     10? ....
d)  .75    "      "      1? ....    m) 875    "      "   1000? ....
e)  .33⅓   "      "      1? ....    n) .16⅔   "      "      1? ....
f)  625    "      "   1000? ....    o) 16⅔    "      "    100? ....
g)  250    "      "   1000? ....    p) .83⅓   "      "      1? ....
h)  7½     "      "     10? ....    q) 37½    "      "    100? ....
i)  .66⅔   "      "      1? ....    r)  6¼    "      "     10? ....

### DIVISION

The following terms are used in division:

*Dividend* is the quantity or number which is to be divided into parts.

*Divisor* is the number by which the dividend is to be divided.

*Quotient* is the result of division.

As we pointed out under multiplication, much of the mechanics can be reduced by using short-cuts wherever possible. Some of these devices are presented below.

1.  To divide by 10, 100, 1000, etc., point off as many decimal places to the left as there are zeros in the divisor.

$$678.5 \div 10 = 67.85$$
$$678.5 \div 100 = 6.785$$
$$678.5 \div 1000 = .6785$$

2. To divide by an aliquot part of a number, divide by the number and multiply the result by the inverted fraction.

Example 1— 480÷2½    2½=¼ of 10
480×4/10=192

Example 2— 480÷25    25=¼ of 100
480×4/100=19.2

Example 3— 480÷250    250=¼ of 1000
480×4/1000=1.92

### PROVING DIVISION

To prove the result, multiply the divisor by the quotient and add the remainder, if any.

To prove the last example:

$$250×1.92=480$$

### Exercise 16

Divide at sight:

| | |
|---|---|
| a. 120 by 2½ | n. 320 by 6¼ |
| b. 90 by 7½ | o. 3000 by 375 |
| c. 600 by 25 | p. 1200 by 16⅔ |
| d. 900 by 75 | q. 5000 by 625 |
| e. 444 by .25 | r. 14000 by 875 |
| f. 90 by 33⅓ | s. 150 by .33⅓ |
| g. 490 by .87½ | t. 3500 by 500 |
| h. 48 by .5 | u. 450 by 50 |
| i. 500 by 16⅔ | v. 400 by 125 |
| j. 480 by .16⅔ | w. 1800 by 750 |
| k. 60 by .83⅓ | x. 900 by .37½ |
| l. 35 by 833⅓ | y. 500 by 12½ |
| m. 24 by .25 | z. 900 by 33⅓ |

### Exercise 17

| | |
|---|---|
| a. 968.75÷6.25 | f. 1342.70÷2.90 |
| b. 43335÷963 | g. 8464÷18 |
| c. 1809÷27 | h. 59832÷72 |
| d. 44160÷128 | i. 1175÷35 |
| e. 19683÷729 | j. 2809÷53 |

# FRACTIONS

An integer is a whole number, like 5. A fraction is a part of a unit like ½ gallon, ½ pound, ¾ yard, and so forth. A fraction indicates division. ¾ means that the unit is divided into four equal parts, each of which is called a fourth.

The number above the line is the *numerator,* and the number below the line, the *denominator*. The denominator expresses the names of the parts, like halves, fourths, sixths, and so forth. The numerator shows the number of parts. In the fraction ¾, the unit is divided into four equal parts and the fraction is three parts of the unit. Which is larger, ⅛ or ¼ of the same unit?

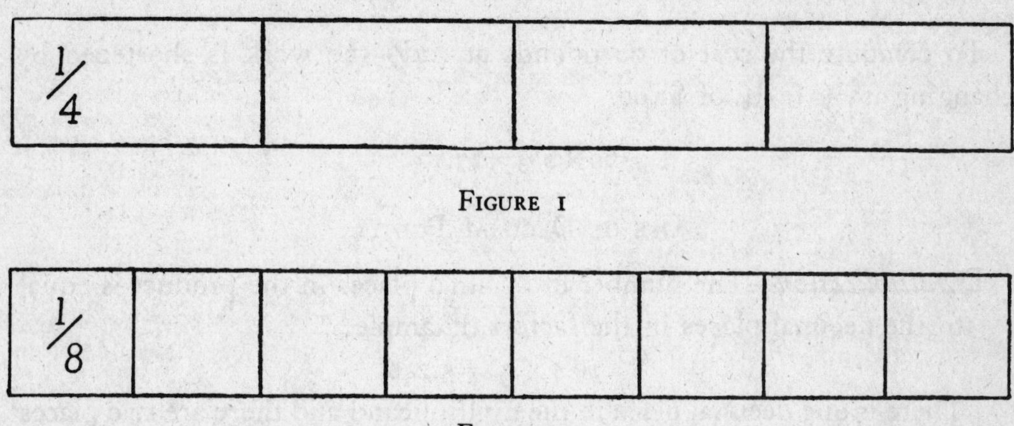

FIGURE 1

FIGURE 2

In Figure 1, the unit was divided into fourths, and in Figure 2, into eighths. When the denominator is increased and the numerator remains the same, the value of the fraction decreases. When the numerator is increased and the denominator remains the same, the value of the fraction increases.

## WRITING FRACTIONS

Fractions may be expressed in two ways:

a.  As a common fraction, with the numerator and denominator separated by the division sign.

Example: ⅔, ⅘, ¾, etc.

b.  To find the decimal equivalence of a common fraction divide the numerator by the denominator. Some common fraction-decimal equivalents are:

| | | | |
|---|---|---|---|
| 1/2 = .5 | 2/5 = .4 | 5/8 = .62-1/2 | 5/10 = .5 |
| 1/3 = .33-1/3 | 3/5 = .6 | 7/8 = .87-1/2 | 6/10 = .6 |
| 2/3 = .66-2/3 | 4/5 = .8 | 1/10 = .1 | 7/10 = .7 |
| 1/4 = .25 | 1/6 = .16-2/3 | 2/10 = .2 | 8/10 = .8 |
| 3/4 = .75 | 1/8 = .12-1/2 | 3/10 = .3 | 9/10 = .9 |
| 1/5 = .2 | 3/8 = .37-1/2 | 4/10 = .4 | 1/16 = .06-1/4 |

The arithmetical calculations may be shortened sometimes by using the common fraction form and at other times by using a decimal fraction form. To compute the cost of 68½ yards at 14¼¢ the multiplication is done more easily if we change the fractions ½ and ¼ to decimal fractions:

$$
\begin{array}{r}
.1425 \\
68.5 \\
\hline
7125 \\
11400 \\
8550 \\
\hline
\$9.76125
\end{array}
\qquad \text{Answer } \$9.76
$$

To compute the cost of 60 pounds at .12½ the work is shortened by changing .12½ to ⅛ of $1.00.

$$60 \times \$\tfrac{1}{8} = \$7.50$$

## Use of Decimal Points

1. *Multiplication*—The number of decimal places in the product is equal to the decimal places in the factors. Example:

$$16.4 \times .32 = 5.248$$

There is one decimal place in the multiplicand and there are two places in the multiplier. Therefore, there should be three decimal places in the product.

2. *Division*—When the divisor has a decimal fraction we move the decimal point as many places as it is necessary to change the fraction to an integer (whole number). Carry the decimal point in the dividend the *same number of places* to the right and if necessary add zeros. Example: 641÷.72

$$
\begin{array}{r}
890.27 \\
72.)\overline{64100.00} \\
576 \\
\hline
650 \\
648 \\
\hline
200 \\
144 \\
\hline
560 \\
504 \\
\hline
56
\end{array}
$$

We move the decimal point two places in the divisor and dividend and add two zeros after the decimal point in the dividend in order to continue the division to two decimal places.

3. *Addition* and *Subtraction*—Write the numbers so that the decimals line up properly and the figures are placed in the proper column one under the other. Example:

$$\begin{array}{r} \textit{Subtract} \\ 658.5 \\ 92.007 \\ \hline 566.493 \end{array}$$

## Exercise 18 (Oral)

Change the following to decimal fractions:

5/10    6/100    5/1000    1/4    1/8    7/8
3/8    1/16    5/8    3/4    1/2    1/3    2/3

Change the following to common fractions:

| | | | |
|---|---|---|---|
| a. | .5 | k. | .015 |
| b. | .05 | l. | .025 |
| c. | .125 | m. | .25 |
| d. | .75 | n. | .8333⅓ |
| e. | .1666⅔ | o. | .005 |
| f. | .6666⅔ | p. | .8 |
| g. | .3333⅓ | q. | .08 |
| h. | .875 | r. | .008 |
| i. | .0125 | s. | .0625 |
| j. | .4 | t. | .375 |

## Exercise 19

Perform the operations indicated:

| | | | |
|---|---|---|---|
| a. | 8.005×68 | h. | 675÷1.5 |
| b. | 94.2×1.45 | i. | 675÷.15 |
| c. | 75.06×405 | j. | 675÷.015 |
| d. | .0916×2.2 | k. | .675÷.015 |
| e. | 64.36×.134 | l. | 6.75÷.15 |
| f. | .8503×.18 | m. | 86.4÷.024 |
| g. | 7.09×.53 | n. | 5.4÷.036 |

What is the value of 413 lbs. @ 60¢ cwt. (cwt. means 100 pounds)
The quantity and the unit price are not alike. Therefore we change 413 lbs. to cwt.

$$413 \div 100 = 4.13 \text{ cwt.}$$
$$4.13 \times .60 = 2.4780 \text{ or } \$2.48.$$

*Principle:* The multiplier must be expressed in terms of the price unit.

### SELLING BY THE THOUSAND

What is the value of 24000 shingles @ 6.40 per M (thousand).
The unit price is M. Therefore we change 24000 to the same unit.

$$24000 \div 1000 = 24 \text{ units}$$
$$\$6.40 \times 24 = \$153.60$$

## Exercise 20

(a) At sight, change the following quantities to units of 100: 300; 6,037; 175; 75; 8,637; 2,637; 4,235; 80,680; 467.5; 83.27.

(b) At sight, change the following quantities to units of 1000: 5000; 65000; 8649; 400; 50; 8496.5; 2840; 93785; 150608; 724.

(c) Find the cost. (Use short cuts wherever possible.)

| | |
|---|---|
| 800 @ .12½ per c | 2,000 @ 4.50 per M |
| 1800 @ .20 per c | 10,000 @ 1.55 per M |
| 450 @ 1.33⅓ per c | 500 @ 8.00 per M |
| 240 @ .87½ per c | 800 @ 5.00 per M |
| 50 @ .80 per c | 625 @ 8.00 per M |

## Exercise 21

Find the total cost.

| | | |
|---|---|---|
| a. | 9980 lbs. of beef | @ 12.50 per cwt. |
| b. | 4672 ft. of lumber | @ 37.00 per M |
| c. | 18400 shingles | @ 4.25 per M |
| d. | 720 lbs. of bran | @ 1.05 per cwt. |
| e. | 1250 fence posts | @ 9.00 per C |
| f. | 14500 tiles | @ 12.25 per M |
| g. | 2500 envelopes | @ 4.10 per M |
| h. | 10250 sheets | @ 3.15 per M |
| i. | 2200 lbs. oats | @ .85 per cwt. |
| j. | 475 lbs. nails | @ 6.00 per cwt. |

A *common fraction* is one whose numerator is less than the denominator.

An *improper fraction* is a fraction whose numerator is larger than the denominator, such as 7/5, 4/3, etc.

A *mixed number* includes an integer and a fraction such as 46⅓, 21⅝, etc.

### CHANGING FRACTIONS TO HIGHER TERMS

A unit may be divided into halves, quarters, eighths, etc.: 1=2/2 or 4/4 or 8/8, etc.

Since all these fractions equal 1 they are equal to each other 2/2=4/4=8/8.

To change halves to quarters, we multiply the numerator and denominator by 2.

$$2/2 \times 2/2 = 4/4$$

In other words we do not change the *value* of a fraction when we multiply the numerator and denominator by the same number.

$$1/4 = ?/12; \qquad 3/4 = ?/12; \qquad 1/5 = ?/20 \qquad 4/5 = ?/20$$

*Rule:* To change a fraction to higher terms, divide the higher denominator by the lower denominator; then using the quotient as a multiplier, multiply the numerator and denominator.

### CHANGING FRACTIONS TO LOWER TERMS

FIGURE 3        FIGURE 4

In Figure 3 the unit is divided into fourths; in Figure 4 the unit is divided into halves. The shaded part in Figure 3 covers 2/4 of the unit and in Figure 4, 1/2 of the unit. It is obvious from the illustration that 2/4=1/2.

To change from fourths to halves we divide the numerator and denominator by 2.

$$2/4 \div 2/2 = 1/2$$

$$\frac{2 \div 2}{4 \div 2} = \frac{1}{2}$$

$$4/8 = ?/2 \qquad 4/6 = ?/3 \qquad 6/15 = ?/5$$

*Rule:* To change a fraction to lower terms, divide the higher denominator by the lower denominator; then using the quotient as a divisor, divide the numerator and denominator.

### Exercise 22

a.  At sight reduce to higher terms:

| | |
|---|---|
| 1/2 to eighths | 2/3 to sixths |
| 1/4 to twentieths | 4/5 to thirtieths |
| 1/6 to twelfths | 3/8 to twenty-fourths |
| 1/3 to twelfths | 3/4 to twelfths |
| 1/5 to fifteenths | 5/6 to twelfths |
| 1/8 to sixteenths | 3/5 to tenths |

b.  At sight reduce to lower terms:

| | |
|---|---|
| 4/8 to fourths | 14/20 to tenths |
| 4/6 to thirds | 15/27 to ninths |
| 5/15 to thirds | 12/16 to eighths |
| 2/16 to eighths | 4/20 to fifths |
| 4/12 to thirds | 6/24 to fourths |
| 14/16 to eighths | 4/32 to eighths |

c.  Reduce to eighths: 1/4, 1/2, 3/4
Reduce to sixteenths: 1/8, 3/8, 5/8, 1/2, 3/4
Reduce to twentieths: 1/2, 1/4, 2/5, 3/10, 3/4, 4/5
Reduce to hundredths: 1/5, 1/4, 1/10, 3/4, 4/5, 10/25, 3/50

### Least Common Denominator

How many feet in 3 yds. and 2 feet? We cannot add yards and feet because the units are different. However, we can change 3 yards to 9 feet and then add 2 feet, making a total of 11 feet.

Add 3/4 and 1/8. We cannot add fourths and eighths. Therefore we change 3/4 to 6/8 and, adding 6/8 and 1/8, we get 7/8.

Add 1/3, 1/2, and 1/4. We must reduce all fractions to a common denominator. 12 is exactly divisible by each denominator, 3, 2, and 4. Therefore we reduce the fractions to twelfths 1/3=4/12, 1/2=6/12, 1/4=3/12, 4/12+6/12+3/12=13/12 or 1 1/12.

The lowest number which is exactly divisible by all the given denominators is called the *least common denominator*.


### Exercise 23

Find the least common denominator:

| | | | |
|---|---|---|---|
| a. | 1/5, 1/6 | h. | 1/5, 1/10, 1/20 |
| b. | 1/3, 1/6, 1/4 | i. | 1/3, 1/6, 1/2, 1/8 |
| c. | 1/2, 1/4, 1/6 | j. | 1/2, 1/4, 1/8, 1/6 |
| d. | 1/4, 1/8, 1/2 | k. | 1/4, 1/8, 1/2, 1/12 |
| e. | 1/2, 1/5 | l. | 1/5, 1/10, 1/4, 1/2 |
| f. | 1/2, 1/5, 1/10 | m. | 1/20, 1/5, 1/10, 1/25, 1/4 |
| g. | 1/6, 1/3, 1/9 | n. | 1/6, 1/4, 1/12, 1/8 |


### ADDITION OF FRACTIONS

*Add:* 1/8, 3/8, 5/8. Answer: 9/8 or 1 1/8. Since all the denominators are alike, we add the numerators, 1, 3, and 5. We added eighths; therefore the result is 9 eighths (9/8).

If the denominators are not alike, we reduce the fractions to equivalent fractions with a *least common denominator* and add numerators.

*Add:* 3/16, 1/4, 5/8, 1/2. The least common denominator is *16.*

$$
\begin{aligned}
&\quad\quad\ \ \textit{sixteenths}\\
3/16 &= \ \ 3\\
1/4 &= \ \ 4\\
5/8 &= \ 10\\
1/2 &= \ \ 8\\
\hline
25/16 &= 1\ 9/16
\end{aligned}
$$


### Exercise 24

Add the following:

| | | | | | | | |
|---|---|---|---|---|---|---|---|
| a. | 1/2<br>+ 1/3 | c. | 1/2<br>7/10<br>+ 3/5 | e. | 5/6<br>+ 7/8 | g. | 6-2/3<br>+ 4 |
| b. | 1/4<br>+ 1/12 | d. | 4/5<br>+ 7/9 | f. | 3/5<br>+ 1/3 | h. | 2-1/2<br>+ 3-3/4 |

Find the difference between 1/2 and 3/8. The denominators are not alike. The first step is to change the fractions to equivalent fractions, having the least common denominator which is 8.  4/8—3/8=1/8.

*Problem:* From 89¼ take 83⅝.

$$\begin{array}{cc} & 8 \\ \hline 89¼ & 2 \\ 83⅝ & 5 \\ \hline \text{Answer: } 5 & ⅝ \end{array}$$

*Explanation:* The least common denominator is 8.

We cannot deduct 5/8 from 2/8. Therefore we take one unit from the integer, and change it to 8/8. 8/8+2/8=10/8. Subtracting 5/8 from 10/8 we get 5/8. 88—83=5.

## *Exercise 25*

Find the difference:

| | | | | | | | |
|---|---|---|---|---|---|---|---|
| a. | 2/3<br>— 1/3 | c. | 5/6<br>— 2/3 | e. | 6-3/4<br>— 4-1/4 | g. | 8-7/10<br>— 4-9/10 |
| b. | 4/5<br>— 1/2 | d. | 2-3/4<br>— 1-5/8 | f. | 5-1/2<br>— 2-3/4 | h. | 7<br>— 3-1/8 |

## MULTIPLICATION OF FRACTIONS

*To multiply an integer by a fraction:*

10×15 feet equals how many feet? 8×2/3 equals how many thirds? 16/3. Since the numerator is larger than the denominator, it is an improper fraction. To change to a mixed number divide the numerator by the denominator. 16/3=5 1/3.

The process of multiplying an integer by a fraction involves two steps:
1. Multiply the integer by the numerator.
2. Divide the product by the denominator.

a. *To multiply a fraction by another fraction:*
$$4/7×3/5=12/35$$
Multiply the numerators to find the new numerator; then multiply the denominators to find the new denominator.

b.  *To multiply a mixed number by a mixed number:*

$$6\tfrac{1}{4} \times 12\tfrac{1}{3}$$

*First Solution:*

$$6\tfrac{1}{4} = 25/4 \qquad\qquad 12\tfrac{1}{3} = 37/3$$

$$25/4 \times 37/3 = 925/12 = 77\ 1/12$$

*Solution:* Change the mixed numbers to improper fractions; multiply the numerators and denominators; then change the improper fraction to a mixed number.

*Second Solution:*

$$
\begin{array}{ll}
6\tfrac{1}{4} & \text{Multiply} \quad 6 \times 1/3 = 2 \\
12\tfrac{1}{3} & \quad\text{``} \qquad\quad 12 \times 1/4 = 3 \\
\hline
2 & \quad\text{``} \qquad\quad 1/4 \times 1/3 = \quad 1/12 \\
3\ 1/12 & \quad\text{``} \qquad\quad 12 \times 6\ \ = 72 \\
72 & \hline \\
\hline
77\ 1/12 & \qquad\qquad\qquad 77\ 1/12
\end{array}
$$

*Third Solution:*

$$6\tfrac{1}{4} = 6.25$$
$$12\tfrac{1}{3} = 12.33\tfrac{1}{3}$$

Change the fractions to equivalent decimals and multiply.

$$
\begin{array}{l}
6.25 \\
12.33\tfrac{1}{3} \\
\hline
208\tfrac{1}{3} \\
1875 \\
1875 \\
1250 \\
625 \\
\hline
77.0833\tfrac{1}{3} = 77\ 1/12
\end{array}
$$

$$625 \times \tfrac{1}{3} = 208\tfrac{1}{3}\ \text{etc.}$$

There are four decimal places in the multiplier and multiplicand; therefore, we point off four decimal places in the product.

### Exercise 26

I.  Find the product mentally and reduce to lowest terms:

|  |  |
|---|---|
| a.  $1/2 \times 1/3$ | f.  $2/3 \times 1/2 \times 3/5$ |
| b.  $3/7 \times 4/5$ | g.  $4/7 \times 2/3 \times 1/2$ |
| c.  $3/4 \times 2/3$ | h.  $4/9 \times 2/5 \times 3/10$ |
| d.  $1/3 \times 5/6$ | i.  $3/5 \times 4/5 \times 2/3$ |
| e.  $3/12 \times 2/5$ | j.  $1/3 \times 9/10 \times 6/7$ |

II. Find the product:

a. 24×5/8
b. 72×5/6
c. 783×4/9
d. 320×11/16
e. 2436×7/12
f. 63×15 1/3
g. 846×20 1/6
h. 42×8 1/4
i. 375×22 2/5

j. 180 1/3×24 1/4
k. 172 1/6×54 2/3
l. 84 1/2×7 1/4
m. 906 2/5×83 1/2
n. 235 1/4×32 7/10
o. 36 5/8×12 1/2
p. 195 2/3×17 1/4
q. 3186 3/5×10 1/10
r. 866 1/2×42 3/8

## ESTIMATING RESULTS

Short cuts may be used to estimate results when we deal with large numbers which cannot be solved mentally. In this way, we avoid absurd answers.

*Example 1.* 77 yds. @ 48¢. Which is the correct amount? $3.70? .37? 369.60? 36.96?

We can estimate the result by using 75 in place of 77, 75=¾ of 100, ¾×100×.48=$36.00. The correct answer is slightly higher, because the quantity is slightly more than 75 yds. Therefore, the correct answer is $36.96.

*Example 2.* Find the cost of 65 dozen @ 35¢. Which is the correct answer? $2.28? $22.75? $227.50?

If we use 37½¢ in place of 35¢, and 64 in place of 65, we can solve the problem mentally, thus: 64×$⅜=$24.00.

The nearest answer given is $22.75, which is correct. In estimating the result we use 64 because it is divisible by the denominator 8. We substitute 37½¢ instead of 35¢ because the former is an aliquot part of a dollar.

## Exercise 27

By the estimating process, select the approximate answer which is nearest the exact answer.

a. 49×32=160? 1600? 16,000?
b. 19×45=90? 9000? 900?
c. 32×126=4000? 400? 40,000?
d. 97×456=456,000? 45,600? 4560?

e. 48×36.50=18,000? 1800? 180?
f. 900÷35=2700? 270? 27?
g. 40,000÷23=16,000? 1600? 160?
h. 3965÷127=320? 32? 3.2?
i. 796÷37=200? 2000? 20?

j. 7972÷250=32? .32? 320? 3200?    m. 51×19=100? 1,000? 10,000?
k. 6397÷71=90? 9000? 900?           n. 480÷22=2500? 250? 25?
l. 8010×63=50,000? 5000?             o. 360×.65=24? 240? 2400?
  500,000?

# PROBLEMS

Thus far the fundamental operations, which include addition, subtraction, multiplication, and division have been reviewed, and practical short cuts explained. These are the arithmetical tools with which you have to work. Complete mastery of these fundamentals is necessary to solve the problems which will be given in this section. To solve a problem you must know three things:

a. What facts are given?
b. What fact or facts must we find?
c. What are the calculations (addition, subtraction, multiplication, division), which numbers are to be grouped, and in what order are the calculations to be performed to solve the problem?

The first two steps, *a* and *b,* are matters of interpretation. If you read the problem *carefully,* you should have no difficulty. The third step requires a knowledge of the fundamental principles of arithmetic. Many problems are patterned after one or more of the following types:

Type 1.   What is ⅔ of $24.00?
Type 2.   ⅔ of what number is $16.00?
Type 3.   What part of $24.00 is $16.00?

*Solution Type 1:*
*Facts given:* The whole number and a fraction.
*Find:* The product.
*Method:* Multiply the multiplicand ($24.00) by the fraction (⅔).
$$⅔×\$24.00=\$16.00$$

*Solution Type 2:*
*Facts given:* A factor (⅔) and a product ($16.00).
*Find:* The other factor. (*Of what number* indicates that we must find a missing factor.)
*Method:* Divide the product by the fraction. (In the section on multiplication we proved the result by dividing the product by either factor.) The product is $16.00 and the given factor is ⅔.
$$\$16.00÷⅔=\$24.00$$
(To divide a number by a fraction, we use the *numerator* as a divisor and the *denominator* as a multiplier; in other words, we *invert* the fraction.)

*Solution Type 3:*

> *Facts given:* A product, $16.00, and one factor, $24.00.
>
> *Find:* The other factor.
>
> *Method:* $16.00 ÷ $24.00 = 16/24 or ⅔.

This type has one thing in common with Type 2, namely, we must find the missing factor. In Type 2 the multiplicand was missing, in Type 3 the multiplier is missing. Therefore, the operation is the same—division.

In Type 3, you must be careful in selecting the numbers as the product and factor respectively. The product is divided by the factor to find the missing factor. The given factor can be easily identified, because it always follows the expression "what part of ......." This is the divisor or denominator of the fraction, 16/24.

PROBLEMS

In the following problems, identify the pattern or type as 1, 2, or 3. List the facts given—what you are required to find—and solve. Always *recheck* the calculations.

1. A retailer's gross profit is ⅓ of the selling price. What is his gross profit on a sale of $1.50?

2. The operating expenses are 1/6 of the sales. If the sales are $24,030.00, what are the operating expenses?

3. The cost of goods is $75.00 and the selling price is $100.00. What part of the selling price is the cost?

4. An employee worked 30 hours and received $90.00 If he had worked 40 hours what amount would he have received?

5. A secretary typed 16 pages of a report, which is 4/5 of the total number. How many pages in the entire report?

6. At the end of a year a clerk's salary was increased 5%. If the new salary rate is $147, what was the old salary?

7. A dealer bought 100 radios @ $300.00 net. He sold ½ of this number at a markup of ½ of cost; 2/5 of the remainder at a markup of ¼ of cost; the remainder at a loss of 1/10 of cost. What was the gross profit or loss on sales?

8. A jobber buys shirts @ $60.00 a dozen and sells them @ $90.00 a dozen. What part of the selling price is the profit? What part of the cost is the profit?

9. A man spends $1,200 for rent, which is 1/10 of his annual income. What is his income per month?

10. In a class of 40 students, 40% received a mark of *B* or better. How many students received a *B* or an *A*?

26

# PERCENTAGE

What part of 28 is 7?

What part of 60 is 45?

The answers may be expressed as *fractions:*

$$7/28=¼ \qquad\qquad 45/60=¾$$

or as *hundredths:*
$$¼=25/100 \qquad\qquad ¾=75/100$$

or as *decimals:* .25; .75

or as *per cents:* 25%; 75%

It simplifies the comparison of two numbers or quantities, if we use *hundredths* as a measure of comparison. Every fraction can be reduced to hundredths by dividing the numerator by the denominator and continuing the division to as many decimal places as the problem requires.

*Example:* Change 24/25 to a decimal.    *Answer:*   .96

$$
\begin{array}{r}
.96 \\
\hline
25.)\overline{24.00} \\
22\;5 \\
\hline
1\;50 \\
1\;50 \\
\hline
\end{array}
$$

Per cent means *by the hundred.* It is usually expressed by this sign "%." Five per cent may be written

$$5/100 \quad \text{or} \quad .05 \quad \text{or} \quad 5\%$$

Do you see any difference between *a.* .1, *b.* 10%, and *c.* .1%? *a* and *b* have the same value, namely 10/100. *c* is 1/10 of 1% or 1/10 of 1/100=1/1000. Whenever the decimal and % are used, it denotes a fractional part of one per cent.

In percentage problems, the basis of comparison is 100/100 or 100%. The method of solving the problems is the same as the problems in fractions solved in the preceding chapter.

## Reading Percentages

Since per cent means hundredths, we use two decimal places, thus 29 is read "twenty-nine per cent." To convert a decimal to per cent form, move the decimal point two places to the right and place % after the number. Conversely, to convert a per cent form to a decimal, point off two places to the left, drop the per cent symbol, and read as a decimal.

.055 is read "five and five-tenths per cent."
.1525 is read "fifteen and twenty-five hundredths per cent."

Read the following expressions as per cent:

| | | | |
|---|---|---|---|
| 1. | 17/100 | 6. | .5% |
| 2. | .95 | 7. | 5/1000 |
| 3. | .9 | 8. | ⅓ |
| 4. | .0775 | 9. | .16⅔ |
| 5. | ¾ | 10. | ⅞ |

## Exercise 28

Change to per cent form (use % after the expression):

| | | | | | |
|---|---|---|---|---|---|
| 1. | .06 | 5. | .96¼ | 9. | .0005 |
| 2. | .72 | 6. | .87½ | 10. | .00 5/100 |
| 3. | .725 | 7. | .0012½ | 11. | .00 1/10 |
| 4. | .005 | 8. | .0175 | 12. | 1.25 |

Change to decimal form:

| | | | | | |
|---|---|---|---|---|---|
| 13. | 70% | 17. | ½% | 21. | 1¼% |
| 14. | 5% | 18. | .75% | 22. | ⅝% |
| 15. | 12½% | 19. | 1/10% | 23. | ⅔% |
| 16. | 33⅓% | 20. | .05% | 24. | 1½% |

Change to decimal and per cent forms:

| | | | | | |
|---|---|---|---|---|---|
| 25. | ¼ | 29. | ⅔ | 33. | 17/85 |
| 26. | ⅛ | 30. | 45/80 | 34. | 5/11 |
| 27. | 1/6 | 31. | 16/80 | 35. | 30/80 |
| 28. | ⅞ | 32. | 35/90 | 36. | 16/25 |

### PROBLEMS IN PERCENTAGE

Learn the following terms:

*Base* is the number or quantity which represents 100/100 or the multiplicand.

*Rate* is the number of hundredths or the multiplier.

*Percentage* is the product of the base and rate.

*Amount* is the sum of the base and rate.

*Difference* is the base less the percentage.

Type 1. *The base and rate are given to find the percentage.*

(a) What is 15% of $880?

Change the rate to a decimal and multiply.

*Solution:*

$$\begin{array}{r} \$880 \\ .15 \\ \hline 4400 \\ 880 \\ \hline \$132.00 \end{array}$$

(b) What is 66⅔% of $1500?

$$66\tfrac{2}{3}\% = \tfrac{2}{3} \qquad\qquad \$1500 \times \tfrac{2}{3} = \$1000$$

Fractions, decimals, and per cents may be reduced from one form to another. Whenever we can convert a per cent to an aliquot part, as in the above example, we simplify the calculation by using the equivalent aliquot part.

### Commutative Law in Multiplication

We may interchange multiplier and multiplicand without changing the result. Thus the problem, 28% of $125, may be converted to 125% of $28.

We converted the multiplicand $125 into the multiplier 125%, and the multiplier 28% was changed to the multiplicand $28. The results of either multiplication is the same:

$$28\% \text{ of } \$125 = \$35.00$$
$$125\% \text{ of } \ \ \$28 = \ \ 35.00$$

*Rule for Type 1.*—Base $\times$ Rate = Percentage.

### Exercise 29

Find the percentage at sight:

| | | |
|---|---|---|
| 1. 80% of $45 | | 6. 125% of $400 |
| 2. 75% of $240 | | 7. 112½% of $1600 |
| 3. 16⅔% of $1800 | | 8. .5% of $660 |
| 4. 62½% of $8000 | | 9. 12½% of $4000 |
| 5. 87½% of $560 | | 10. 83⅓% of $2400 |

11.  27% of $3333.33
12.  45% of $2000
13.  16% of $1250
14.  66% of $1666.66
15.  56% of $125

16.  32% of $250
17.  36% of $2500
18.  18% of $666.66
19.  40% of $750
20.  35% of $6000

Type 2. *The base and percentage are given to find the rate.*

$40. is what part of $120?

$40. is what per cent of $120? or what per cent of $120. is $40.?

$120.$\times$?%=$40.

The base is $120. The percentage is $40. Rate?

*Solution:* $40.÷$120.=Rate.

$40/120=\frac{1}{3}=33\frac{1}{3}$% Proof: $120.$\times\frac{1}{3}$=$40.

*Rule for Type 2:* To find the rate, divide the percentage by the base.

*Note:* The number after "per cent of ......" is the base.

## Exercise 30

What per cent of:

1.  $45 is $18?
2.  $96 is $16?
3.  $960 is $120?
4.  $.50 is $.20?

5.  $2.00 is $.75?
6.  $1.50 is $.30?
7.  $40.80 is $8.16?
8.  $335.00 is $97.50?

9.  $410.00 is $287.00?
10.  $31.00 is $15.50?

Type 3. *The rate and percentage are given to find the base.*

84 is $\frac{1}{3}$ of what number?

84 is $33\frac{1}{3}$% of what number? or, ?$\times 33\frac{1}{3}$%=84.

We are given the rate $33\frac{1}{3}$% and the percentage 84. The missing number is the *base*.

This is similar to Type 2 of problems in fractions.

*Solution:* 84÷$\frac{1}{3}$=252. (In division by fractions, the denominator is the multiplier.) Proof: $\frac{1}{3}$ of 252=84.

*Rule for Type 3:* Percentage divided by the rate equals the base.

## Exercise 31

Find the amount of which

1.  $ 90.00 is 15%
2.  696.00 is 30%
3.  480.00 is $66\frac{2}{3}$%

4.  $735.00 is $87\frac{1}{2}$%
5.  32.00 is $12\frac{1}{2}$%
6.  96.00 is $6\frac{1}{4}$%

| 7. | $30.00 is 75% | 14. | $ 20.00 is 1/6% |
| 8. | 720.00 is 40% | 15. | 6.90 is 23% |
| 9. | 60.00 is 125% | 16. | 7.20 is 18% |
| 10. | 20.00 is 133 1/3% | 17. | 168.00 is 42% |
| 11. | 45.00 is .5% | 18. | 10.80 is 12% |
| 12. | 90.00 is 3/4% | 19. | 16.50 is .33% |
| 13. | 777.00 is .87 1/2% | 20. | 11.20 is 6 1/4% |

**Type 4.** *Per cent of Increase.*

> *Problem:* A number increased by 25% equals 150. What is the number?
>
> *Solution:* The missing number is the base or 100%. When we increase it by 25%, we get 125% of the number. Therefore the rate is 125%.

$$? \times 125\% = 150$$
$$150 \div 5/4 = 120$$

> *Proof:* $120 \times 5/4 = 150$.

*Rule for Type 4:* When the problem indicates an increase, be sure to add the increase to 100%.

**Type 5.** *Per cent of Decrease.*

> *Problem:* A number decreased by 10% equals 810. What is the number?
>
> *Solution:* The missing number is the base or 100%. Deducting 10% from the base, we get 90%.

$$? \times 90\% = 810$$
$$810 \div 9/10 = 900$$

> *Proof:* $900 \times 90\% = 810$.

*Rule for Type 5:* When the problem indicates a decrease, deduct the per cent of decrease from 100% and proceed in accordance with the solution for Type 2 problems.

*Exercise 32*

What number increased by

| 1. | 25% of itself is 300? | 6. | 62½% of itself is 65? |
| 2. | 10% of itself is 242? | 7. | 87½% of itself is 900? |
| 3. | 33⅓% of itself is 98? | 8. | 5% of itself is 1050? |
| 4. | 40% of itself is 9800? | 9. | 30% of itself is 910? |
| 5. | 100% of itself is 36? | 10. | 250% of itself is 1050? |

What number decreased by

1. 25% of itself is 9?
2. 10% of itself is 90?
3. 33⅓% of itself is 120?
4. 40% of itself is 120?
5. 50% of itself is 45?

6. 62½% of itself is 300?
7. 87½% of itself is 14?
8. 15% of itself is 1700?
9. 30% of itself is 560?
10. 12½% of itself is 56?

## How to Solve Problems in Percentage

Five types of problems in percentage have been presented. To solve the problems that follow, it is necessary to recognize the type in order to get the correct result. You will find it helpful to arrange your solution in this form:

    a. Facts given:
    b. Find:
    c. Solution:

Each type of problem is illustrated below.

*Type 1 Problem:* An investor realized a profit of 8% in his investment of $4850.00. What was his profit?
    *Facts given:* Base, $4850.00. Rate, 8%.
    *Find:* Profit (percentage).
    *Solution:* Base×Rate=Percentage.
        $4850×.08=$388.

*Type 2 Problem:* January sales were $10,500. February sales were $787.50 less than January. What was the per cent of decrease?
    *Facts given:* Base (January sales).
            Percentage (February *decrease of sales*).
    *Find:* The rate (per cent of decrease).
    *Solution:* Percentage÷Base=Rate.
        $787.50÷$10,500=.075 or 7½%.
    *Proof:* $10,500.×.075=$787.50.

*Type 3 Problem:* The operating expenses of a retail store for one year were $10,547. This is 26½% of the net sales. What were the sales?
    *Facts given:* Percentage (operating expenses).
            Rate (per cent of net sales).
    *Find:* The base (net sales).

*Solution:* Percentage ÷ Rate = Base.

$$1\% \text{ of sales is } \$10,547 \div .265 = \$398.$$
$$100\% \text{ of sales is } \$398 \times 100 = \$39,800.$$

*Proof:* $\$39,800 \times .265 = \$10,547.$

*Type 4 Problem:* A salesman's salary was increased from $60 to $70 per week. What was the rate of increase?

    *Facts given:* Base (old salary).

                 Amount: (new salary).

    *Find:* The per cent of increase.

    *Solution:* Increase ÷ Base = Rate.

$$\text{The increase} = \$70 - \$60 = \$10.$$
$$\text{The rate} = \$10 \div \$60 = 1/6 \text{ or } 16\,2/3\%.$$

*Type 5 Problem:* A suit marked $35 was reduced to $29.75. What was the mark-down per cent?

    *Facts given:* Base (original sales price).

                 Difference (marked down price).

    *Find:* The per cent of decrease.

    *Solution:* Decrease ÷ Base = Rate.

$$\text{The decrease is } \$35 - \$29.75 = \$5.25.$$
$$\$5.25 \div \$35 = 15\%.$$

## PROBLEMS IN PERCENTAGE

1.   An automobile depreciates 25% in value in its first year. What is the value of an automobile that sold new at $3,800 after one year?

2.   Mrs. Smith paid $45 for a dress which was marked down 33⅓%. What was the original price?

3.   The school enrollment at Jackson High School increased in one year from 1,500 students to 1,875 students. What was the percent of increase?

4.   Mr. Jones pays $21.00 per month for Blue Cross. This represents a 14% increase from last year. What did he pay last year?

5.   During April the operating expenses of a variety store were 20% of the sales. If the sales were $6,500, what were the expenses?

6.   Mr. Johnson received a 7% increase on a weekly salary of $142. What is his new salary?

7.   A lawyer's income in 1946 was 18% more than in 1945. If his income in 1946 was $7,457.60, how much did he earn in 1945?

8.   During March the operating expenses of a department store were 19% of the sales. If the expenses were $5,440.84, what were the sales?

9.  The sales were $4352 and the cost of sales, $2720. What was the per cent of gross profit on sales?

10.  In problem 9 what was the per cent of gross profit on cost?

11.  A commission merchant made sales as follows:

       1015 bunches of bananas @ $2.10
        970   "   "   "   @ $1.80
      1425   "   "   "   @ $1.50

His commission is 7½% of sales. What were his commissions?

12.  A salesman who works on a straight commission basis earned $3600. If his rate is 7½% on sales, what were his sales for the period?

13.  Mr. Frohm sold a building for $126,500. The original cost to Mr. Frohm was $95,000. He spent $32,500 on permanent improvements and had a net income of $4,850 during the period of ownership. What was the per cent of profit or loss on this transaction?

14.  A and B are in the retail grocery business. A's average mark-up is 33⅓% on cost, while B's average mark-up is 30% on sales. Assuming that each has net sales of $3,000 for January, which one has a greater gross profit, and what is the difference?

15.  Mr. Franklin purchased 100 motors @ $10.00 less 5%. He sold 50% of them at a mark-up of 50% on cost; 30% of the remainder at a mark-up of 25% on cost and the rest of the lot at a loss of 15% on cost. What was his gross profit or loss on the entire lot?

# TRADE DISCOUNTS

In some industries it is customary to issue catalogues with list prices subject to *trade discounts.* When the market prices fluctuate upward or downward, the discounts are changed. This arrangement makes it possible to continue using the same catalogue indefinitely. *Trade discounts* are deductions from the list price.

*Problem 1*

An article is listed at $20 and the trade discount is 40%. What is the net selling price?

The list price is the base or 100%.

    40% of $20.00=$8.00  Trade Discount
    $20.00—$8.00=$12.00  Selling Price.

*Problem 2*

The list price is $75.00 less 20%, 10% and 10%. Find the net selling price.

When there are two or more trade discounts, it makes no difference in what order the discounts are taken. To illustrate this point, we offer two solutions, one deducting the discounts in the order given, 20%, 10%, 10%, the other following the reverse order of discounts, 10%, 10%, and 20%.

| *Solution 1* | | *Solution 2* |
|---|---|---|
| 20% of $75.00=$15.00 | *The first discount* | 10% of $75.00=$7.50 |
| $75.—$15.=$60. | The price after the first discount | $75.00—$7.50=$67.50 |
| 10% of $60.00=$6.00 | *The second discount* | 10% of $67.50=$6.75 |
| $60.—$6.=$54.00 | The price after the second discount | $67.50—$6.75=$60.75 |
| 10% of $54.00=$5.40 | *The third discount* | 20% of $60.75=$12.15 |
| $54.00—$5.40=$48.60 | *Net Selling Price* | $60.75—$12.15=$48.60 |

Note that after the first discount is deducted, the following discounts are computed on the last remainder or the price after the previous discount is deducted. In other words, each discount is based on a different amount.

*Exercise 34*

Find the net selling price.

| | List Price | Trade Discounts | | List Price | Trade Discounts |
|---|---|---|---|---|---|
| a. | $8.00 | 25%, 10% | f. | $4.40 | 25%, 12½%, 5% |
| b. | $45.00 | 33⅓%, 10%, 5% | g. | $30.00 | 50%, 10%, 3% |
| c. | $16.00 | 40% and 12½% | h. | $40.00 | 15%, 10%, 5% |
| d. | $2.40 | 20%, 16⅔% | i. | $6.00 | 12½%, 5%, 5% |
| c. | $15.00 | 30%, 10%, 10% | j. | $18.00 | 33⅓%, 16⅔%, 10% |

*To find a single rate of discount equal to a discount series.*

To shorten the calculation, we find a single rate of discount which is equivalent to a series of discounts.

*Example:* What single discount is equal to 15%, 10% and 10%?

    Let  $1.00   =the list price

          .15   =the first discount

         .85   =the remainder after deducting the first discount

      .085 =the second discount (10% of .85)

      .765 =the remainder after deducting the second discount

    .0765=the third discount (10% of .765)

      .6885=the net selling price

  1.00—.6885=.3115 or 31.15%

Find the single rate of discount equivalent to:

a.  25% and 10%

b.  33⅓%, 10% and 5%

c.  40% and 12½%

d.  20% and 16⅔%

e.  30%, 10% and 10%

f.  25%, 12½% and 5%

g.  50%, 10% and 3%

h.  15%, 10% and 5%

i.  12½%, 5% and 5%

j.  33⅓%, 16⅔% and 10%

Discounts are also offered for payment of a bill within the discount period, which is indicated in the terms of the invoice. They are called *time discounts*. The retail merchants occasionally try to stimulate sales by offering goods at marked down prices. These reductions in price are known as discounts or "Mark-down." The computation for finding the net selling price is based on Type 1 of percentage.

$$\text{Base} \times \text{Rate} = \text{Percentage}$$
$$\text{Base} - \text{Percentage} = \text{Net Selling Price}$$

## PROBLEMS

1.  A watch is listed at $45.00 less 40% and 5%. The cash discount is 2%. What is the net cost to the retailer?

2.  Refrigerators are invoiced at $225.00 less 30% and 10%. What is the net invoice cost?

3.  Typewriters are listed at $100.00 less 20%, 10% and 2% for cash. Find the net cost if the dealer pays cash.

4.  A diamond ring that sells for $800 has discounts of 40% and 15%. What is the net cost to the retailer?

5.  A desk cost the retailer $60 less 33⅓% and 5%. What should the marked price be to yield a gross profit of 33⅓% on cost?

6.  A radio is listed at $50.00 less 15% and 20%. What would a buyer have to pay for 6 radios?

7.  The net cost of an alarm clock is $7.00. If the trade discount is 28%, what is the list price?

8.  A bicycle listed at $40 less 15%, 10% and 10% was changed to $40 less 33⅓%. Was the net invoice amount increased or decreased and how much?

9.  The marked down price of stockings was 76¢. If the discount was 20%, what was the original selling price?

10.  A valise is to be sold for $16.20 net. If the manufacturer is to offer a trade discount of 40% and 10%, at what price should it be listed?

# PROFIT AND LOSS

*Cost* is the net price to the seller.

*Selling Price* is the amount the buyer pays for the goods.

*Gross Profit* is the difference between the selling price and the cost.

*Overhead* or *Operating Expenses* include the expenses incurred in the management of a business such as rent, salaries, electric and telephone service, supplies, depreciation charges, etc.

*Net Profit* or *Loss* is the difference between gross profit and operating expenses.

If a camera costing $30. retails for $50., what is the gross profit per cent?

This is similar to Type 2—percentage.

The gross profit is $20.

To find per cent of gross profit, divide the percentage $20. by the base. The problem does not indicate whether per cent of gross profit is based on cost or selling price. In accordance with sound business practice, per cent of profit is usually computed on selling price. Sales are the basis. Gross profit is generally compared with sales, not with cost.

$20/$50=40% *gross profit on selling price.*

Profit and Loss problems are similar to the types in percentage and are solved in the same manner.

The base is usually the selling price.

The per cent of profit on sales is the rate.

The profit or loss is the percentage.

## Exercise 36

Fill in the gross profit and per cent of gross profit on sales.

| | Selling Price | Cost | Gross Profit | % Gross Profit on Sales |
|---|---|---|---|---|
| 1. | 2.40 | 1.20 | .......... | .......... |
| 2. | 20.00 | 15.00 | .......... | .......... |
| 3. | 5.40 | 3.60 | .......... | .......... |
| 4. | 10.00 | 7.50 | .......... | .......... |
| 5. | 1.75 | 1.26 | .......... | .......... |
| 6. | .75 | .45 | .......... | .......... |
| 7. | 1.25 | .75 | .......... | .......... |
| 8. | 5.50 | 3.50 | .......... | .......... |
| 9. | 8.75 | 6.25 | .......... | .......... |

A retailer buys hats at $24.00 a dozen. If his mark-up rate is 33⅓% on sales, what is the resale price per hat?

*Facts Given:* Cost per dozen and the mark-up rate on sales.

*Find:* Selling price per hat.

| *Solution:* | *Explanation:* |
|---|---|

*Solution:*

Sales     = 1.00
Mark-up = .33⅓
Cost     = .66⅔

$\dfrac{33⅓}{66⅔}=$ ½ or 50% on Cost

$24.00 ÷ 12 = $2.00 Cost of 1 hat
$2.00 × 50% = $1.00 Profit
$2.00 + $1.00 = $3.00 Selling Price
*Proof:* $1.00 ÷ $3.00 = 33⅓%

*Explanation:*

Sales is the base, 100%. Cost is 66⅔% of Sales. We do not know the sales. However we can convert the per cent rate on sales to an equivalent per cent rate based on cost by dividing the mark-up by the cost.

33⅓% on Sales = 50% on Cost
Base × Rate of Profit = Profit

*Summary:* To find the selling price when the cost and per cent of gross profit on sales are given:

1.   Find the complement of the mark-up rate on sales (the difference between $1.00 and the mark-up rate).

2.   Form a fraction with the given mark-up rate as the numerator and its complement as a denominator.

3.   Multiply the cost by the result of Step 2.

## Exercise 37

The complement of a % is the difference obtained by subtracting the given % from 100%. The complement of 25% is therefore 75%.

What is the complement of the following per cents?

| | | |
|---|---|---|
| 1.   20% | 6.   50% | 11.   37½% |
| 2.   40% | 7.   30% | 12.   14 2/7% |
| 3.   12½% | 8.   10% | 13.   28 4/7% |
| 4.   33⅓% | 9.   16⅔% | 14.   62½% |
| 5.   35% | 10.   45% | 15.   66 2/3% |

The per cents shown above represent per cent gross profit on Sales. Find the equivalent rates based on Cost.

*Illustration:* Per cent of gross profit on sales is 25%.

The complement is 75%. 25/75 = ⅓ = 33⅓%.

The equivalent per cent of gross profit on cost is 33⅓%.

Using the equivalent rates computed in Exercise 36, find the gross profit and selling price. Prove all results.

| | Cost | Mark-up Rate based on S. P. | Equivalent Rate based on Cost | Profit | Selling Price |
|---|---|---|---|---|---|
| 1. | 4.00 | 20% | .......... | .......... | .......... |
| 2. | .75 | 40% | .......... | .......... | .......... |
| 3. | 2.10 | 12½% | .......... | .......... | .......... |
| 4. | 5.00 | 33⅓% | .......... | .......... | .......... |
| 5. | .65 | 37½% | .......... | .......... | .......... |
| 6. | .85 | 50% | .......... | .......... | .......... |
| 7. | 7.00 | 30% | .......... | .......... | .......... |
| 8. | 1.08 | 10% | .......... | .......... | .......... |
| 9. | 1.50 | 16⅔% | .......... | .......... | .......... |
| 10. | .66 | 45% | .......... | .......... | .......... |
| 11. | .45 | 37½% | .......... | .......... | .......... |
| 12. | 1.74 | 14 2/7% | .......... | .......... | .......... |
| 13. | 3.00 | 28 4/7% | .......... | .......... | .......... |

*Given cost, per cent of operating expenses, and per cent of net profit. Find the selling price. (Note per cents are based on selling price.)*

*Problem:* A retailer buys tooth brushes @ $1.80 per dozen. His operating expenses are 30% of sales. If he desires to make a net profit of 10% on sales, at what price each must he sell the tooth brushes?

*Given:* Cost per dozen, per cent of operating expenses and per cent of desired profit on sales.

*Find:* Selling price per tooth brush.

*Solution:*

Selling Price = 100%
$1.80 + 30% + 10% = Selling Price
100% − 30% − 10% = 60%
$1.80 = 60% of Selling Price
$1.80 ÷ .6 = $3.00 Selling Price per doz.
$3.00 ÷ 12 = $.25 S. P. per brush

*Proof:* 30% of 3.00 = .90
10% of 3.00 = .30

*Explanation:*

All per cents are based on selling price.

Deduct the rate of expenses and rate of profit from selling price to find the per cent of cost. Apply the formula: Percentage ÷ Rate = Base
$1.80 + .90 + .30 = $3.00

Find the selling price.

|  | Cost | Operating Expenses | Desired Net Profit | Selling Price |
|---|---|---|---|---|
| 1. | $18.00 | 25% | 15% | . . . . . . . . . . . |
| 2. | 1.50 | 37½% | 12½% | . . . . . . . . . . . |
| 3. | 1.05 | 20% | 10% | . . . . . . . . . . . |
| 4. | .95 | 33⅓% | 16⅔% | . . . . . . . . . . . |
| 5. | 1.60 | 12% | 8% | . . . . . . . . . . . |
| 6. | 8.50 | 10% | 5% | . . . . . . . . . . . |
| 7. | 156.00 |  | 15% | . . . . . . . . . . . |
| 8. | 2430.00 | 13% | 6% | . . . . . . . . . . . |
| 9. | 28.70 | 25% | 5% | . . . . . . . . . . . |
| 10. | 125.00 | 12½% | 10% | . . . . . . . . . . . |

## FINDING THE LIST PRICE

*Problem:* A manufacturer produces lawn mowers at a cost of $12.00. He desires to make a gross profit of $6.00 after allowing a trade discount of 40% on the list price. Find the list price.

*Given:* Cost, gross profit and trade discount.

*Find:* List price.

*Solution:*

1. $12+$6=$18 Selling Price.

2. List Price=100%.
   100%—40%=Selling Price.

3. 60% of List Price=Selling Price.
   60% of the List Price=$18.

4. $18÷.6=$30 List Price.

*Explanation:*

1. Cost+Gross Profit=Selling Price.

2. List Price—Trade Discount= Selling Price.
   Since the trade discount is computed on list price, the latter equals 100% of the amount which we are required to find.

3. In line 1 we determined the selling price to be $18, which is 60% of the list price.

4. P÷R=B (Percentage divided by the rate equals the base).

*Proof:* 40% of $30=$12 Trade Discount.
$30.00—$12.00=$18.00 Selling Price.

Find the List Price.

| | Cost | Gross Profit | Selling Price | Trade Disc. | List Price |
|---|---|---|---|---|---|
| 1. | $ 1.50 | .50 | ...... | 33⅓% | ...... |
| 2. | 4.50 | 2.25 | ...... | 10% | ...... |
| 3. | 15.00 | 6.00 | ...... | 25% | ...... |
| 4. | 3.00 | 1.20 | ...... | 30% | ...... |
| 5. | 20.00 | 10.00 | ...... | 40% | ...... |
| 6. | 33.00 | 12.50 | ...... | 35% | ...... |
| 7. | 12.00 | 16.80 | ...... | 20% | ...... |
| 8. | 2.60 | 1.30 | ...... | 37½% | ...... |
| 9. | 1.50 | .90 | ...... | 60% | ...... |
| 10. | 3.50 | 1.50 | ...... | 16⅔% | ...... |

# COMMISSION AND BROKERAGE

When a farmer brings his fruit or vegetables to the market place and disposes of his products, he sells directly to the customer. Because of distance from markets or other inconveniences, the grower frequently sells through an agent called a commission merchant. The goods are shipped to the commission merchant, but the title or ownership remains with the shipper until the merchandise is sold. A few of the terms used in this type of business are briefly explained:

A *consignor* or *shipper* is the principal who ships the goods.

A *consignee* is the agent to whom the goods are forwarded.

A *consignment* or *shipment* refers to the goods to be sold by the commission merchant for the shipper.

A *broker* is an agent who buys or sells for the principal without handling the goods.

*Commission* or *brokerage* is the agent's compensation for his services.

*Net proceeds* is the difference between the sales and charges.

An *account sale* is an itemized statement of sales and charges which the commission merchant sends to his principal.

*Problem:* The Liberty Fruit Distributors received 800 bags of coconuts from The Mayaguez Trading Company to be sold on their account. The consignee sold 400 bags @ $4.10; 300 @ $3.75; and 100 @ $3.25. Freight and insurance was $.50 a bag, trucking $.25 a bag, and storage charges $40.00. Advertising costs were $15.00; commission 5%. What are the net proceeds?

*Given:* Consignment; sales; charges; rate of commission.

*Find:* Net proceeds.

*Solution:*

Sales:

| | | |
|---|---|---|
| 400 bags @ $4.10 | = | $1640.00 |
| 300 bags @ 3.75 | = | 1125.00 |
| 100 bags @ 3.25 | = | 325.00 |

Total: 800     $3090.00

*Charges:*

| | | |
|---|---|---|
| Freight | .50 × 800 = | $400.00 |
| Trucking | .25 × 800 = | 200.00 |
| Storage | | 40.00 |
| Advertising | | 15.00 |
| Commission | $3090 × .05 = | 154.50 |
| Total charges | | 809.50 |

Net proceeds     $2280.50

## Exercise 41

| | Selling Price | Rate Comm. | Expenses | Net Proceeds |
|---|---|---|---|---|
| 1. | 1360.50 | 5% | 148.25 | ......... |
| 2. | 3471.00 | 2% | 420.75 | ......... |
| 3. | 546.40 | 7½% | 49.10 | ......... |
| 4. | 2684.70 | 2½% | 328.50 | ......... |
| 5. | 1965.15 | 3% | 248.95 | ......... |
| 6. | 4175.00 | 2% | 816.30 | ......... |
| 7. | 627.60 | 8% | 59.10 | ......... |
| 8. | 1382.40 | 5% | 322.80 | ......... |
| 9. | 916.25 | 7½% | 88.00 | ......... |
| 10. | 1844.65 | 2% | 428.35 | ......... |

1. Mr. Jones sells automobiles. If his commission is 5% of total sales, how much does he earn for selling an automobile at $4,200?

2. A salesman's total sales for the day were $965. If his commission is 8%, how much did he earn?

3. A real estate salesman received 3% commission for selling a home at $35,000. How much commission did he receive?

4. A salesman received a commission of $1,200 for the total sales of one month. If this amount represents 5% of total sales, how much did he sell?

5. A broker received $400 for selling a piece of land worth $8,000. What was the rate of commission?

# INTEREST

In profit and loss, marking goods, commission and brokerage problems the rules of percentage were applied. In the solution of the problems we used one of the rules of percentage.

$$Base \times Rate = Percentage$$
$$Percentage \div Base = Rate$$
$$Percentage \div Rate = Base$$

Interest problems belong to this group. However, there is a new factor in computing interest, namely the interest period.

Thomas Brown borrowed $1000 from the bank for 60 days at 6%. Alfred Coyne borrowed $2000 for 30 days @ 6%. Michael Dunn borrowed $2000 for 60 days @ 3%. How much interest does Brown pay? Coyne? Dunn?

The factors to be considered in each problem are (a) the sum of money (b) the time (c) the interest rate. The money borrowed is called the *principal*. The unit of time is a year. Interest rate is expressed as a *per cent* for a year. The interest rates in the preceding problem are 6% and 3% for one year. The rule for computing interest is:

$$P \times R \times T = I$$
P—Principal; R—Rate; T—Time; I—Interest.

Bankers and business men compute interest on the basis of 360 days to the year, because of convenience. For example, 90 days, 60 days, 30 days, may be readily changed to simple fractions of a year, thus:

$$90/360 = 1/4 \text{ of a year}$$
$$60/360 = 1/6 \text{ of a year}$$
$$30/360 = 1/12 \text{ of a year}$$

For the same reason business men also use 30 days to the month instead of the exact number of days. Banks, however, use the exact number of days in the calendar month.

### To Find the Interest

The solutions for the above problems are shown below:

*Given:* Principal, time and rate

*Find:* Interest

THOMAS BROWN

*Solution:* $\$1000 \times 6/100 \times 60/360 = \$10.00$

ALFRED COYNE

*Solution:* $\$2000 \times 6/100 \times 30/360 = \$10.00$

MICHAEL DUNN

*Solution:* $\$2000 \times 3/100 \times 60/360 = \$10.00$

Why is the result the same in each case?

When the time is one year, the formula uses 1 (360/360) as the time factor. The interest for $250 @ 2% for 1 year is $\$250 \times 2/100 \times 1 = \$5.00$.

To shorten the calculations, use simple fractions of a year.

| *Days* | *Year* |
|---|---|
| 30 | 1/12 |
| 45 | 1/8 |
| 60 | 1/6 |
| 90 | 1/4 |
| 120 | 1/3 |

No. of days to the year = 360

Find the interest:

| | Principal | Time | | 2% | 3% | 4% | 6% |
|---|---|---|---|---|---|---|---|
| 1. | $500.00 | 1 | year | . . . . . . . | . . . . . . . | . . . . . . . | . . . . . . . |
| 2. | $800.00 | 90 | days | . . . . . . . | . . . . . . . | . . . . . . . | . . . . . . . |
| 3. | $600.00 | 60 | " | . . . . . . . | . . . . . . . | . . . . . . . | . . . . . . . |
| 4. | $2400.00 | 30 | " | . . . . . . . | . . . . . . . | . . . . . . . | . . . . . . . |
| 5. | $240.00 | 75 | " | . . . . . . . | . . . . . . . | . . . . . . . | . . . . . . . |

The *amount* is the principal plus the interest. Find the amounts in the preceding exercise.

## THE 60-DAY METHOD

Business men usually borrow money from banks for 30-, 60-, or 90-day periods. The 60-day method is a short-cut for computing interest for periods less than a year. The basis of this method is: 60 days=1/6 of a year. When the interest is 6% for one year, we multiply 6/100 by 1/6 to find the equivalent rate for 60 days.

$$6/100 \times 1/6 = 1\%.$$

*Rule:* To find the interest on any sum of money for 60 days at 6% take 1% of the principal.

*Example:* What is the interest on $1328.25 for 60 days at 6%?

*Answer:* $13.28 (1% of $1328.25).

*Proof:* $1328.25 \times 6/100 \times 60/360 = $13.28.

If the period of time is a multiple of 60 days, find the interest for 60 days and multiply result by the multiple of 60 days. For example:

$$120 \text{ days} = 60 \times 2$$
$$180 \text{ days} = 60 \times 3$$
$$240 \text{ days} = 60 \times 4$$

For periods less than 60 days, we use an aliquot part of 60, thus:

$$6 \text{ days} = 1/10 \text{ of } 60$$
$$15 \text{ " } = \tfrac{1}{4} \text{ of } 60$$
$$20 \text{ " } = \tfrac{1}{3} \text{ of } 60$$
$$30 \text{ " } = \tfrac{1}{2} \text{ of } 60$$

*Illustrations:*

a.  What is the interest on $400.00 for 240 days at 6%?

Interest for 60 days=$4.00
" " 240 " =$4.00×4=$16.00

b.  What is the interest on $400.00 for 15 days at 6%?

Interest for 60 days=$4.00
" " 15 " =$4.00×¼=$1.00

c.  What is the interest on $400.00 for 90 days at 6%?

Interest for 60 days=$4.00
" " 30 " =$2.00
" " 90 " =$6.00

d.  What is the interest on $400.00 for 18 days at 6%?

Interest for 60 days=$4.00
" " 6 " = .40
" " 12 " = .80
" " 18 " =$1.20

To facilitate the calculation, break up the time into periods which are aliquot parts of 60, thus:

$$72=60+12$$
$$54=60-6$$
$$24=30-6$$
$$36=30+6$$
$$80=60+20 \text{ etc.}$$

## Exercise 43

Find the interest at 6% on $1500.00 for

| | | | | | | |
|---|---|---|---|---|---|---|---|
| 1. | 66 days | 5. | 90 days | 9. | 70 days | 13. | 39 days |
| 2. | 120 " | 6. | 6 " | 10. | 45 " | 14. | 72 " |
| 3. | 180 " | 7. | 36 " | 11. | 20 " | 15. | 90 " |
| 4. | 240 " | 8. | 10 " | 12. | 50 " | 16. | 18 " |

Break up the following into periods which are multiples or aliquot parts of 60.

| | | | | | | | |
|---|---|---|---|---|---|---|---|
| 17. | 66 days | 21. | 90 days | 25. | 70 days | 29. | 39 days |
| 18. | 40 " | 22. | 3 " | 26. | 76 " | 30. | 150 " |
| 19. | 36 " | 23. | 10 " | 27. | 57 " | 31. | 186 " |
| 20. | 75 " | 24. | 96 " | 28. | 21 " | 32. | 42 " |

### THE 60-DAY METHOD AT OTHER RATES

When the interest rate is more or less than 6%, the interest can be computed in the following manner:

First compute interest at 6%. Divide the interest at 6% by 6 and multiply by the required rate.

*Example:* Find the interest on $1800.00 for 30 days at 4%.

$$\text{Interest for 60 days at } 6\% = \$18.00$$
$$\text{"}\quad\text{"}\quad 30 \quad\text{"}\quad\text{"}\quad 6\% = 9.00$$
$$\text{"}\quad\text{"}\quad 30 \quad\text{"}\quad\text{"}\quad 1\% = \$9.00 \div 6 = \$1.50$$
$$\text{"}\quad\text{"}\quad 30 \quad\text{"}\quad\text{"}\quad 4\% = \$1.50 \times 4 = \$6.00$$

### Exercise 44

Find the interest by using the 60-day method:

| | Principal | Time | 6% | 5% | 7% | 4% | 2% |
|---|---|---|---|---|---|---|---|
| 1. | $ 900.00 | 60 days | | | | | |
| 2. | $1500.00 | 72 " | | | | | |
| 3. | $2400.00 | 120 " | | | | | |
| 4. | $ 300.00 | 36 " | | | | | |
| 5. | $ 800.00 | 66 " | | | | | |

### COMPOUND INTEREST

If you place a sum of money in a savings bank, it draws a certain amount of interest at the end of the first interest date. This interest is now added on to the original amount, and the interest at the end of the next interest date is computed on this larger amount. You are now receiving interest on the interest. This is known as *compound interest*. If the interest is added once a year, it is compounded annually. If it is added twice a year, it is compounded semi-annually; if it is added 4 times a year, it is compounded quarterly. Compound interest may be computed as illustrated below. However, most banks use tables for this purpose.

*Illustration:*

Find the amount of $600.00 for 3 years at 6% compounded annually.

| | |
|---|---|
| Principal at beginning | $600.00 |
| Interest first year | 36.00 |
| Amount at end of first year | $636.00 |
| Interest second year | 38.16 |
| Amount at end of second year | $674.16 |
| Interest third year | 40.4496 |
| Amount at end of third year | $714.6096 |
| Answer to the nearest cent | $714.61 |

$714.61—$600.00=$114.61, compound interest

# BANK DISCOUNT

John Doe needs to pay for his purchases. He applies at his bank for a loan of $1500 for three months. The bank, having agreed to make the loan, asks John Doe to fill in a promissory note. John Doe fills in the note as follows:

No. 52            New York, March 15, 19—

Three months after date I promise

To pay to the order of ....MYSELF.....$1500

Fifteen hundred...........................dollars

JOHN DOE (signed)

John Doe endorses the note and gives it to the bank.

Banks usually deduct from the face value of the note the charge for their services. In this case, the bank will charge John Doe interest on $1500 for the period of the loan. This charge is called Bank Discount. It is customary for banks to figure the exact number of days from the date of discount to the maturity date of the note. This interval is called the Term of Discount.

### HOW TO COMPUTE THE TERM OF DISCOUNT

Suppose the discount date in the above transaction is March 15, 1946. The note becomes due three months after March 15, or June 15. The exact number of days from March 15 to June 15 is arrived at in the following manner:

| *Term of Discount* | | *Bank Discount* | |
|---|---|---|---|
| March 15–31 | 16 days | Int. for 60 days | $15.00 |
| April has | 30 " | "   "   30   " | 7.50 |
| May has | 31 " | "   "   2   " | .50 |
| June 1–15 | 15 " | "   "   92   " | $23.00 |
| (Total term of discount) | 92 days | | |

The bank discount on $1500 for the 92 days at 6% is $23.00. After deducting the bank discount from the face value of the note, you get the net amount which will be credited to John Doe's account.

$1500—$23.00=$1477. This is called the net proceeds.

Exercise 45

Compute the term of discount:

|  | Date of Discount | Maturity Date | Term of Discount |
|---|---|---|---|
| 1. | Jan. 5 | March 5 | . . . . . . . . . . . . . |
| 2. | Feb. 10 | May 10 | . . . . . . . . . . . . . |
| 3. | March 20 | Apr. 19 | . . . . . . . . . . . . . |
| 4. | Apr. 2 | June 1 | . . . . . . . . . . . . . |
| 5. | May 25 | July 10 | . . . . . . . . . . . . . |
| 6. | June 9 | Sept. 9 | . . . . . . . . . . . . . |
| 7. | July 17 | Aug. 16 | . . . . . . . . . . . . . |
| 8. | Aug. 5 | Nov. 3 | . . . . . . . . . . . . . |
| 9. | Sept. 30 | Dec. 5 | . . . . . . . . . . . . . |
| 10. | Oct. 1 | Nov. 30 | . . . . . . . . . . . . . |

### How to Compute the Date of Maturity

**a.** *When time is expressed in months:*

A note dated April 10, becomes due three months after date. What is the date of maturity?

April 10 plus three months equals July 10. The number of months is added to the date of the note. The due date falls on the corresponding date of the note. If the maturity date falls on Saturday, Sunday, or a legal holiday, the maturity date is on the following business day.

**b.** *When the time is expressed in days:*

A note dated April 10, will be due 90 days after date. What is the date of maturity?

| | |
|---|---|
| Number of days left in April (Apr. 30—15) | 15 days |
| May | 31 " |
| June | 30 " |
| | 76 days |
| July | 14 " |
| Total number of days from April 10 to July 14 | 90 days |

Note that we took a total after June 30 because we approached the required number of days. Fourteen additional days are required in July to bring the total up to 90.

50

Find the maturity date:

|  | Date of<br>Note | Time | Maturity<br>Date |
|---|---|---|---|
| 1. | Jan. 5 | 60 days | . . . . . . . . |
| 2. | Feb. 10 | 90 " | . . . . . . . |
| 3. | March 20 | 20 " | . . . . . . . . |
| 4. | Apr. 2 | 60 " | . . . . . . . . |
| 5. | May 25 | 90 " | . . . . . . . |
| 6. | June 9 | 90 " | . . . . . . . . |
| 7. | July 17 | 40 " | . . . . . . . |
| 8. | Aug. 5 | 50 " | . . . . . . . |
| 9. | Sept. 30 | 90 " | . . . . . . . |
| 10. | Oct. 1 | 80 " | . . . . . . . |

## INTEREST-BEARING NOTES

No. 10   New York, N. Y., May 20, 19—

Ninety days. . . . . . . . . .after date I promise to pay to
the order of. . . . . WILLIAM STRAUSS. . . . .$1000.00
One Thousand 00/100. . . . . . . . . . . . . . . . . . . .Dollars
Value received with interest at 6%

JOHN HENDERSON (signed)

Payable at Commercial Bank and Trust Co.
150 Broadway, New York.

John Henderson is called the *maker* or drawer, and William Strauss the
*payee*.

How much should the payee of the above note collect from John Henderson on the date of maturity? Since the note bears interest at 6%, the maker must pay in addition to the face value the interest on $1000.00 for ninety days. The amount is computed thus:

| | |
|---|---|
| Face Value | $1000.00 |
| Interest (on $1000 for 90 days) | 15.00 |
| Maturity Value | $1015.00 |

If this were a non-interest bearing note, the maker would pay $1000.00.

Let us assume that on June 19, the payee, William Strauss, is in need of funds. If his credit standing is satisfactory, he can discount the note at his bank. To transfer the note to the bank, William Strauss endorses his name. The endorsement guarantees to the bank that the signature of the maker is bona fide, and that the note will be paid by the endorser if the maker fails to pay. What are the net proceeds if the bank charges at the rate of 6%?

*Given:* The face value, time of note, date of discount, interest rate, discount rate.

*Find:* Discount, and Net Proceeds.
*Solution:*

$$P \times T \times R = \text{Interest}$$
$$P + I = \text{Maturity Value}$$
$$M.V. \times \text{Term of Discount} \times R = \text{Discount}$$
$$M.V. - D = \text{Net Proceeds (Present Value)}$$

Banks compute the discount on the maturity value of the note. They figure the exact number of days from the date of discount to the maturity date. The routine for computing the net proceeds follows.

1. *Find the Date of Maturity.*

   May 20 + 90 days . . . . . . . . . . . . . . . . . . . . . . . . . August 18

   | | | |
   |---|---|---|
   | May (31—20) | 11 days | (If August 18 falls on Sat- |
   | June | 30 " | urday or Sunday, the note |
   | July | 31 " | matures on the following |
   | August | 18 " | business day.) |
   | Total | 90 " | |

2. *Compute the Maturity Value.*
   Interest for 90 days at 6% on $1000 is $15.00.
   Principal, $1000 + Interest, $15.00 = $1015.
   (The interest is computed for the time of the note at the specified rate of interest.)

3. *Find the Term of Discount.*
   From the date of discount, June 19, to the maturity date, August 18, there are 60 days.

   June (30—19) 11 + July 31 + August 18 = 60 days

4. *Compute the Discount* (on the maturity value).
   Interest on $1015.00 for 60 days at 6% . . . . . . . . $10.15

5. *Compute the Discount.*

Maturity Value  $1015.00
Discount                10.15
__________
Net Proceeds  $1004.85

When the time of the note is expressed in months, the date of maturity is computed by adding the number of months to the date of the note.

## Exercise 47

Find the maturity value of the following notes bearing interest at 6%.

|    | Face of Note | Time |
|----|-------------|---------|
| 1. | $1500.00 | 90 days |
| 2. | 4500.00 | 3 mos. |
| 3. | 500.00 | 60 days |
| 4. | 5000.00 | 2 mos. |
| 5. | 3600.00 | 1 mo. |

## Exercise 48

Find the term of discount.

|    | Date of Note | Time | Date of Discount |
|----|--------------|---------|------------------|
| 1. | Jan. 15 | 60 days | Jan. 25 |
| 2. | Feb. 1 | 90 " | Mar. 15 |
| 3. | Mar. 30 | 30 " | Apr. 9 |
| 4. | Apr. 10 | 60 " | May 15 |
| 5. | May 5 | 90 " | May 15 |

# TAXES

Who pays the salaries of public school teachers, policemen, firemen, judges of municipal and county courts? Who pays for the construction of public buildings, the maintenance of health service, parks and recreation centers, and highway department? What are the sources of income for the town or city in which you reside?

Every resident is subject to one form of tax or another. A direct tax is a sum of money levied against an individual, his property or his business for the support of the government. Examples of direct taxes are taxes on real estate, personal property, and income. Indirect taxes are taxes levied on tobacco, liquor, gasoline, imported goods, etc. What taxes do you pay directly or indirectly?

In this section we shall concern ourselves with one type of tax—real estate taxes. Most of the money needed to run the state, county, and city government is collected from this source. First, the various units of government determine the sum of money which will be needed for the following year for government expenses and construction of buildings. This estimate of expenses is called a budget. A discussion of the legal procedure involved is beyond the scope of arithmetic.

Let us assume that Rosedale Manor has adopted a budget of $50,000 for next year. How much should be levied against each property owner? In order to distribute the tax on an equitable basis, each lot and building is valued for tax purposes. This value is known as an *assessed valuation,* and is usually less than the resale value of the property. Let us further assume that the total valuation of all real estate in Rosedale Manor is $2,000,000. The tax rate is computed by dividing the budget total by the total assessed valuation.

$$\$50,000 \div \$2,000,000 = .025$$

This rate may be expressed as

$$
\begin{aligned}
&25 \text{ mills per dollar, or}\\
&\$2.50 \quad\quad\text{ `` hundred dollars, or}\\
&\$25.00 \quad\quad\text{ `` thousand dollars.}
\end{aligned}
$$

To change the tax rate from a dollar basis to a hundred dollar basis, move the decimal point in the tax rate two places to the right. Why?

To change the tax rate from a dollar basis to a thousand dollar basis, move the decimal three places to the right. Why?

A's property (which is situated in Rosedale Manor) is assessed at $15,000. What is the amount of tax levied against him?

*Given:* Assessed valuation and the tax rate.
*Find:* The tax.

*Solution:* Base$\times$Rate$=$Tax

$$\$15,000\times.025=\$375.00$$

*Proof:* $\$375.\div\$15,000.=.025$

Care must be exercised to point off the correct number of decimal places in the answer. In this problem, there are three decimal places in the rate, therefore, we point off three decimal places to the left in the result. When the rate is per hundred dollars, divide the assessed valuation by 100 and proceed as above. When the rate is per thousand dollars, divide the assessed valuation by 1000 and proceed in the same manner.

### Exercise 49

Find the tax rate:

| | Assessed valuation | Amount of tax | Rate per dollar | Rate per $100 | Rate per $1000 |
|---|---|---|---|---|---|
| 1. | $8,000,000 | $120,000 | ........ | ........ | ........ |
| 2. | 70,000,000 | 350,000 | ........ | ........ | ........ |
| 3. | 40,000,000 | 700,000 | ........ | ........ | ........ |
| 4. | 200,000,000 | 2,500,000 | ........ | ........ | ........ |
| 5. | 100,000,000 | 3,000,000 | ........ | ........ | ........ |

### Exercise 50

Change the tax rates per dollar to equivalent tax rates per hundred and per thousand dollars.

| | Rate per dollar | Rate per $100 | Rate per $1000 |
|---|---|---|---|
| 1. | .03½ | ........ | ........ |
| 2. | 35 mills | ........ | ........ |
| 3. | 20 mills | ........ | ........ |
| 4. | 2¾ cents | ........ | ........ |
| 5. | 27.5 mills | ........ | ........ |
| 6. | 18.64 mills | ........ | ........ |
| 7. | 82.25 mills | ........ | ........ |
| 8. | 75 mills | ........ | ........ |
| 9. | .075 | ........ | ........ |
| 10. | .01864 | ........ | ........ |

Note 1 mill is 1/10 of a cent and may be decimally expressed as .001 or .1¢.

Compute the tax.

| | Assessed valuation | Tax rate | Tax |
|---|---|---|---|
| 1. | $6,500 | 27.5 mills | . . . . . . . . . . . . |
| 2. | 12,000 | $1.758 per $100 | . . . . . . . . . . . . |
| 3. | 25,000 | $8.254 per $1000 | . . . . . . . . . . . . |
| 4. | 14,600 | 25 mills | . . . . . . . . . . . . |
| 5. | 10,500 | $1.952 per $100 | . . . . . . . . . . . . |
| 6. | 30,000 | $12.581 per $1000 | . . . . . . . . . . . . |
| 7. | 5,000 | $1.5724 per $100 | . . . . . . . . . . . . |
| 8. | 7,500 | $14.079 per $1000 | . . . . . . . . . . . . |
| 9. | 8,000 | 26.9 mills | . . . . . . . . . . . . |
| 10. | 6,000 | $1.426 per $100 | . . . . . . . . . . . . |

The formulas explained in the chapter on Percentage may be applied to tax problems, if you substitute the terms used in property taxes for the terms used in percentage.

| *Percentage* | *Taxes* |
|---|---|
| Base | Assessed Valuation |
| Rate | Tax Rate |
| Percentage | Tax |

The type problems illustrated below indicate how the percentage formulas are applied:

Type 1. Assessed Valuation $\times$ Tax Rate $=$ Tax. This type has already been illustrated.

Type 2. Tax $\div$ Assessed Valuation $=$ Tax Rate.
*Problem.* The tax levied on a building assessed at $6500 was $178.75. What was the tax rate?
*Solution:* $178.75 $\div$ $6500 $=$ .0275 or $2\frac{3}{4}\%$
*Proof:* $6500 $\times$ .0275 $=$ $178.75

Type 3. Tax $\div$ Tax Rate $=$ Assessed Valuation.
*Problem.* At 1.426 per hundred dollars the tax amounts to $85.56. What is the assessed valuation?

*Solution:* $\$85.56 \div \dfrac{1.426}{100} = \$6000$

*Proof:* $\dfrac{\$6000}{100} \times 1.426 = \$85.56$

Fill in the missing number in the following problems:

|  | Assessed valuation | Tax rate | Tax levy |
|---|---|---|---|
| 1. | $14,500 | . . . . . . . . . . . | $253.75 |
| 2. | . . . . . . . . | 17.5 mills | $560.00 |
| 3. | $125,500 | 1.875 per 100 | . . . . . . . . |
| 4. | $1,500,000 | . . . . . . . . . . . | $1,875.00 |
| 5. | . . . . . . . . | 12.582 per 1000 | $10,694.70 |

# DENOMINATE NUMBERS

Quantities are measured by standard units of measure established by law or custom, like a pound, a yard, a gallon, a bushel. A number used apart from a unit is abstract, such as 3. A number of articles, such as 3 desks, 3 typewriters, is concrete. A number of units such as 3 yards, 3 pounds, 3 dollars is a denominate number. When the numerical expression denotes one kind of unit, it is a simple number, such as 5 gallons. When the expression denotes two or more units, such as 5 gallons, 3 quarts, 1 pint, it is a compound number.

In the following list, state whether the numbers are abstract or concrete:

| | | |
|---|---|---|
| a.  15 | e.  5 tons | i.  25 |
| b.  8 hours | f.  25 houses | j.  1 year 4 months |
| c.  10 chairs | g.  40 quarts | k.  3 yds. 2 ft. 5 in. |
| d.  9 pounds | h.  $100 | l.  1000 sq. miles |

This division presents problems in denominate numbers. A knowledge of tables of weights and measures is essential to solve these problems.

## LINEAR MEASURE

Linear measure is used for measuring distances.

12 inches (in.) = 1 foot (ft.)
3 feet = 1 yard (yd.)
5½ yards = 1 rod (rd.)
320 rods
1760 yards } = 1 mile (mi.)
5280 feet

1 fathom=6 feet (used in measuring depths at sea)
1 knot   =1.15266 miles or 6080.27 ft. (used in measuring
distances at sea)
3 miles  =1 league

## SQUARE MEASURE

Square measure is used for measuring areas of surfaces.

144 square inches (sq. in.)=1 square foot (sq. ft.)
9 square feet          =1 square yard (sq. yd.)
30¼ square yards       =1 square rod (sq. rd.)
160 sq. rd.            =1 acre (A)
640 acres             =1 square mile (sq. mi.)
1 square             =100 sq. ft.

The *square* is the unit used for measuring roofing material.
The *acre* is the unit used for measuring land outside of cities.

## CUBIC MEASURE

Cubic measure is used to measure volume of solids.

1728 cubic inches       =1 cubic foot (cu. ft.)
27 cubic feet          =1 cubic yard (cu. yd.)
128 cubic feet         =1 cord (cd.)
1 cubic yard (of earth)=1 load

1 perch of stone is 1 rod long, 1½ ft. wide, 1 ft. high.
1 cord of wood is a pile 8 ft. long, 4 ft. wide, 4 ft. high.
1 cubic foot of water weighs 62½ lb. (avoirdupois).

## LIQUID MEASURE

Liquid measure is used to measure liquids and capacities of tanks,
reservoirs, etc.

4 gills       =1 pint (pt.)
2 pints       =1 quart (qt.)
4 quarts      =1 gallon (gal.)
1 wine gallon=231 cubic inches
1 gallon of water weighs approximately 8⅓ lb. (avoirdupois)
1 cu. ft. of water weighs 62½ lb.

Apothecaries' fluid measure is used by druggists.

$$
\begin{aligned}
60 \text{ minims (m.)} &= 1 \text{ fluid drachm} \\
8 \text{ fluid drachms} &= 1 \text{ fluid ounce} \\
16 \text{ fluid ounces} &= 1 \text{ pint} \\
8 \text{ pints} &= 1 \text{ gallon}
\end{aligned}
$$

1 gallon of the apothecaries' measure is the same as 1 wine gallon.

## DRY MEASURE

Dry measure is used for measuring grain, fruit, and produce.

$$
\begin{aligned}
2 \text{ pints (pt.)} &= 1 \text{ quart (qt.)} \\
8 \text{ quarts (qt.)} &= 1 \text{ peck (pk.)} \\
4 \text{ pecks (pk.)} &= 1 \text{ bushel (bu.)}
\end{aligned}
$$

The unit of dry measure is the bushel, which contains 2150.42 cubic inches, or a cylinder 18½ inches in diameter and 8 inches deep.

## MEASURES OF WEIGHT

Jewelers use troy weight, the druggist uses apothecary weight, and others use avoirdupois weight.

### TROY WEIGHT

$$
\begin{aligned}
24 \text{ grains (gr.)} &= 1 \text{ pennyweight (pwt.)} \\
20 \text{ pennyweights} &= 1 \text{ ounce (oz.)} \\
12 \text{ ounces} &= 1 \text{ pound (lb.)} \\
1 \text{ carat} &= 3.168 \text{ grains}
\end{aligned}
$$

The carat is used to measure diamonds. When used in connection with gold, it denotes fineness and means 1/24 part. Gold marked 14K (14 carat) means 14/24 of the weight is pure gold and 10/24 alloy.

### APOTHECARIES' WEIGHT

$$
\begin{aligned}
20 \text{ grains} &= 1 \text{ scruple (sc.)} \\
3 \text{ scruples} &= 1 \text{ dram (dr.)} \\
8 \text{ drams} &= 1 \text{ ounce (oz.)} \\
12 \text{ ounces} &= 1 \text{ pound (lb.)}
\end{aligned}
$$

16 ounces = 1 pound (lb.)
100 pounds = 1 hundredweight (cwt.)
2000 pounds = 1 ton (T.)
2240 pounds = 1 ton (long)

Coal is sold at the mines by the long ton. The government uses the long ton to compute the duty on goods taxed by the ton.

Other common measures:

A bushel (bu.) of wheat, potatoes, or peas weighs     60 pounds
A barrel (bbl.) of beef or pork weighs     200 pounds
A firkin of butter weighs     56 pounds
A barrel (bbl.) of flour weighs     196 pounds
A keg of nails weighs     100 pounds

## Reduction of Denominate Numbers

Add 5 gallons and 10 gallons. Answer: 15 gallons.

Add 5 yards and 10 feet. We cannot add these quantities because the units are not alike. However, we can change 5 yards to 15 feet (without changing the value) and then add 10 feet, which gives a total of 25 feet.

*Reduction* of denominate numbers means changing the unit or denomination without changing the value, as in the above example.

Principle: Denominations that are unlike cannot be added.

*Descending Reduction* means changing from a higher to a lower unit, as from yards to feet, from pounds to ounces, etc.

*Ascending Reduction* means changing from a lower to a higher unit, as from quarts to gallons.

## Reduction Descending

*Example:* Reduce 8 gallons, 3 quarts, 1 pint to pints.

8 gallons = 32 quarts     (4 quarts = 1 gallon)
Add     3 "
———
35 quarts
35 quarts = 70 pints     (2 pints = 1 quart)
Add     1 pint
———
Answer     71 pints

Reduce:

1. 150 rods to yards.
2. 15 square miles to acres.
3. 20 gallons to pints.
4. 30 ounces to drachms.
5. 10 ounces to pennyweight.
6. 12 bushels to quarts.
7. 20 ounces to drams (apothecaries' weight).
8. 15 bushels potatoes to pounds.
9. 5 bbl. flour to pounds.
10. 3 carats to grains.
11. 5 bu., 2 pks., 6 qts., to pints.
12. 4 oz., 15 pwt., 19 grains to grains.
13. 2 pts., 12 oz., 7 drams to drams.
14. 1 gal., 2 qts., 1 pt. to pints.
15. 4 cu. yd., 20 cu. ft. to cubic inches.
16. 15 sq. yds., 6 sq. ft., 130 sq. in. to square inches.
17. 6 miles, 800 yds., 50 ft. to feet.
18. 1 yr., 3 wks., 5 days to days.

## REDUCTION ASCENDING

*Example:* Change 57 pints to higher denominations. The denominations in ascending order are pints, quarts, gallons.

$$\begin{array}{r} 2\,|\,57 \\ \hline 4\,)\,28 \text{ qts. 1 pt.} \\ \hline 7 \text{ gal.} \end{array}$$

Answer:  7 gal. 1 pt.

## *Exercise 54*

Change to higher denominations:

1. 5000 in.
2. 400 sq. ft.
3. 3600 sq. rods.
4. 465 pts. (liquid measure).
5. 320 qts. (dry measure).
6. 560 grains (troy weight).

7.  3400 drachms (apothecaries' fluid measure).
8.  300 cu. ft.
9.  775 rods.
10. 250,000 ounces (avoirdupois).

## Addition and Subtraction of Denominate Numbers

To enhance terms arrange the units, writing the highest unit at the left. Remember, you can only combine like terms.

*Example:*    Addition

Subtraction

<table>
<tr><td>2 feet</td><td>8 inches</td></tr>
<tr><td>10 feet</td><td>6 inches</td></tr>
<tr><td>12 feet</td><td>14 inches =</td></tr>
<tr><td>13 feet</td><td>2 inches or</td></tr>
<tr><td>4 yd., 1 ft. 2 in.</td><td></td></tr>
</table>

|         |       |
|---------|-------|
| 5 lb.   | 8 oz. |
| − 3 lb. | 4 oz. |
| 2 lb.   | 4 oz. |

Sometimes in subtraction borrowing is necessary as in the following example:

|         |          |     |         |          |
|---------|----------|-----|---------|----------|
| 6 hr.   | 40 min.  | =   | 5 hr.   | 100 min. |
| − 4 hr. | 50 min.  | =   | − 4 hr. | 50 min.  |
|         |          |     | 1 hr.   | 50 min.  |

## Exercise 55

Add or subtract as indicated:

1.     3 gal. 1 qt. 1 pt.
     +5 gal. 2 qt. 1 pt.

2.     2 wk. 4 da.
     +7 wk. 3 da.

3.     2 yd. 1 ft.  9 in.
     4 yd. 2 ft.  6 in.
     +6 yd.       11 in.

4.     4 lb.  9 oz.
     6 lb. 13 oz.
     +10 lb.  5 oz.

5.     10 bu. 2 pk. 6 qt.
     +25 bu. 3 pk. 5 qt.

6.     41 yd. 1 ft.
     − 30 yd. 2 ft.

7.     10 hr. 15 min.
     − 5 hr. 30 min.

8.     19 cu. yd.  6 cu. ft.
     − 11 cu. yd.  2 cu. ft.

9.     35 lb.
     − 24 lb. 9 oz.

10.     7 wk. 3 da. 6 hr.
     − 2 wk. 5 da. 8 hr.

# MEASURING DISTANCES, AREAS, AND VOLUMES

In the last division the units of measurements were listed in connection with denominate numbers. Problems relating to measurement of distances, areas, and volumes will now be discussed.

## MEASURING DISTANCES

The distance from one point to another is measured by units listed in linear measure. The tailor uses a tape measure, which indicates inches and subdivisions of inches: the retailer uses a yardstick, the builder a steel tape (which is usually made in five ft., six ft., 50 ft., and 100 ft. lengths) and the surveyor measures by rods and chains. Custom and practice in each industry determine the basic unit of measurement. The symbol used to denote feet is ′ to the right of the number; thus, 5′ means five feet. The symbol for inches is ″. 10″ means ten inches. 5′10″ is read "Five feet ten inches."

*Problem 1:* Frank Falk wants to put a fence on the limits of his property, which borders on the public highway. The distance measures 500 feet. Find the cost, if the price is $7.95 a hundred lineal feet. Find the cost of posts at $.55 if the posts are 20 feet apart. Find the total cost of materials.

*Given:* The measurement of the fence, cost per hundred feet, spacing of posts, and cost per post.

*Find:* The cost of wire, of posts, and total cost of materials.

*Solution:*

1. $\dfrac{500}{100} \times \$7.95 = \$39.75$ cost of fence

2. $500 \div 20 = 25$

   $\dfrac{1}{\phantom{0}}$

   26 Posts required

3. $26 \times 55¢ = \$14.30$ Cost of posts
4. $\$39.75 + 14.30 = \$54.05$ Total cost

*Explanation:*

The price is quoted per hundred feet; therefore the length is divided by 100.

Posts are placed 20 ft. apart. An extra post is needed at the end.

Add cost of fence and posts.

## PERIMETERS

The *perimeter* is the distance around an area. The perimeter of a plot of ground is the total of the measurements of all sides. If the area is a square, the perimeter is the total of the four sides. If the area is a circle, the perimeter is the circumference.

The measurement of circumference is based on the formula D$\times$3.1416 =C or 2R$\times$3.1416.

D is the diameter of the circle.

C is the circumference.

R is the radius.

3.1416 is approximately 3 1/7. When exact measurements are not required, the work may be shortened by using 3 1/7 in place of 3.1416.

The symbol $\pi$ (read "pie") is frequently used in place of the factor 3.1416 in expressing formulas for circular measurements.

*Problem 2:* What is the distance around a circular reservoir, if the radius is 750 feet?

*Given:* Radius of reservoir.

*Find:* The circumference.

*Solution:*

*Explanation:*

1.   2$\times$750$\times$3.1416=4712.4 feet     Apply the formula 2R$\times$3.1416.

*Problem 3:* What is the radius of a circle whose circumference is 2827.44 feet?

*Given:* Circumference of circle.

*Find:* The radius.

*Solution:*

*Explanation:*

2827.44 divided by (2$\times$3.1416) =450$'$

*Proof:* 2$\times$450$'\times$3.1416=2827.44

If the radius were one foot, the circumference would be 2$\times$3.1416 which equals 6.2832 (according to the formula given above).

Since the circumference is 2827.44, the length of the radius is determined by dividing by the circumference of a circle whose radius is one foot.

In measurement problems the geometric figures commonly used include the following:

A *rectangle* is a figure bounded by four straight lines and having four right angles.

A *square* is a rectangle whose sides are all equal.

A *triangle* is a figure having three sides.

A *circle* is a figure bounded by a curved line every point of which is equally distant from the center.

A *radius* is the distance from the center to the circumference.

*Diameter* is any line that passes through the center and whose terminals are in the circumference of a circle.

*Altitude* refers to the height of a figure.

## PROBLEMS

1. At 5¢ a foot, what will it cost to paint a rail which encloses a rectangular field 450′ long and 210′ wide?

2. How many rolls of chicken wire are required to enclose a rectangular yard 165 feet long, 210 feet wide? There are 100 feet to a roll and the dealer does not sell less than a roll.

3. What is the distance around a race track, if the diameter is 843 feet?

4. How many feet of moulding will be required for four rectangular rooms whose measurements are 13′ 6″×11′ 4″; 18′ 2″×14′ 6″; 14′ 4″× 15′ 6″ and 12′ 6″×16′.

5. The rear wheels of a wagon are 3′ in diameter. If they make 1000 revolutions, how far has the wagon traveled?

## MEASURING AREAS

### RECTANGLES

Study the terms:

The *base* is the horizontal line at the bottom of a figure.

The *altitude* is the vertical line or the height of the figure.

The area is the surface of a figure. Lateral surfaces are the areas of the sides of a figure like the walls of a building. The area of Figure 5 is 15 sq.′. Square units are used to measure areas. The tables should be reviewed. (See page 774)

FIGURE 5

The area of a rectangle is found by multiplying base×altitude. The formula is b×a=area. In Figure 5 the base and altitude are 5 and 3 units each; therefore the area=3×5 or 15 sq.′.

*Problem 4:* Find the cost to carpet a room which is 14′ wide and 18′ long. The carpet is 36″ wide and is laid lengthwise.

*Given:* Length and width of room.

Width of carpet and cost per yard.

*Find:* Cost to carpet the room.

*Solution:* 1. $14' \div 3' = 4\frac{2}{3}$ or 5 strips.

2. $5 \times \dfrac{18}{3} = 30$ yds.

3. $\$3.75 \times 30 = \$112.50$ Cost.

*Explanation:* 1. Since the carpet is laid lengthwise, we divide the width of the room by the width of the carpet to find the number of strips. (Dealers do not sell fractions of a width, therefore the nearest number is 5 strips.)

2. Each strip is 18′ long. Divide by 3 to change to yards.

3. Multiply the yardage by the unit price to find cost.

## TRIANGLES

The area of the rectangle ABCD$=4'' \times 2''$ or 8 sq. in. By drawing a

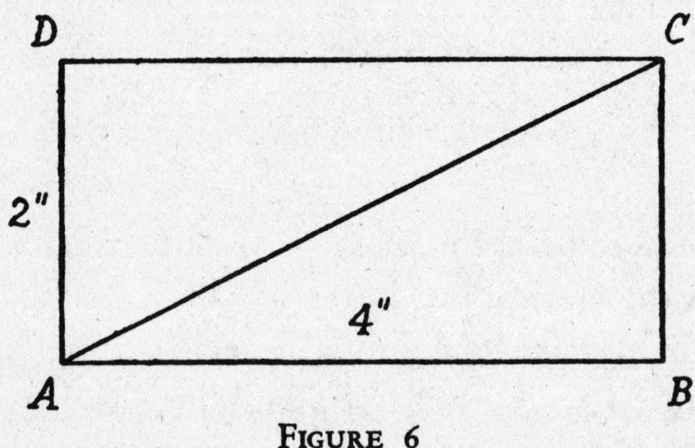


FIGURE 6

diagonal AC, we divide the area in half; therefore the triangle ABC or ADC$=\frac{1}{2}$ of the area of the rectangle.

The formula for computing areas of triangles therefore is

$$\frac{b \times a}{2} = A$$

b—base

a—altitude

A—area

*Problem 5:* The gable end of a house (shaped like an inverted V) has a base of 20′ 3″ and a height of 2 yds. What is the area?

*Given:* Base and altitude

*Find:* Area of triangle

*Solution:*

1. 20′ 3″=20¼′
   2 yds.=6′

2. $\dfrac{20\frac{1}{4}'\times 6'}{2}=60\frac{3}{4}$ sq. ft.

*Explanation: 1.* Reduce all measurements to a common unit. In this case our unit is feet. Change 3″ to a ¼′ and 2 yds. to 6′.

2. Apply the formula to find the area of triangles. ½b✕a.

## Circular Measurements

### CIRCLES

The formula to find the area of a circle is 3.1416✕square of the radius. The square of a number is found by multiplying the number by itself. The square of 4 is 4✕4 or 16. The square of 10 is 100, etc.

*Problem 6:* A tank has a diameter of 30″. What is the area of the cover?

*Given:* Diameter of tank
*Find:* Area of cover

*Solution: 1.* ½ of 30″=15″ Radius
2. 3.1416✕15″✕15″=707.86 sq.″

*Explanation: 1.* To find the radius we take ½ of the diameter.

2. Apply the formula for finding the area of a circle. The radius is repeated as a factor to square it.

### CYLINDERS

Figure 7 is a cylinder with a diameter of 1″ and an altitude of 1½″. The lateral surface is a rectangle. This is obvious when we cut the cylinder vertically and unroll it as in Figure 8. The diameter is 1″, therefore, the circumference of the cylinder is 1✕3.1416. What is the base of the rectangle? The formula for the area of a rectangle is b✕a. The formula for the

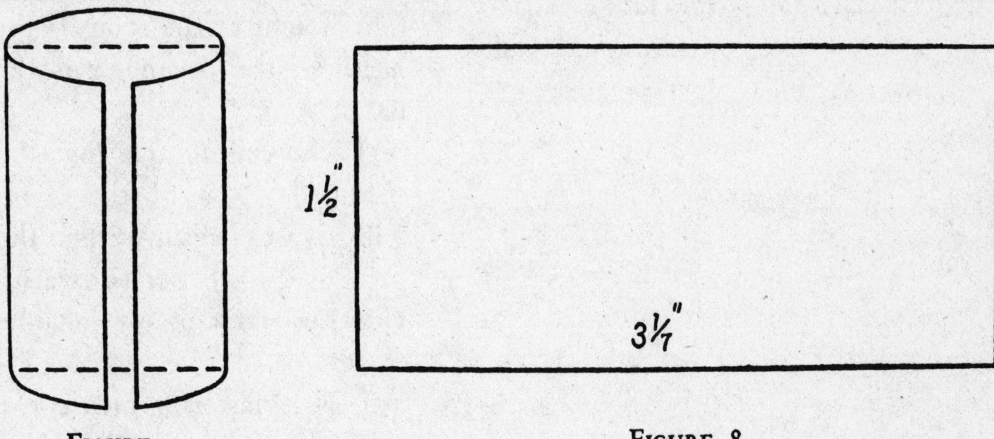


FIGURE 7     FIGURE 8

lateral area of a cylinder is c$\times$a. To find the base of a cylinder use the formula of a circle. 2R$\times$3.1416 or D$\times$3.1416=C.

*Problem 7:* Find the cost of painting the sides of a water tank measuring 6′ in diameter and 12′ in height at 40¢ a sq. yd.
*Given:* Diameter, altitude, price per sq. yd.
*Find:* Area in sq. yds. and cost of painting.

*Solution:*
1. 6′=2 yds.
   12′=4 yds.
2. 2$\times$3.1416=6.2832 yds. Base
3. 4$\times$6.2832=25.1328 sq. yds. Area
4. 40¢$\times$25.1328=\$10.05. Cost

*Explanation:* 1. Change feet to yds. because the price is given in yds.

2. The formula to find the circumference is D$\times$3.1416.

3. Find the area of the lateral surface by formula b$\times$a =A.

4. The area and price have the same unit, viz., sq. yds.; therefore, multiply the area by the unit price to find the cost.

*Problem 8:* Find the cost of plastering the walls and ceiling of a room 18′ x 15′ and 11′ high @ 30¢ sq. yd. (no allowance for openings).
*Given:* Length, width, height, and cost per sq. yd.
*Find:* Areas of walls and ceiling and cost of plastering.

*Solution:*
1. 2(18′+15′)=66′=22 yds.
2. $22\times\dfrac{11}{3}=80\frac{2}{3}$ sq. yds. Area of four walls.
3. $\dfrac{18\times15}{9}=30$ sq. yds. Area of ceiling
4. $80\frac{2}{3}+30=110\frac{2}{3}$ sq. yds. Area of ceiling and walls.
5. $110\frac{2}{3}\times.30=\$33.20$.

*Explanation:* 1. To find the perimeter, we add the length and width and multiply by 2. The four walls measure 66′ or 22 yds.

2. The formula to find the area of a rectangle is b$\times$a. The height of the room is the altitude; the perimeter is the base.

3. The ceiling area must be included. l$\times$w of the room will give the result. Since the price is quoted per yd. we divide the result by 9 to change to yds.

4. The plastering area is the total of the 4 walls and ceiling.

5. Multiply the total area by
the unit price to find total cost
of plastering.

**PROBLEMS**

1. How many yards in the 4 walls and ceiling of a room 17′×14′×9′.

2. The ridge of a gabled roof is 64′ and the rafters are 29′ 8″. How many bundles of shingles are required to cover the roof if each bundle covers 100 sq.′? (Dealers do not sell a fraction of a bundle.)

3. Find the cost of painting the sides of a water tank if the diameter is 10′ and the height is 15′, and the cost 30¢ sq. yd.

4. Find the cost of carpeting the room mentioned in problem 1, allowing for a border of 1′ on each side. The carpet is laid lengthwise, is 1 yd. wide, and costs $3.50 yd.

5. Find the cost of covering with tile a circular area with a diameter of 12′ @ $1.25 a sq. yd.

6. Find the cost of painting the walls and ceilings of the following rooms and corridors @ 25¢ a sq. yd., no allowance being made for windows and doors: 20′×15′; 12′ 6″×15′; 12′ 6″×9′; 30′×6′. The height of all the rooms is 9′.

7. Find the cost of carpeting rooms in problem 6 if the carpet is 1 yd. wide, is laid lengthwise, and costs $3.85 a yd.

## SQUARE ROOT

What is a square? How many square feet in a square with sides 5 feet long? What is the length of a square with an area of 25 square feet?

When a number contains 2 equal factors it is a perfect square. 25 is a perfect square because the two factors are 5 and 5. The process of breaking down a number into equal factors is called "extracting the square root." The square root of 100 is 10. Proof: 10×10=the number.

### How to Compute Square Root

*Problem 1:* Find the square root of 729.

*Solution:*

$$
\begin{array}{r}
2\ \ 7 \\
\overline{2)7{,}29} \\
4 \\
\overline{47)3{,}29} \\
3{,}29 \\
\hline
\end{array}
$$

Proof: 27×27=729

1. Beginning at the right end of the number, group the digits by pairs. The quotient will have one digit for each group in the dividend. There are two groups: the quotient will have two digits.

2. The largest perfect square contained in seven is four. The square root of 4 is 2. Write 2 in the quotient. Subtract the square of 2, which is 4, from the partial dividend, 7: the remainder is 3.

3. Bring down the next pair to get the next partial dividend: result 329. The trial divisor is found by doubling the partial quotient 2: answer 4. This means that the trial divisor will be forty something because the partial quotient is in the 10 column. The divisor will be somewhere between 40 and 49. Forty something goes into 329 approximately 7 times. Write 7 in the quotient and trial divisor.

4. Multiply the last digit in the quotient, 7, by the trial divisor, 47 and deduct the result from the last remainder. The square root of 729 is 27.

## To Find the Square Root of a Number Which Is Not a Perfect Square

*Problem 2:* Find the square root of 800 and carry it out to 2 decimal places.

*Solution:*

```
          2 8. 2 8
       2)8,00.00,00
         4
     48)4,00
        3,84
    562)  16,00
         11,24
   5648)  4,76,00
         4,51,84
           24,16
```

*Explanation:*

1. Beginning at the decimal point and moving to the right and left of the decimal point, group the digits by pairs as in the preceding example. Note that two pairs of zeros were added after the decimal point because we are required to carry out the answer to two decimal places.

2. Proceed as in the first illustration. Remember to double the partial quotient each time to find the trial divisor. Thus the first partial quotient is 2. Therefore the following trial divisor is 4. The second partial quotient is 28; therefore the trial divisor is 56. The third partial quotient is 28.2; therefore the partial divisor is 564.

## Application of Square Root to Triangles

Square root is used in connection with problems based on triangles.

A right triangle is one which has one right angle. Figure 9 illustrates a right-angle triangle. The base is four inches, the altitude 3 inches. The side

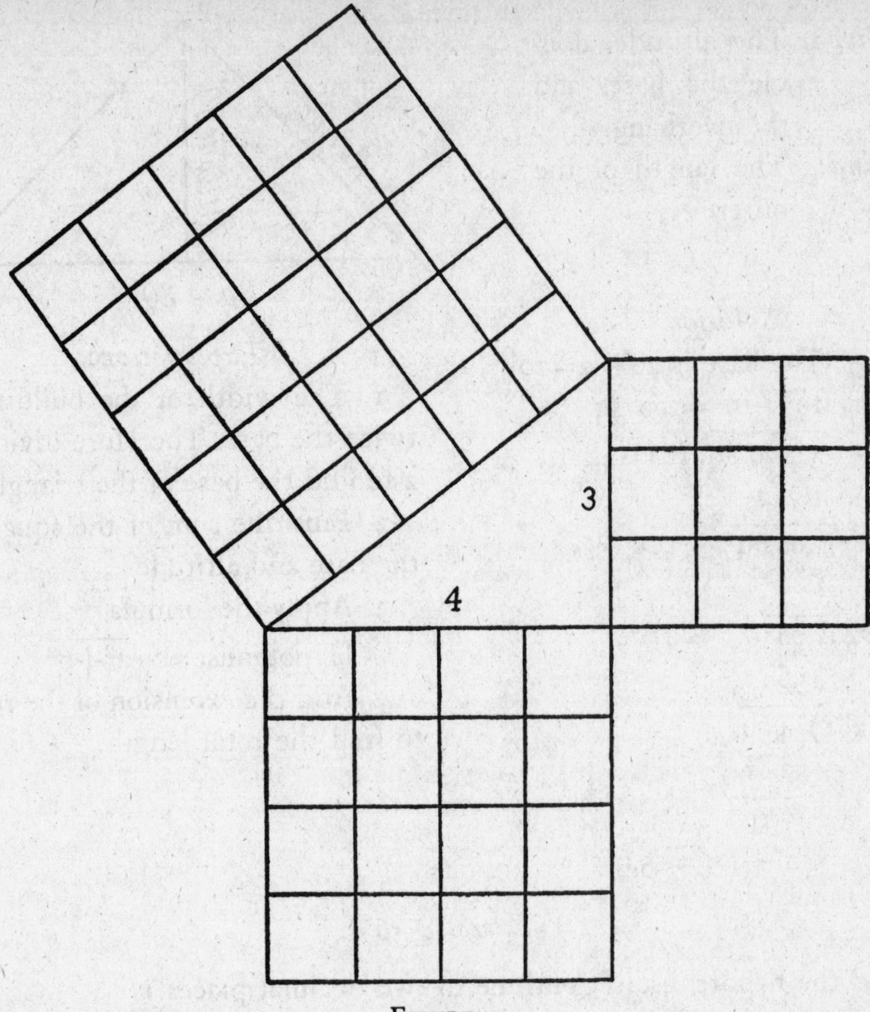


FIGURE 9

opposite the right angle is called a *hypotenuse*. In Figure 9 the length of the hypotenuse can be determined by the following method:

1.  Square the base: $4 \times 4 = 16$.
2.  Square the altitude: $3 \times 3 = 9$.
3.  The square of the hypotenuse is equal to the sum of the squares of the base and altitude. The relationship among base, altitude and hypotenuse is expressed briefly thus: $A^2 + B^2 = H^2$ or $\sqrt{A^2 + B^2} = H$. In this formula A means altitude, B means base, H means hypotenuse. The sign $\sqrt{\phantom{-}}$ means square root.
4.  Applying the formula, we get the following result: $16 + 9 = 25$ square inches. To find the length of the hypotenuse we take the square root of 25 which is 5.

*Problem 3:* The distance from the ridge to the base of the gable is 10′ and the building is 20′ wide. The rafters extend 1.5′. What is the length of the rafters?

*Given:* The altitude, double the base, and the overhang.

*Find:* The length of the rafter.

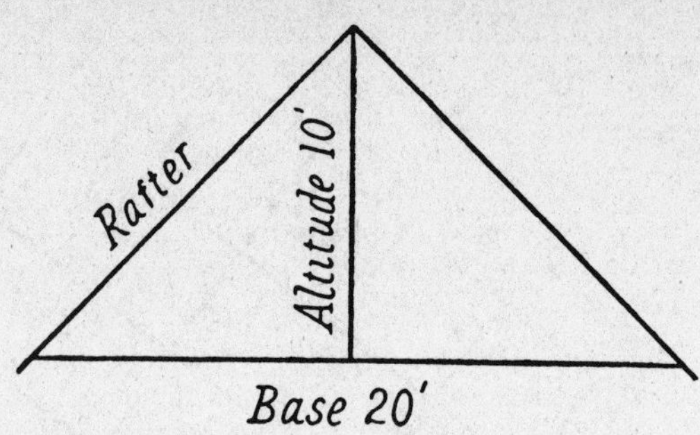


*Solution:*

1. The base is $20' \div 2 = 10'$
2. $10^2 + 10^2 = 200$ sq. ft.
3. $\sqrt{200}$ sq. ft. $= 14.1$ ft.

$$
\begin{array}{r}
1\ 4.1 \\
\overline{)2,00.00} \\
1 \\
\hline
24)1\ 00 \\
96 \\
\hline
281)\ 4\ 00 \\
2\ 81 \\
\hline
1\ 19
\end{array}
$$

4. $14.1' + 1.5' = 15.6'$

*Explanation:*

1. The width of the building is twice the base. Therefore divide by 2 to find the base of the triangle.

2. Find the sum of the square of the base and altitude.

3. Apply the formula

$$\text{Hypotenuse} = \sqrt{a^2 + b^2}$$

4. Add the extension of the rafter to find the total length.

## Exercise 56

Find the hypotenuse: (Continue to two decimal places.)

|    | Base | Altitude |    |    | Base | Altitude |
|----|------|----------|----|----|------|----------|
| 1. | 14″  | 7″       |    | 3. | 12′  | 6′       |
| 2. | 20′  | 25′      |    | 4. | 12′  | 8′       |

Find the squares:

| 5. | 42  | 7. | 75  |
|----|-----|----|-----|
| 6. | 105 | 8. | 125 |

Find the square root:

| 9.  | 6.869   | 11. | 42.25   |
|-----|---------|-----|---------|
| 10. | 375.769 | 12. | 10.3684 |

# MEASURING VOLUME

What is the difference between a square and a cube? How many dimensions does the square have? the cube?

To measure volumes or solids we must know length, width, and breadth or thickness. The method of measuring rectangular solids, cylinders, and cones will be explained in this section. Study the following terms:

A rectangular solid is a solid that has six rectangular surfaces like a brick.

A cylinder is a solid that is bounded by two circles parallel to each other and a uniformly curved surface, like a circular smokestack.

A cone is a solid that is bounded by one circle and a lateral surface which tapers uniformly to a point like the top of a witch's hat.

Use the following formulas to find volume or capacity:

| Solid | Formula |
|---|---|
| Rectangular Solids | Length$\times$width$\times$thickness |
| Cylinder | Area of circle$\times$height |
| Cone | ⅓ of area of circle$\times$height |

Units commonly used in business are listed below:

A *cord* of wood is a pile 8′ long, 4′ wide, and 4′ high. This equals 128 cubic feet.

A *foot* of lumber, or board foot, is a board 1′ long, 12″ wide, and 1″ thick. Boards less than 1″ in thickness are measured as boards 1″ in thickness.

A *perch* of stone is a mass 16½′ long, 1½′ wide, and 1′ high. This equals 24¾ cubic ft. (In some areas, the perch contains 16½ cu. ft.)

In measuring stone work, such as walls of buildings, the outside of the wall is measured for length. This is called the *girth*.

To compute *capacity of tanks,* we use the volume of 1 gallon which equals 231 cu. in. One cubic foot contains approximately 7.48 gal.

*Problem 1:* How many gallons does a rectangular vat contain which measures 6′$\times$4′ 2″$\times$10′?

*Given:* Measurements of a rectangular vat.

*Find:* Capacity in gallons.

| Solution: | Explanation: |
|---|---|
| 1.  $6' \times \dfrac{25'}{6} \times 10' = 250$ cu. ft. | 1. Formula to find volume is l$\times$w$\times$t. |
| 2.  $250' \times 1728 = 432,000$ cu. in. | 2. Change cu. ft. to cu. in. |
| 3.  $432,000 \div 231 = 1870$ gallons. | 3. A gallon equals 231 cu. in. Divio volume by 231 to find number of gallons. |

*Problem 2:* How many gallons does a cylindrical tank contain, which measures 10′ in diameter and 6′ in height?

| Solution: | Explanation: |
|---|---|
| 1.  $\dfrac{10'}{2} = 5'$ | 1. To find the radius, take ½ of the diameter. |
| 2.  $3.1416 \times 25 \times 6 = 471.24$ cu. ft. | 2. The area of the circle is 3.1416 |

3. $471.24 \times 1728 = 814{,}302.72$ cu. in.
4. $814{,}302.72 \div 231 = 3526.85$ gal.
5. $.85 \times 4 = 3.4$ qts.
6. $.4 \times 2 = .8$ pts.

Ans. 3526 gals. 3 qts. .8 pts.

$\times 25$. The formula to find the volume of a cylinder is area of circle $\times$ height.

3. To change cu. ft. to cu. in. multiply volume by 1728.

4. 1 gal. 231 cu. in. To find the number of gallons in the cylinder divide its volume in cu. in. by 231.

5. and 6. Reduce gallons to qts. and pts.

*Problem 3:* How many cu. ft. are there in a cone whose diameter is 8' and whose altitude is 15'?

*Given:* Measurements of the diameter and base of a cone.

*Find:* Volume in cu. ft.

*Solution:*

1. $8' \div 2 = 4'$

2. $\dfrac{3.1416 \times 16' \times 15}{3} = 251.328$ cu. ft.

*Explanation:*

1. To find the radius divide the diameter by 2.

2. The radius squared is 16. The formula to find the volume of a cone is ⅓ of area of circle $\times$ height. The area of the circle is $3.1416 \times 4^2$ or $3.1416 \times 16 \div 3$.

*Problem 4:* A pile of wood contains 12 cords. If it is 4' wide and 8' high, how long is it?

*Given:* Width, height, and volume.

*Find:* Length.

*Solution:*

1. $12 \times 128 = 1{,}536$ cu. ft. vol.

2. $4' \times 8' = 32$ sq. ft.

3. $1536 \div 32 = 48'$ long.

*Explanation:*

1. One cord equals 128 cu. ft. To find the volume of the pile multiply 5 cords by 128.

2. To find the area of a rectangle, use the formula base $\times$ altitude.

3. If the length were 1' the pile would contain 32 cu. ft. Since the pile contains 1536 cu. ft. the length is equal to the quotient of $1536 \div 32$.

$1536 \div 128$ cu. ft. $= 12$ cords

*Proof:* $4' \times 8' \times 32' = 1536$ cu. ft.

*Problem 5:* Find the cost of 36 planks, $3'' \times 10'' \times 16'$ @ $36 per M (thousand feet). (3 in. in thickness, 10 in. in width, 16 ft. in length).

*Given:* The number and measurements of planks and the cost per thousand feet.

*Find:* The cost.

<table>
<tr><td>Solution:</td><td>Explanation:</td></tr>
</table>

1. $$\frac{36\times3\times10\times16}{12}=1440 \text{ board ft.}$$

1. There are 36 pieces. One board ft. is a board 1 ft. wide, 1 ft. long, 1 in. thick. We multiply the number of pieces by the thickness, width, and length of each piece. Since the width is expressed in inches, we divide by 12 to change it to feet.

2. $1440\div1000\times36=51.84$.

2. Since the price is quoted at $36 per M, we divide 1440 by 1000 to find how many thousands we have. Then we multiply by the price.

NOTE: When the thickness is not mentioned, we assume it is 1″ or less and omit it in the calculation.

The width of lumber is always expressed in inches, therefore we always divide it by 12 to change to feet.

## Exercise 57

Find the approximate number of gallons in the following vats:

| | | | | | |
|---|---|---|---|---|---|
| 1. | $8'\times8'\times4'$ | 3. | $4'\times6'\times8'$ | 5. | $2'4''\times2'4''\times6'$ |
| 2. | $10'\times5'\times6'$ | 4. | $5'3''\times4'8''\times9'$ | 6. | $10'\times8'\times5'$ |

Find the approximate number of gallons in the following cylindrical tanks:

| | *Diameter* | *Height* | | *Diameter* | *Height* |
|---|---|---|---|---|---|
| 7. | $8'$ | $8'$ | 10. | $2'$ | $8'$ |
| 8. | $10'$ | $8'$ | 11. | $6'$ | $12'$ |
| 9. | $4'$ | $6'$ | 12. | $1'6''$ | $6'$ |

Find the volume of the following cones:

| | *Diameter* | *Altitude* | | *Diameter* | *Altitude* |
|---|---|---|---|---|---|
| 13. | $4''$ | $9''$ | 16. | $4'$ | 3 yds. |
| 14. | $4'$ | $10'$ | 17. | $3'$ | $8'$ |
| 15. | $6'$ | $14'$ | 18. | $14'$ | $12'$ |

Find the number of cords in the following piles of wood:

| | | | | | |
|---|---|---|---|---|---|
| 19. | $20'\times4'\times4'$ | 21. | $32'\times4'\times6'$ | 23. | $12'\times4'\times6'$ |
| 20. | $12'\times8'\times4'$ | 22. | $16'\times6'\times8'$ | 24. | $18'\times6'\times10'$ |

# SETS

<u>Basic Set Theory</u>

1a. A set — By a <u>set</u> we mean a collection of objects or things called <u>elements</u>. For example—all of the students in your classroom (is) a set and each student is an element of that set of students in your classroom. All General Motors cars (is) the set of General Motors cars and each General Motors car is an element of that set. We have just defined two sets of elements and each set is considered "the universal set."

1b. The symbol used for a set is braces $\{\ \ \}$. The elements within a set are represented by· numbers, letters of the alphabet or other designs. A capital letter of the alphabet is usually used to represent the set once it has been defined.

*Example:*     Set A = $\{2, 4, 6, 8\}$     D = $\{*1, *2, *3\}$
                  B = $\{a, b, c\}$

Other symbols used for sets or subsets are:

brackets [     ], parentheses (     ), or the bar ———— (placed over members of a set as $\overline{a,\ b,\ c}$.

Cardinality — The <u>cardinality</u> of a set gives the number of elements in a set. If I should ask you the <u>cardinality</u> of the set A= $\{2, 4, 6, 8\}$ , the reply would be 4 because there are 4 elements in the set A. Therefore, the "cardinality" of set A is 4. The "cardinality" of the set B= $\{a, b, c\}$ is 3 because there are 3 elements in B.

*Exercise* 58

What is the cardinality of each of the following sets:

(1) $\{2, 6, 8\}$      (2) $\{1, 3, 7, 4, 6\}$      (3) $\{a, b, c, d\}$

(4) $\{21, 26\}$      (5) $\{*, *, *, *, *, *\}$

Check your answers with the key.

2a. A subset — If we designated a set of elements by S= $\{3, 5, 7, 9, 11\}$ , then the set of elements T= $\{5, 7, 11\}$ is a <u>subset</u> of S, if every element of T is also an element of S. The set of all convertible General Motors cars is a "subset" of the set of all General Motors cars.

2b. The symbol for "subset" is represented by $\subset$ , T $\subset$ S which is read T is contained in S or T is a subset of S.

*Exercise* 59

Write a subset of each of the following sets:

(1) $\{13, 15, 17, 19\}$      (2) $\{d, e, f, g\}$      (3) $\{a, c, d\}$

(4) $\{a, b, c, d, e\}$      (5) $\{27, 28, 29, 30, 31\}$

Check your answers with the key.

## <u>Set Operations and Their Symbols</u>

3a. Intersection — Consider two sets:

$$E = \{2, 3, 5, 7, 11\} \quad \text{and} \quad F. = \{1, 3, 5, 7, 9\}$$

We can form a new set by selecting the elements which are common to the two sets. For example, the numbers 3, 5, and 7 are elements of both sets, therefore they are said to be common to the two sets. This new set consisting of the common elements is called the "intersection" of sets E and F. The symbol for "intersection" is $\cap$ , thus E $\cap$ F =3, 5, 7.

Other examples are:

(a)　　A = $\{1, 2, 3, 4\}$　　　　B = $\{0, 2, 4, 6\}$

　　　　A $\cap$ B = $\{2, 4\}$

(b)　　C = $\{q, x, y, z\}$　　　　D = $\{w, x, y, z\}$

　　　　C $\cap$ D = $\{x, y, z\}$

Another condition can occur when we find the "intersection" of two sets.

Consider the sets:　　G = $\{1, 6, 8\}$　　and　　H = $\{2, 4, 7\}$

From our definition of intersection we know that an intersection is formed from those elements common to both sets. In sets G and H we can clearly see that there are no elements common to both sets. So, these sets are said to be "disjoint" sets and the intersection of two "disjoint" sets yields what is known as an "empty" or "null" set.

*Example:*　　　　G $\cap$ H = $\{\quad\}$ ____ empty set

Word approach:

Bob, Dick, John, Frank, and Pete are on the school's hockey team. (H)

Carl, Dick, Ed, Frank, and Sam are on the basketball team. (B)

Which boys are on both teams?

Dick and Frank are.

H $\cap$ B = Dick and Frank

3b.　Union — Consider the two sets, G= $\{1, 6, 8\}$ and H= $\{2, 4, 7\}$. Another new set can be formed from G and H by selecting all the different elements which occur in either set G or H or both. This new set is called the "union" of sets G and H, written G $\cup$ H.

Thus G $\cup$ H= $\{1, 2, 3, 6, 7, 8\}$ and is the second set operation that we have discussed.

Another example of the union of two sets is:

Consider the two sets: A= $\{$a, b, c, d, e$\}$ and B= $\{$c, e, g, i$\}$ , then
A $\cup$ B= $\{$a, b, c, d, e, g, i$\}$

*Exercise* 60

Find the union of the following sets:

(1)  E= $\{$a, b, c, d$\}$          (2)  C= $\{$w, x, y, z$\}$
       and                                  and
     F= $\{$c, d, e$\}$                D= $\{$t, u, v, w$\}$

     E $\cup$ F=                       C $\cup$ D=


(3)  A= $\{$1, 2, 3, 4, 5$\}$     (4)  I= $\{$27, 29, 31$\}$
       and                                  and
     B= $\{$0, 2, 4$\}$               K= $\{$26, 28, 30, 32$\}$

     A $\cup$ B=                       I $\cup$ K=


(5)  O= $\{$11, 12, 15, 16, 19, 20$\}$
                    and
     P= $\{$9, 10, 13, 14, 16, 17$\}$

     O $\cup$ P=

Check your answers with the key.


## Subsets of the Real Number System

1a. <u>The set of natural numbers</u> — The numbers 1, 2, 3, 4 and all
    numbers that follow, without including fractions, form the set of
    <u>natural numbers</u>. Thus, 2, 23, 345 and 12,471 are examples of
    <u>natural numbers</u>. In symbolic set notation, the set of <u>natural</u>
    <u>numbers</u> = 1, 2, 3, 4, . . . . The three dots after the number 4
    in the set notation represent all of the numbers that follow 4,
    based on the pattern established with 1, 2, 3 and 4, in a counting
    sequence. With this in mind, then, the symbolic set notation
    representing the set of <u>whole numbers</u> defined in an earlier chapter
    is: the set of <u>whole numbers</u> = 0, 1, 2, 3, 4, . . . . Now, from

this we can clearly see, based on our definition of a <u>subset</u>, that the set of <u>natural</u> <u>numbers</u> is a <u>subset</u> of the set of <u>whole</u> <u>numbers</u>.

2a. <u>The set of integers</u> — Let us now become familiar with a <u>number line</u>. To this point we have only considered those sets of numbers that begin with the number 0 and 1:

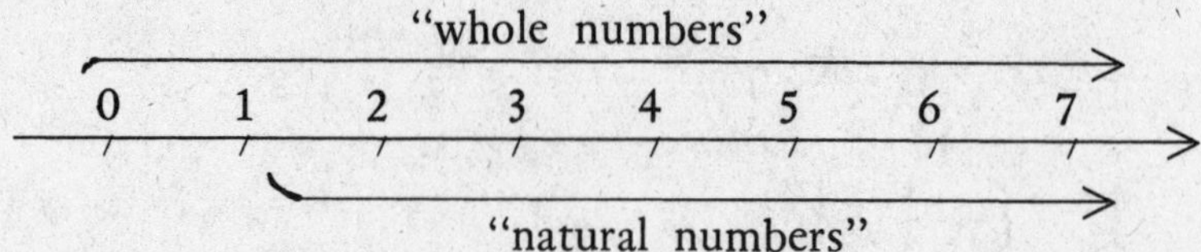


To perform the operation of subtraction with $5 - 2$, we would get as a <u>difference</u>, 3, which belongs to our previously defined sets of number systems. But to perform the operation of subtraction with $2 - 5$, we would no longer get a member of one of our previously defined sets of number systems as a difference. Instead, our difference of $2 - 5$ would be $-3$ (negative 3). This then calls for the need to extend our number line and system to include <u>negative</u> numbers.

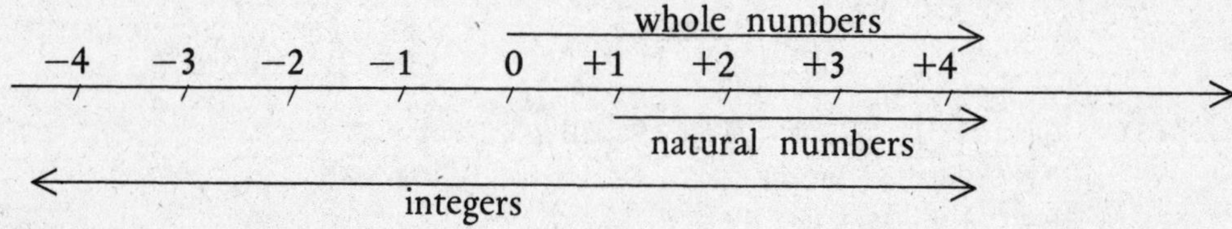


When this is done, the new set of numbers is referred to as the set of <u>integers</u>. In symbolic set notation,

the set of <u>integers</u>= . . ., −4, −3, −2, −1, 0, 1, 2, 3, 4, . . . ,

and includes all negative numbers, without fractions, <u>all positive numbers</u>, without fractions, and the 0. So from this we can clearly see that the set of <u>whole</u> <u>numbers</u> and the set of <u>natural</u> <u>numbers</u> are both <u>subsets</u> of the set of <u>integers</u>. When writing one of the integers, it is a help to write negative integers ⁻5 , etc. and the positive integers ⁺5 , with the signs raised to distinguish the notation for integers from that for the operations of subtraction and addition.

2b. Addition — The operation of addition with integers can be interpreted simply as the answer to the question. Starting at ⁺2 , what is the final position of a movement of ⁻5 ? (A negative movement is a movement from right to left and a positive movement is from left to right.)

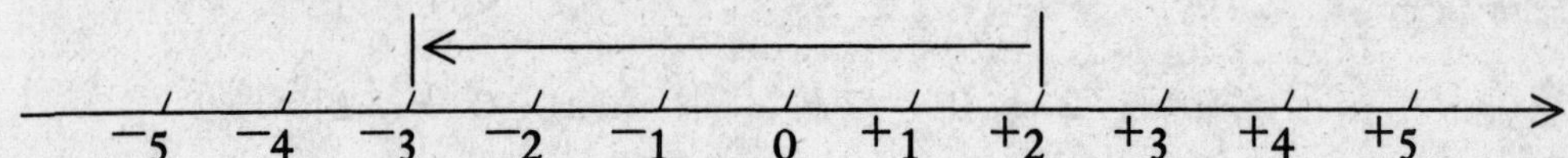

$$^+2 \; + \; ^-5 \; = \; ^-3$$



Other examples are:

(a)     $^-2 \; + \; ^-5 \; = \; ^-7$



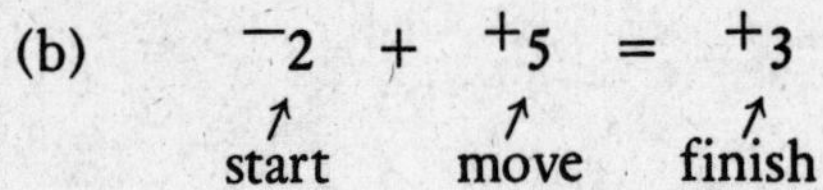

(b)     $^-2 \; + \; ^+5 \; = \; ^+3$



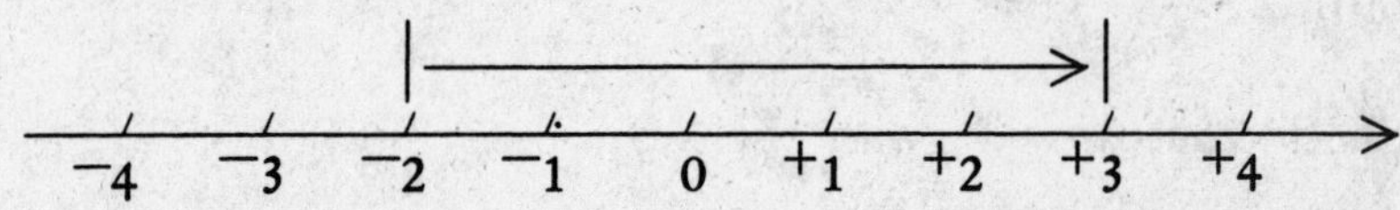

(c)     $^+2 \; + \; ^+5 \; = \; ^+7$



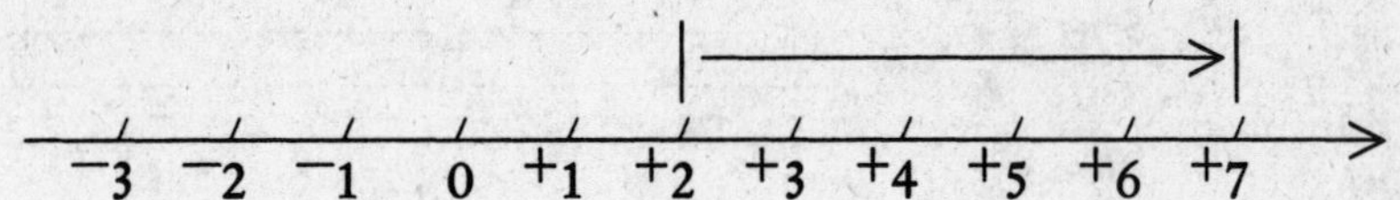

The <u>identity</u> element for addition is 0. This element is sometimes called the <u>additive</u> <u>identity</u> or the <u>zero</u> element; since adding it to a number leaves the number unchanged.

*Examples:*     (a)   $^-2 + 0 = {}^-2$       (c)   $0 + {}^-2 = {}^-2$

                 (b)   $^+2 + 0 = {}^+2$       (d)   $0 + {}^+2 = {}^+2$

The <u>inverse</u> element for addition is any element which, when added to another element, will yield a sum of 0 or the <u>identity</u> element for addition.

*Examples:*  (a) $^-2 + {}^+2 = 0$    (b) $^+6 + {}^-6 = 0$    (c) $^-7 + {}^+7 = 0$

Therefore, adding any number to its inverse results in 0.

## Exercise 61

Perform the operation of addition with the following integers:

(1)   $^-5 + {}^-4 =$       (2)   $^+10 + {}^-2 =$      (3)   $^+5 + {}^-4 =$

(4)   $^-7 + {}^+7 =$       (5)   $^+3 + {}^-1 =$       (6)   $^-8 + {}^+9 =$

(7)   $^-1 + {}^+7 =$       (8)   $^+8 + {}^-4 =$       (9)   $0 + {}^-2 =$

(10)   $^-2 + {}^-3 =$

Check your answers with the key.

2c.   Subtraction — The operation of subtraction with integers is the inverse of the operation of addition and can be interpreted as the answer to the question: Starting at $^-5$, how many positions must I move to get a final position of $^+2$?

$$^+2 - {}^-5 = {}^+7$$

finish   start   move

moved $^+7$ positions (left to right is +)

$$^-5 \quad {}^-4 \quad {}^-3 \quad {}^-2 \quad {}^-1 \quad 0 \quad {}^+1 \quad {}^+2 \quad {}^+3 \quad {}^+4$$

Other examples are:

(a)  $^-2 - ^-5 = ^+3$

    finish   start   move

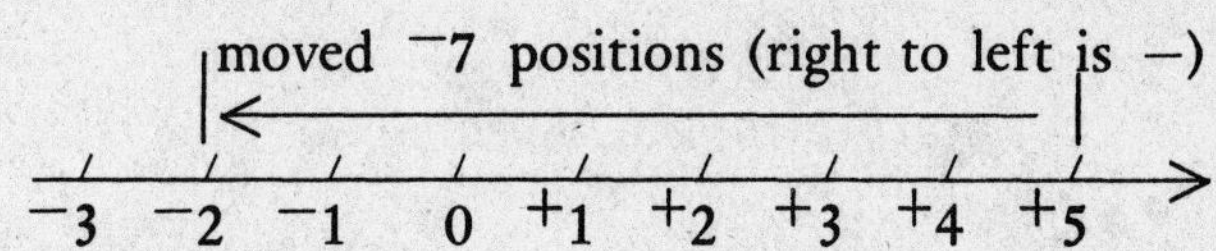


(b)  $^-2 - ^+5 = ^-7$

    finish   start   move



(c)  $^+2 - ^+5 = ^-3$

    finish   start   move



**Exercise 62**

Perform the operation of subtraction with the following integers:

(1)  $^-3 - ^-7 =$     (2)  $^+3 - ^+7 =$     (3)  $^-8 - ^+2 =$

(4)  $^-8 - ^-2 =$     (5)  $^-2 - ^+8 =$     (6)  $^+2 - ^+8 =$

(7)  $^-2 - ^-8 =$     (8)  $^-5 - ^+3 =$     (9)  $^+5 - ^-3 =$

(10)  $^-3 - ^-8 =$

Check your answers with the key.

2d. Multiplication — The operation of multiplication with integers differs from the operation of multiplication with whole numbers in only one respect and that is the sign of the product. The procedure is simplified if we remember this principle — When the multiplier and multiplicand have like signs, the product is always positive and when the multiplier and multiplicand have different signs, the product is always negative.

*Examples:*

$$\text{(a)} \quad {}^-2 \cdot {}^+5 = {}^-10$$

$$\text{(b)} \quad {}^+2 \cdot {}^-5 = {}^-10$$

$$\text{(c)} \quad {}^-2 \cdot {}^-5 = {}^+10$$

$$\text{(d)} \quad {}^+2 \cdot {}^+5 = {}^+10$$

So, we are simply saying that:

$$\text{(a)} \quad - \cdot + = -$$

$$\text{(b)} \quad + \cdot - = -$$

$$\text{(c)} \quad - \cdot - = +$$

$$\text{(d)} \quad + \cdot + = +$$

The <u>identity</u> element for multiplication is ${}^+1$. That is, multiplying any number by ${}^+1$ will leave that number unchanged.

*Examples:* $\quad$ (a) $\quad {}^-6 \cdot {}^+1 = {}^-6 \qquad\qquad$ (b) $\quad {}^+6 \cdot {}^+1 = {}^+6$

The <u>inverse</u> element in multiplication, called the <u>multiplicative inverse</u>, is any number when multiplied by its <u>reciprocal</u> results in a product of ${}^+1$. The <u>reciprocal</u> of 3 is $\frac{1}{3}$; the <u>reciprocal</u> of $\frac{3}{4}$ is $\frac{4}{3}$, etc., therefore, the reciprocal of any number is that number simply turned up-side-down or inverted.

So,

$$ {}^+3 \cdot \frac{{}^+3}{{}^+3} = \frac{{}^+3}{{}^+3} = {}^+1 $$

and

$$ \frac{{}^+3}{{}^+4} \cdot \frac{{}^+4}{{}^+3} = \frac{{}^+3 \cdot {}^+4}{{}^+4 \cdot {}^+3} = \frac{{}^+12}{{}^+12} = {}^+1 $$

Since we know that the integer $^+6$ is the same as $\frac{^+6}{^+1}$, then the inverse or reciprocal of $^+6$ is $\frac{^+1}{^+6}$, and when we multiply $^+6$ by its inverse or reciprocal, our product is $^+1$, the identity element in multiplication:

$$^+6 \cdot \frac{^+1}{^+6} = \frac{^+6}{^+6} = {^+1}$$

*Exercise* **63**

Find the products of the following integers:

(1) $^+6 \cdot {^-1} =$       (2) $^-4 \cdot {^-3} =$       (3) $^-2 \cdot {^+1} =$

(4) $^-6 \cdot {^+5} =$       (5) $^+10 \cdot {^-1} =$       (6) $^-8 \cdot {^-7} =$

Find the inverse or reciprocal of the following integers:

(7) $^+4$       (8) $^+9$       (9) $^+50$       (10) $^+13$

Check your answers with the key.

3a. The set of rational numbers — We have seen that the set of <u>natural</u> <u>numbers</u> is a subset of the set of <u>whole</u> <u>numbers</u> and the set of <u>natural</u> <u>numbers</u> and <u>whole</u> <u>numbers</u> are both subsets of the set of <u>integers</u>. Now we will see how the set of integers, in turn, form a subset of a still larger set of numbers. If we let a and b represent elements of the set of integers, with the restriction that b cannot be equal to 0 (b≠0), then

$$\frac{a}{b} = \text{rational numbers}$$

that is to say, the set of all integers that can be expressed in the form $\frac{a}{b}$ is our new set called <u>rational</u> <u>numbers</u>. Therefore, all integers plus the fractions, both positive and negative, form the set of <u>rational</u> <u>numbers</u>.

*Examples:*

(a) $\frac{^+2}{^+3}$       (b) $\frac{^-6}{^+8}$       (c) $^+2$       (d) $^-4$

3b. Division — The operation of division with rational numbers differs from the operation of division with whole numbers in only one respect and that is the sign of the quotient. This procedure is a simple matter to understand if we remember the principle: When the divisor and dividend have like signs, the quotient is always positive and when the divisor and dividend have unlike signs, the quotient is always negative. (We now know that the divisor and denominator are the same and also the dividend and the numerator are the same.)

*Examples:*

(a) $\dfrac{^+6}{^+2} = {}^+3$  or  $^+2\overline{\smash)^+6} \;\; {}^+3$

(b) $\dfrac{^+6}{^-2} = {}^-3$  or  $^-2\overline{\smash)^+6} \;\; {}^-3$

(c) $\dfrac{^-6}{^+2} = {}^-3$  or  $^+2\overline{\smash)^-6} \;\; {}^-3$

(d) $\dfrac{^-6}{^-2} = {}^+3$  or  $^-2\overline{\smash)^-6} \;\; {}^+3$

So, we are simply saying that:

(a) $\dfrac{+}{+} = {}+$

(b) $\dfrac{+}{-} = {}-$

(c) $\dfrac{-}{+} = {}-$

(d) $\dfrac{-}{-} = {}+$

*Exercise* 64

Find the quotient of the following:

(1) $^-12 \div {}^-3 =$

(2) $^-24 \div {}^+8 =$

(3) $^+6 \div {}^-1 =$

(4) $^+14 \div {}^-2 =$

(5) $^-18 \div {}^+3 =$

(6) $\dfrac{^-4}{^-3} \div \dfrac{^+1}{^+3} =$

(7) $^+16 \div {}^-16 =$

(8) $^-20 \div {}^+4 =$

(9) $^+18 \div {}^-3 =$

(10) $^-6 \div {}^-3 =$

Check your answers with the key.

# GRAPHS & CHARTS

## INTRODUCTION

The study of graphs is twofold: to learn to read a graph and interpret the facts represented, and to learn to make a graph from data supplied. Interpretation of data, as comparisons, and changes in increase and decrease can be made at a glance.

### Line Graphs

A line graph is used to show how a quantity changes, when it is increasing and decreasing and the trend that the change follows.

*Illustration:* Jim kept a record of his earnings for five weeks. Here is a broken line to show his earnings:

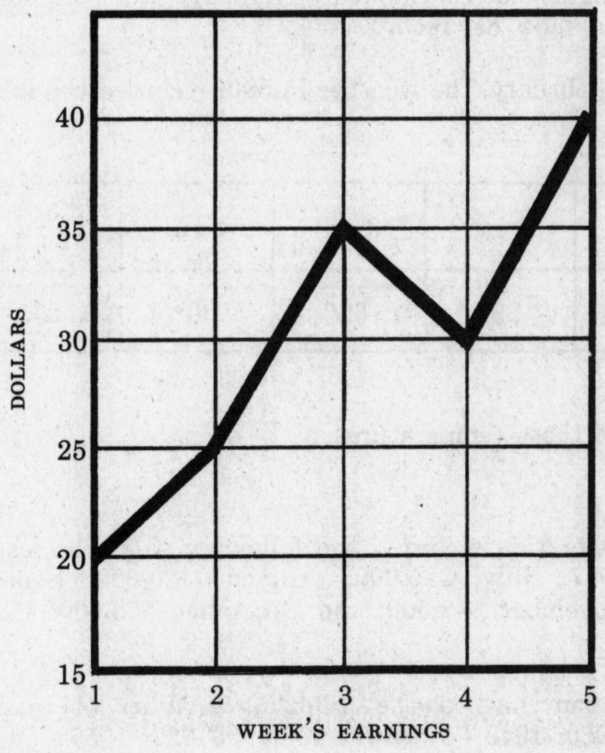


1) During which week did Jim make the least earnings?

2) What was the greatest amount he earned?

3) During which week did his earnings drop?

4) What is the general trend of his earnings?

# Suggestions on How to Make a Line Graph

1) Obtain the necessary data.

2) Plan the vertical and horizontal scales. Mark off the scales—the scale need not begin at zero.

3) Place a point on the graph for each set of numbers in the given data.

4) Connect the consecutive points with straight lines.

5) Give the graph a title.


## Exercise 1

1) Susan's marks in English for the month of January were 80, 85, 90, 87 and 82. Make a line graph to show her record.

2) On a certain day in February, the weather bureau recorded the following temperatures:

| HOUR | 1 PM | 2 PM | 3 PM | 4 PM | 5 PM | 6 PM |
|------|------|------|------|------|------|------|
| TEMP. | 28° | 29° | 32° | 30° | 27° | 22° |

Make a line graph of these temperatures.


3) The Apex Sales Corporation recorded the following sales the last six months of the year during 1957: July, $25,000; August, $20,000; September, $35,000; October, $40,000; November, $42,500; and December, $50,000. Make a line graph to show the sales.

4) The Star Cab Company owned the following number of taxis in the years between 1940 and 1960: 1940 - 5; 1945 - 15; 1950 - 22; 1955 - 35; and 1960 - 40. Make a broken-line graph showing this data.

5) The population of the U.S. from 1900 to 1940 was as follows: 1900, 75 million; 1910, 90 million; 1920, 105 million; 1930, 120 million; 1940, 132 million. Show this information on a line graph.

# Bar Graphs

A bar graph is used to show comparisons between numbers. The bars on the graph may be placed vertically or horizontally.

## Suggestions on How to Make a Bar Graph

1) Obtain the necessary data.

2) Decide whether to make a vertical or horizontal bar graph.

3) Find a suitable scale. When the numbers to be compared are large in value, it will be necessary to round off these numbers first.

4) Mark off the scale starting at *zero*.

5) Make the bars.

6) Give the graph a title.

*Illustration:* Joan had a spelling test every day for a week. Here is a graph to show the scores for a week.

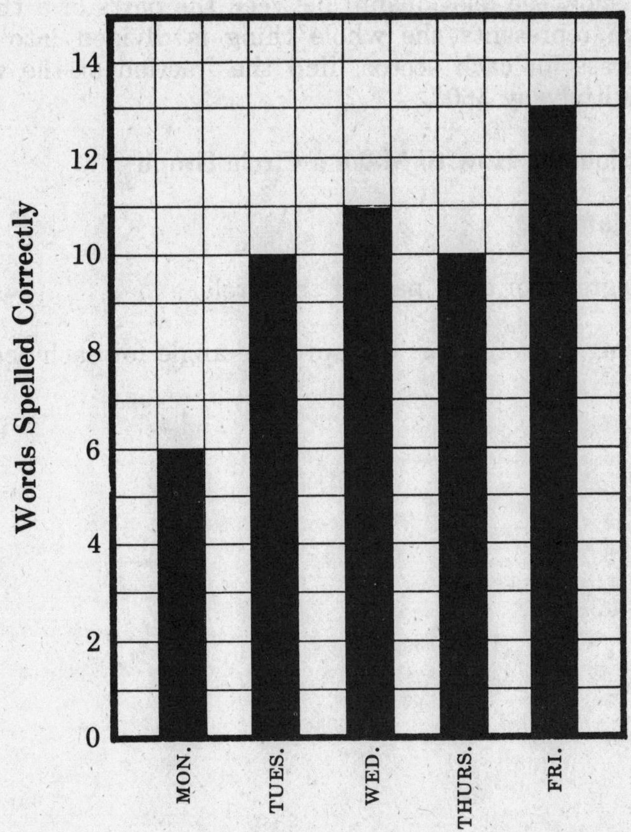



**Joan's Weekly Spelling Record**

1) What was the highest score she received? On what day did this occur?

2) What was her score on Monday?

3) On two days she received the same score. What was the score?

*Exercise 2*

1) The enrollment at East Junior High School is as follows: Grade 7, 250; Grade 8, 200; Grade 9, 175. Construct a bar graph to show the information.

2) At the end of the first term, Karl received the following scores: Mathematics - 80; English - 75; Chemistry - 85; Physics - 85; History - 70. Make a bar graph to compare this information.

3) Construct a bar graph showing the annual rainfall for Somerset for the years 1969-1972. 1969-25 in.; 1970-27 in.; 1971-21 in.: 1972-14 in.

4) The population of Baysville for the years 1955, 1960, 1965, and 1970 was: 1955 - 22,000; 1960 - 24,000; 1965 - 25,500; 1970 - 26,500. Construct a bar graph to represent this information.

## Circle Graphs

A circle graph is used to show the relationship between the parts of a thing and the whole thing. The circle which represents the whole thing is divided into sectors. To determine the number of degrees for each sector, find the fraction of the whole which each sector represents and multiply by 360°.

### Suggestions on How to Make a Circle Graph

1) Obtain the necessary data.

2) Find the number of degrees for each part of the circle.

3) Draw a circle, and, using a protractor, measure the angle for each sector.

4) Label each sector.

5) Give the graph a title.

*Illustration:* Mary James is planning her travel allowance. Here is a circle graph to show how she allots her money.

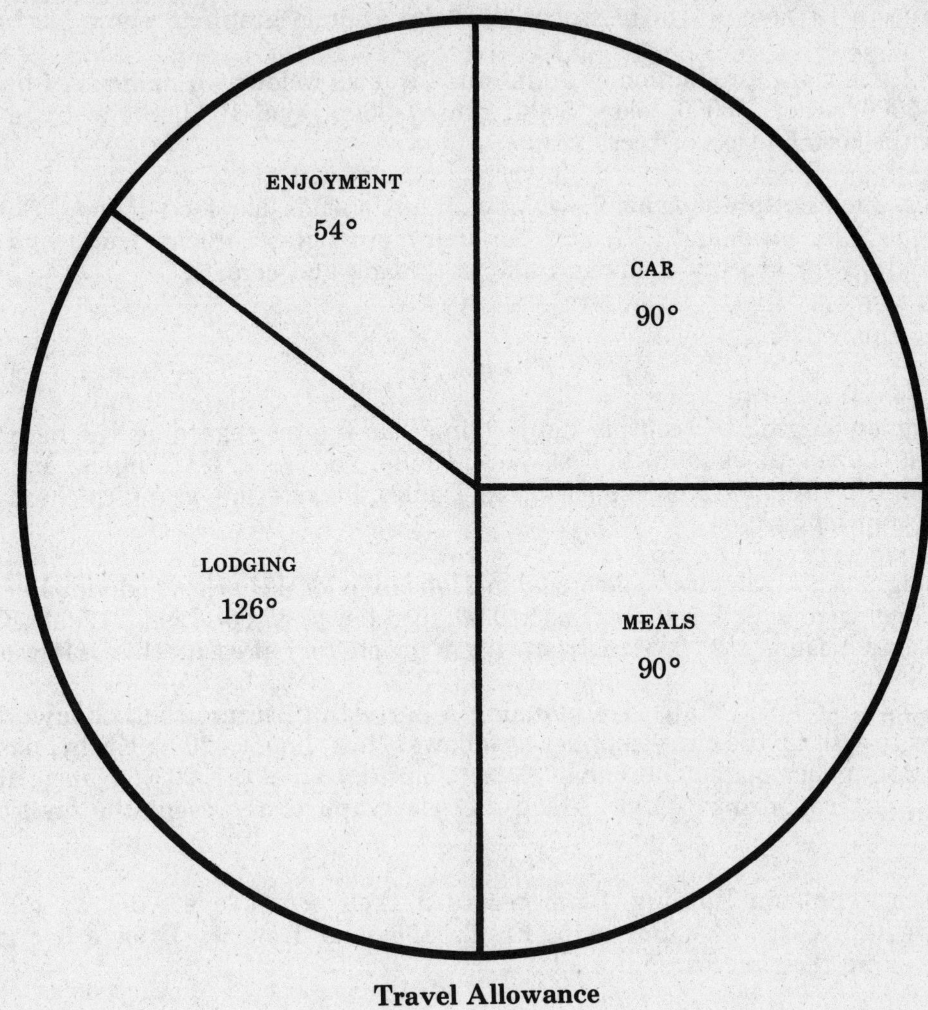

**Travel Allowance**

1) What percent does she spend for lodging?

2) She allots the same amount for two parts of her allowance. Which two are the same?

3) What percent is allotted for pure enjoyment?

1) Mr. Abrams has planned the following budget: rent 25%; food 35%; expenses 35%. He expects to save 5% of his income. Make a circle graph to show his budget.

2) In 1942, the world production of grain crops was as follows, in millions of bushels: corn, 5000; wheat, 6000; oats, 5000; barley 3000; rye, 1000. Show by a circle graph the distribution of these crops.

3) Make a circle graph showing how Mrs. Jones spends her food money. She estimates 30% for meat and fish; 25% for dairy products; 25% for fruits and vegetables; 15% for grocery items and 5% for breads and cereals.

*Exercise 4*

1) Jon started jogging to keep his figure trim. The figures regarding the number of miles he jogged are as follows: first week, 1 mile; 2nd week, 2-1/2 miles; 3rd week, 4 miles; 4th week, 6-1/2 miles; 5th week, 7 miles. Make a line graph to chart Jon's progress in jogging.

2) Five neighborhood children collected donations for a local charity. Individually their collections were as follows: Shawn, $10.00; Kimberly, $7.00; Lisa, $12.00; Karly, $6.00; and Leanne, $9.00. Construct a bar graph to represent this information.

3) Members of an office staff were planning a party to celebrate the holidays. They decided to split up the party supplies as follows: Nick, liquor - 20%; Kathy, pastry - 25%; Mae, paper plates and cups - 10%; Charlie, cold cuts - 20%; Nancy, rolls - 15%; Doug, soft drinks - 10%. Make a circle graph to represent the division of these party items.

4) The Ace Candlepin Bowling Team recorded their scores one week as follows: Freddie, 120; Gene, 110; Bob, 115; Frank, 105; and Tom, 95. Draw a bar graph which shows their scores.

5) A survey was done in the Acme Travel Agencies in New York City. It showed that New Yorkers in this survey had the following preferences for vacation spots: Bermuda, 40%; Europe, 30%; South America, 10%; Canada, 20%. Construct a circle graph indicating the survey's findings.

# ALGEBRA

# ALGEBRA

## THE BASIS OF ALGEBRA

In arithmetic we learned to add, subtract, multiply, and divide *numbers*.

In algebra we learn to apply all these operations (and two new ones) to *letters* as well as numbers. We shall learn to add, subtract, multiply, and divide with these letters and numbers just as we did in arithmetic.

In algebra, instead of saying that we walked 5 miles or spent 10 dollars, we are just as apt to say that we walked $a$ miles or spent $b$ dollars. The letters $a$ and $b$ are used to represent numbers. (In this case $a$ stands for 5 and $b$ stands for 10.)

It is easily seen that if someone else walked 20 miles and spent 35 dollars, we could also say that he walked $a$ miles and spent $b$ dollars, only in this case $a$ stands for 20 and $b$ stands for 35.

Again, let us suppose that we want to say in the language of algebra that a certain thing, *a*, is twice as much as another thing, *b*. We simply write

$$a = 2 \times b$$

Now, no matter what number we assign to *b*, *a* will always be twice as great. If $b = 2$, $a = 2 \times b = 2 \times 2 = 4$; if $b = 16$, $a = 2 \times 16 = 32$; and so on.

We see then that letters used in algebra *always represent numbers*. The first letters of the alphabet (*a, b, c, d*, etc.) are used to represent known numbers or numbers to which we can give any value we choose. The last letters of the alphabet (*x, y*, and *z*) are used to represent unknown numbers. Whenever we have no idea of the value of a certain number, we say "let *x* equal the value of that number," and work the problem to find the value of *x*. We shall learn how to do this.

Let us pause for a moment and see what the advantage is of using letters instead of numbers. Let us look at this simple principle: We know that the distance an express train travels equals the speed of the train times the length of time it travels. If it travels at the rate of 60 miles per hour for 2 hours, the distance it travels is $2 \times 60$ miles $= 120$ miles. In other words,

$$\text{distance} = \text{speed} \times \text{time of traveling}$$

If we abbreviate this we can say,

$$d = s \times t$$

If the speed is 45 miles per hour and the time it travels is 3 hours, then $s = 45$ and $t = 3$ and

$$d = 45 \times 3 = 135 \text{ miles}$$

We can name any speed we choose (letting *s* equal the number of miles per hour) and any length of time we choose (letting *t* equal that many hours), and we can always get the distance (*d*) by multiplying *s* by *t*.

The use of numbers gives only *one* solution to a given condition, while the use of letters gives as many solutions as we wish because the letters can represent any numbers we choose to let them represent.


## NEGATIVE NUMBERS

There is another difference between algebra and arithmetic. In arithmetic we worked with numbers which were always greater than zero. In algebra we shall work with numbers which are less than zero as well as those which are greater than zero.

Any number that is less than zero is a *negative number*, and is always a minus quantity.

At first it seems as though anything less than zero were foolish. How can anything be less than nothing? Suppose you have absolutely no money. You are in a bad fix, to be sure, for your wealth is at zero; you have nothing. But cheer up! You are much better off than if you had borrowed $100 and spent it, for then you would owe $100 or, in the language of algebra, you would have *minus* $100. Your wealth would then be $100 less than zero, and only by earning $100 and paying your debt could you bring yourself back to zero.

Negative numbers always mean that something is lacking. They imply that something must be supplied to bring conditions back to normal. In a square hole 10 feet deep and 10 feet square, there are *minus* 1,000 cubic feet of dirt. This is like saying that 1,000 cubic feet of dirt are necessary to bring that hole back (fill it in) to its original state.

Negative numbers are always written with a minus sign (—) in front of them, thus:

$$-4, \ -6, \ -10, \ -a, \ -d, \ -x, \ -14a$$

Later on we shall learn how to add, subtract, multiply, and divide with these negative numbers.


## POWERS AND ROOTS

There are only four processes in arithmetic: addition, subtraction, multiplication, and division. When we first studied arithmetic, we learned these four fundamental processes and used them only with *whole* numbers. Later on, when we were more advanced, we learned how to apply these four processes to fractions.

Now, in algebra, we learn to use the same four processes with letters as well as numbers, and find that in doing this we are obliged to use two new processes, called "raising to powers" and "extracting roots."

Whenever a number is multiplied by itself one or more times, it is raised to a power. If it is multiplied by itself once, it is "squared." If it is multiplied by itself twice, it is "cubed." If it is multiplied by itself three times, it is "raised to the 4th power," and so on. The power to which a number is raised is written smaller to the upper right of the number, thus:

$$3 \times 3 = 3 \text{ squared or } 3^2 = 9$$
$$5 \times 5 \times 5 = 5 \text{ cubed or } 5^3 = 125$$
$$a \times a \times a \times a = a \text{ to the 4th power or } a^4$$

We are somewhat familiar with squares and cubes from arithmetic. We may recall some of those problems which called for the area of a square whose side was 5 inches, or the number of cubic inches in a cube whose side was 10 inches. These were very simple problems in arithmetic, and they are just as simple in algebra, except that in algebra we go much farther with this operation.

The extraction of roots is just the opposite of raising to powers. To find the square root of 81, for example, we must find some number which, when multiplied by itself once, will give us 81. Since $9 \times 9$ or $9^2 = 81$, we say that the square root of 81 is 9. For the same reason, since $5 \times 5 \times 5$ or $5^3 = 125$, we say that the cube root of 125 is 5.

## SIGNS USED IN ALGEBRA

There are a number of signs and symbols used in algebra which we should memorize at once. These are the following:

$+$(plus): the same as in arithmetic; $a+b$.

$-$(minus): the same as in arithmetic; $a-b$.

$\times$(multiplied by): the multiplication sign ($\times$) is seldom used in algebra. Either a dot is used or nothing at all. Thus

$$a \times b \text{ is written } ab \text{ or } a \cdot b$$
$$4 \times a \times c \text{ is written } 4ac \text{ or } 4 \cdot a \cdot c$$

The old familiar sign of division ($\div$) is seldom used in algebra. Instead of $17 \div 3$ we write $\dfrac{17}{3}$. Instead of $a \div b$ we write $\dfrac{a}{b}$.

We have seen that numbers raised to powers have the power written smaller to the upper right of the number. Thus, $a^2$ is read "$a$ squared"; $b^{12}$ is read "$b$ to the 12th power."

The sign $\sqrt{\phantom{x}}$ means square root. If there is a small number in front of it, it means the root indicated by that number; thus, $\sqrt[3]{\phantom{x}}$ means cube root; $\sqrt[4]{\phantom{x}}$ means 4th root; etc.

### How to Express Yourself in Algebraic Signs

As a matter of practice it might be well to "translate" some ordinary terms into algebraic signs.

For example:

$a$ times $b$ times $c$ times $d$ minus $a$ plus $c$, would be

$$abcd - a + c$$

The 5th root of 7 divided by $a$ times the cube of $b$, would be written

$$\frac{\sqrt[5]{7}}{ab^3}$$

$a$ minus $b$ plus the square root of 12 divided by 2, would be written

$$\frac{a-b+\sqrt[2]{12}}{2}$$

EXERCISE 1

*Now see whether you can write the signs for the following:*

1. $b$ times $c$ divided by $a$.
2. $d$ times $e$ plus the cube root of $a$.
3. 4 times $b$ times $c$ divided by $b$ squared.
4. $a$ plus 3 times $b$ minus $b$ cubed divided by 10.
5. minus $b$ plus the square root of $b$ squared divided by 2 times $a$.
6. the cube root of $a$ times $b$ times $c$.

*See whether you can find the numerical value of each of the following:*

7. $6^2+8^2$
8. $3^2\times2^3$
9. $\sqrt{256}$
10. $8^2-\sqrt{36}$
11. $\sqrt{72}+3^4-\sqrt[3]{27}$
12. $\sqrt{3^2+4^2}$

# FINDING VALUES BY SUBSTITUTION

Now let us go a step farther by substituting numbers for letters and finding the value of various expressions.

Let $a=2$ and $b=3$ and $c=4$ and $d=5$ in the following problems:

Find the value of $abcd$.

Substituting the values: $2\times3\times4\times5=120$.

Find the value of $\dfrac{cb}{a}-\sqrt[2]{c}$.

Substituting the values:

$$\frac{4\times3}{2}-\sqrt[2]{4}=\frac{12}{2}-2=6-2=4.$$

Find the value of $cd^2-a+b^2$.

Substituting the values: $4\times5^2-2+3^2$

$$4\times25-2+9$$

$$100-2+9=107$$

99

*Now see whether you can find the values of the following* (remember that $a=2$, $b=3$, $c=4$, and $d=5$):

1. $\dfrac{cd}{a}$    3. $\sqrt{b^2+c^2}$    5. $\sqrt{10ad}$    7. $\sqrt{4abc+4}$

2. $b^2+c^2$    4. $a+b-c+\dfrac{da}{2}$    6. $\dfrac{c^2+4ac}{2a}$    8. $\dfrac{cd-a}{b^2}$

## POSITIVE AND NEGATIVE NUMBERS

Negative numbers are always less than zero and are always written with a minus sign in front of them. We must now learn how to add, subtract, multiply, and divide negative numbers.

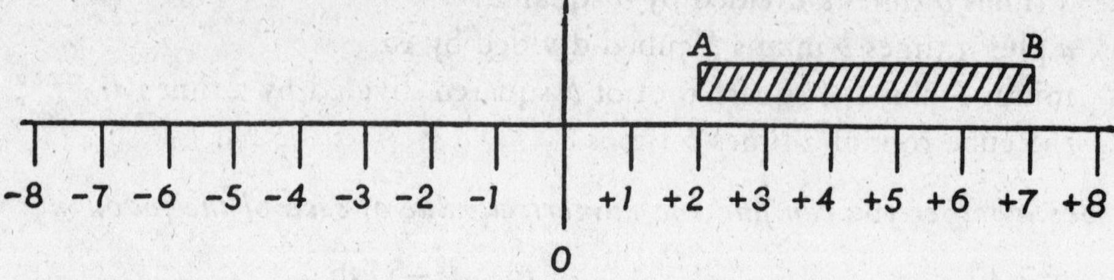

The diagram above is a straight line marked off with numbers. You will notice that zero is in the center and all the numbers to the *right* of zero are + (positive) while all the numbers to the *left* of zero are — (negative). Suppose we place a ruler (AB) 5 units long on the line so that A (the left end of the ruler) is over +2; then the other end, B, will be right over +7, or 2+5 (length of the ruler)=+7. As long as we read from A to B, we *add* 5 to whatever number the A end of the ruler is placed over. If A were moved up to 4, B would be over 9 (4+5=9). If we read from B to A, we *subtract* 5 from the number B is over. In the diagram, B is over 7 and A is over 2, or 7—5=2. If B were moved to the left so that it came over 5, then A would be right over 0, or 5—5=0.

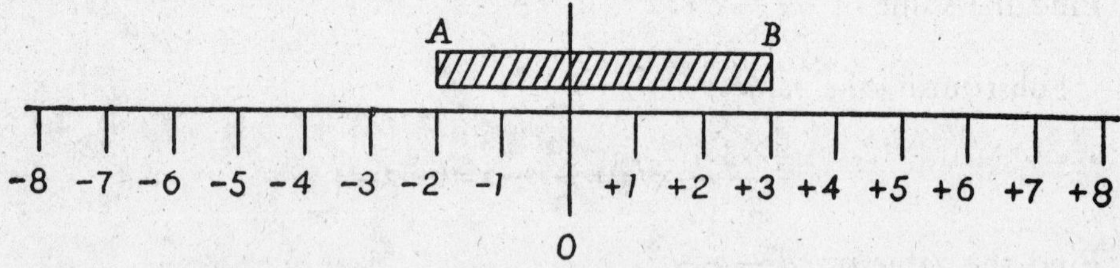

Now let us move the ruler still farther to the left so that B comes over 3. Where is A now? We see that A is over —2. Then 3—5=—2. Suppose B were moved over zero, then A would be over —5, or 0—5=—5.

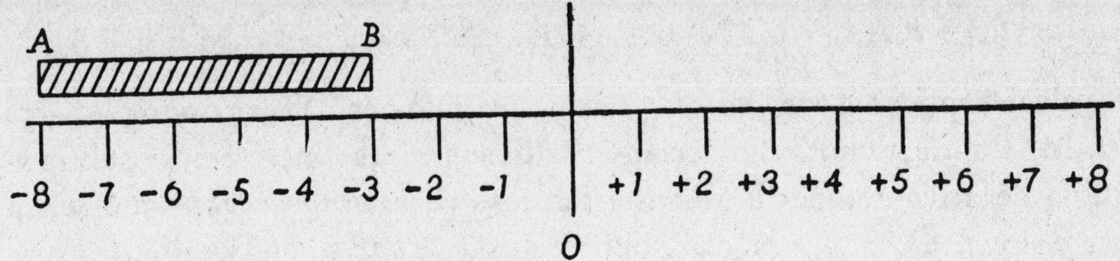

Now suppose B were moved over —3; then A would come over —8, or —3—5=—8. Note the following examples:

$$4-6=-2 \qquad\qquad -5-3=-8$$
$$17-21=-4 \qquad\qquad 7+3-16=-6$$
$$-4+8=+4 \qquad\qquad -2+6-8-2=-6$$

**EXERCISE 3**

*See whether you can do the following:*

1. 5—8=?
2. 3—17=?
3. —7+12=?

4. —3+8=?
5. —5—2—2+10=?
6. —6+18—21—14=?

It is extremely important to note right here that there are two ways of writing a positive number. We may write it either with or without the (+) sign in front of it. +8 is just the same as 8. 8 means +8.

Now, let us look at one of the previous examples:

$$4-6=-2$$

This really means that

$$+4-(+6)=-2$$

In other words, we have *subtracted* +6 from +4. We could just as well *add* —6 to +4 and get the same result.

So *subtracting* +6 from +4 is just the same as *adding* —6 to +4:

$$4-(+6)=-2$$
$$4+(-6)=-2$$

There is no difference between *subtracting* a positive number and *adding* the same negative number. For instance:

$$5-(+6) \text{ is the same as } 5-6$$
$$5+(-6) \text{ is the same as } 5-6$$
$$10-(+4) \text{ is the same as } 10-4$$
$$10+(-4) \text{ is the same as } 10-4$$

# SUBTRACTION OF NEGATIVE NUMBERS

What happens if we *subtract a negative* number? What does 5—(—5) equal? Subtraction means decrease; addition means increase. So subtracting a negative number is just the same as *decreasing a debt*—and when we *decrease* a debt, we *increase* our wealth—we *add* to our wealth. If I owe you $5, I have —$5 in my pocket. —$5 is the debt. To subtract from that —$5 is to decrease that debt by $5, or, in other words, to wipe out the debt and be even. To wipe out the $5 debt is to be $5 richer than you were before, or you have added $5 to your wealth.

This can be shown even more clearly when we listen to an uneducated person using the double negative. We may overhear someone say, "I haven't nothing." This statement really means he has *something*, because if he had *not nothing* he must have *something*.

We see, then, that in subtracting a minus we always get a positive. We see also that subtracting a negative (minus) is the same as adding the same positive number. For example:

$$\text{Take } -6 \text{ from } +4. \text{ Answer: } +10$$
$$\text{Take } -10 \text{ from } -10. \text{ Answer: } 0$$
$$\text{Take } -14 \text{ from } +3. \text{ Answer: } +17$$

It follows, then, that whenever we subtract a negative number we change the — to + and add.


# MULTIPLICATION OF POSITIVE AND NEGATIVE NUMBERS

Let a friend represent a positive number, and let an enemy represent a negative number. We know that:

The friend of the friend is a friend.
*a plus times a plus = a plus.*
The friend of the enemy is an enemy.
*a plus times a minus = a minus.*
The enemy of the friend is an enemy.
*a minus times a plus = a minus.*
The enemy of the enemy is a friend.
*a minus times a minus = a plus.*

It would be well to memorize the following:

$$+\times+=+$$
$$+\times-=-$$
$$-\times+=-$$
$$-\times-=+$$

For example:

$$+3\times+6=+18 \quad (+\times+=+)$$
$$+3\times-6=-18 \quad (+\times-=-)$$
$$-3\times+6=-18 \quad (-\times+=-)$$
$$-3\times-6=+18 \quad (-\times-=+)$$

When the signs are the same, the answer is $+$; when the signs are different, the answer is $-$; like signs $+$, unlike $-$.

EXERCISE 4

*See whether you can do the following:*

| | | |
|---|---|---|
| 1. $-3\times-4=?$ | 11. $(-62)\times(-1)=?$ | 21. $(-3)(3)(-3)=?$ |
| 2. $+5\times-3=?$ | 12. $(3)(-4)(-3)=?$ | 22. $(2)(-2)(2)=?$ |
| 3. $+7\times-2=?$ | 13. $(9)(-2)(1)=?$ | 23. $(1)(1)(-1)=?$ |
| 4. $-5\times+5=?$ | 14. $(-1)(-1)(1)=?$ | 24. $(2)(-4)(6)=?$ |
| 5. $-2\times-2=?$ | 15. $(10)(-1)(-1)=?$ | 25. $(-1)(-3)(-5)=?$ |
| 6. $-3\times-3=?$ | 16. $(-8)(+8)=?$ | 26. $(1)(6)(-9)=?$ |
| 7. $+4\times-2=?$ | 17. $(-2)(1)(-2)=?$ | 27. $(-4(-5)(-6)=?$ |
| 8. $-6\times+1=?$ | 18. $(1)(2)(3)=?$ | 28. $(5)(-10)(15)=?$ |
| 9. $-11\times-11=?$ | 19. $(4)(-3)(2)=?$ | 29. $(-2)(-3)(-1)=?$ |
| 10. $-6\times1=?$ | 20. $(-9)(-8)(-1)=?$ | 30. $(2)(-3)(-1)=?$ |

If you were asked what the square root of 9 is, you would say 3 and let it go at that. This is true, but it is only partly true. $-3$ is also a square root of 9 because $-3\times-3$ also equals 9 ($-\times-=+$). Other negative numbers multiplied by themselves give positive numbers. In other words, the square root of any positive number is both a positive and a negative number. For example, the square root of 4 is both $+2$ and $-2$; the square root of 25 is both $+5$ and $-5$; and so on.

But if you should ask what is the square root of $-9$, the answer would involve an entirely different system of numbers, known as imaginary numbers. These are vitally important in higher mathematics and engineering, and require much more advanced knowledge than we can present here.

# DIVISION OF POSITIVE AND NEGATIVE NUMBERS

The same laws hold true for the division of negative and positive numbers as for multiplication, thus:

$$\frac{+4}{+2}=+2 \qquad\qquad \frac{+6}{-2}=-3$$

$$\frac{-8}{+2}=-4 \qquad\qquad \frac{-6}{-3}=+2$$

# ADDITION AND SUBTRACTION

### ADDITION

Suppose I had 10 apples, and you gave me 5 apples and your brother gave me 7 apples. I would have a total of 22 apples.

Now suppose I had 10 apples and you gave me 5 bananas and your brother gave me 7 apples. I would have 17 apples and 5 bananas. Let us abbreviate this, letting $a$ stand for apples and $b$ for bananas. Then, in the first instance,

$$10a+5a+7a=22a$$

and in the second instance,

$$10a+5b+7a=17a+5b$$

Suppose now that you had 3 apples, 2 bananas, and 14 cherries, and that I gave you 5 bananas, 6 cherries, and 3 dates. You would then have 3 apples, 7 bananas, 20 cherries, and 3 dates, or

$$\begin{array}{r} 3a+2b+14c\phantom{+3d} \\ +5b+\phantom{0}6c+3d \\ \hline 3a+7b+20c+3d \end{array}$$

It is clear, then, that in adding algebraic numbers we must separate them into similar terms and add up all those terms separately.

It is just like taking inventory in a store. You add up in separate columns the number of pounds of the various items, like tea, sugar, coffee, etc., and the total will consist of your entire stock. Instead of saying that you have so many pounds all together of tea, coffee, sugar, etc., you say that you

have so many pounds of tea *and* s[o]         [l]s of coffee *and* so many
pounds of sugar, etc.

Of course, this all applies to positi[ve]       t also applies to negative
numbers, and from what we have           [t] negative numbers we
should have no trouble in adding t[hem.]   [exa]mple, to add:

$$6a-2b+3c \text{ a}[\text{nd}]\ [4a+3b-4]c$$

we write the following:

$$
\begin{array}{r}
6a-2b+3c \\
4a+3b-4c \\
\hline
10a+\ b-\ c
\end{array}
$$

Note these examples:

$$-12a+6a=-6a$$
$$5r-8r=-3r$$
$$ax+2ax-ax+4ax=6ax$$

EXERCISE 5

*See whether you can add:*

1. $-11a+9a-12a-2a+31a=?$
2. $16b-3b+7b-15b=?$
3. $10bc-6bc+12bc-8bc=?$
4. $2a-5b+3a+2b=?$
5. $-4c+6b+5c-3b+2c-b=?$
6. $4a-2b+c+5b-3a-2c=?$

## DEFINITIONS

In algebra a single term not added to or subtracted from any other term is called a *monomial*. For example: $6$, $b$, $a^2$, $12a$, $2ax$, $8bc$, etc.

If two terms are indicated to be added or subtracted, the resulting expression is called a *binomial*. For example: $a+b$, $2x+4y$, $a^2-2b$, etc.

A *trinomial* is an expression of three terms. For example: $a+b-c$, $x+y-z$, $a+2b^2-5c$, etc.

*Binomials* and *trinomials* are also known as *polynomials*, a polynomial being an expression consisting of two or more terms. For example: $6a-12b+11c^2-4d+e$, $x-2y+3z-4$, etc.

## ADDITION OF POLYNOMIALS

To add the following polynomials:

$$3a-2b+bc^2,\ 4b+2bc^2,\ 3a+7bc^2+11, \text{ and } 6b-8$$

the problem should be arranged so that similar terms are in the same column; thus:

$$
\begin{array}{l}
3a-2b+\ bc^2 \\
\quad\ 4b+\ 2bc^2 \\
3a\quad\ +\ 7bc^2+11 \\
\quad\ 6b\qquad\ -\ 8 \\
\hline
6a+8b+10bc^2+\ 3
\end{array}
$$

Add the following polynomials:

$$a+k-x+5,\ 3a-2x+4,\ 7-3k+x,\ 6-3x-5a+k.$$

$$
\begin{array}{l}
a+\ k-\ x+\ 5 \\
3a\qquad\ -2x+\ 4 \\
\quad\ -3k+\ x+\ 7 \\
-5a+\ k-3x+\ 6 \\
\hline
-\ a-\ k-5x+22
\end{array}
$$

In the polynomial $2x^2+3x-4$, you will see that the terms $2x^2$ and $3x$ appear. Just as square inches and inches are different things and cannot be added to each other, so $x^2$ and $x$ are different and must be considered as different objects. Therefore, if we add $2x^2+3x-4$, $x^2-3x+6$, $3x^2-2x-2$, $2x^2-x-1$, we arrange as follows:

$$
\begin{array}{l}
2x^2+3x-4 \\
\ x^2-3x+6 \\
3x^2-2x-2 \\
2x^2-\ x-1 \\
\hline
8x^2-3x-1
\end{array}
$$

and add thus:

The answer cannot be made simpler by further addition.

EXERCISE 6

*See whether you can add the following:*

1. $8x+7y-4z$, $5x+3z$, and $5x+7y-6z$.
2. $5d+4d^2+6$, $d^2+2d-1$, and $5d+3d^2-8$.
3. $5x-8y+8z$, $12y-12z+2x$, and $10z-5y$.
4. $2x-10z$, $5x+2y$, $3z-y$, and $3x-4y+z$.

SUBTRACTION

Subtraction is extremely simple. You will remember that the subtraction of a positive number was the same as the addition of the same negative number. If you will memorize one simple rule, you will know how to subtract. The rule is as follows: In subtracting one algebraic expression from another, *change signs in the subtrahend and add*.

From $10a$ subtract $4a$.

$$\begin{array}{r} +10a \\ +\ 4a \text{ (subtrahend)} \\ \hline 6a \end{array}$$

We *changed the sign* of $4a$ to $-4a$ and *added* $10a$ and $-4a$, and obtained $6a$ as the result.

This process should be looked upon not as subtraction but as addition. *All subtraction must be looked upon as addition with the sign changed in the subtrahend.* This is necessary because there is no other way of subtracting negative numbers except by adding the same positive numbers. Inasmuch as algebraic expressions involve both negative and positive numbers and we cannot add some while subtracting others, there is this general rule for adding instead of subtracting in all cases.

1. From $10a$ subtract $-4a$.

$$\begin{array}{r} +10a \\ -\ 4a \text{ (subtrahend)} \\ \hline +14a \end{array}$$

We changed $-4a$ to $+4a$ and added $10a + 4a = 14a$.

2. Subtract $-3ax$ from $-7ax$.

$$\begin{array}{r} -7ax \\ -3ax \text{ (subtrahend)} \\ \hline -4ax \end{array}$$

We changed $-3ax$ to $+3ax$ and added it to $-7ax$.

3. Subtract $9ab^3$ from $-3ab^3$.

$$\begin{array}{r} -\ 3ab^3 \\ 9ab^3 \\ \hline -12ab^3 \end{array}$$

We changed $+9ab^3$ to $-9ab^3$ and added it to $-3ab^3$.

4. Subtract $3a-4b-5c+4$ from $a+7b-4c$.

$$\begin{array}{r} a+\ 7b-4c \\ 3a-\ 4b-5c+4 \\ \hline -2a+11b+\ c-4 \end{array}$$

We changed the signs in the subtrahend and added thus:

$$a+\ 7b-4c$$
$$\underline{-3a+\ 4b+5c-4}$$
$$-2a+11b+\ c-4$$

EXERCISE 7

1. Subtract $2x-3y+4$ from $3x+2y-8$.
2. Subtract $2x^2-4x+6$ from $3x^2+7x-3$.
3. Subtract $2a-2c-4$ from $a+3c+2$.
4. Subtract $3x-2y+z$ from $4x-3y+2z$.
5. Subtract $4x^2+7y^2-2z$ from $-6x^2-14y^2+3z$.

# EQUATIONS

Whenever something equals something else, we have an *equation*. An equation is an equality. The following are three distinct equations:

$$6+4=10$$
$$3+7-2=4+4$$
$$11-2=20-2-9$$

Every equation has two parts: a left member or left side and a right member or right side. These two members or sides are separated by the *equals* sign ($=$); thus:

$$\text{left member} = \text{right member}$$
$$18+2=20$$

The equals sign in any equation is like a fence. It is necessary to move terms from one side of the "fence" to the other side. Before a number can "jump over the fence" its sign must be changed. If it is plus it becomes minus, and if it is minus it becomes a plus:

$$18+2=20 \begin{cases} +2=20-18 \\ 18\ \ =20-2 \end{cases}$$

Moving a term from one side of the "fence" to the other is called *transposing*. What we really do here is to add the same number to both sides of the equation. (This does not change the value of the equation.) In the preceding example we first added $-18$ to both sides and got $+2=20-18$; we then added $-2$ to both sides and got $18=20-2$. The $-18$ canceled the

+18 in the first instance, leaving +2 on the left side. And the —2 canceled the +2, leaving 18 on the left side.

$$26+4=30$$

$$26 = 30-4$$

$$41-16=25$$

$$41 = 25+16$$

$$a+b=c$$

$$a = c-b$$

If $x-10=7$
Then $x=7+10$ or $x=17$.

If $x+3=6$
Then $x=6-3$ or $x=3$

If $x-2=0$
Then $x=2$

### EXERCISE 8

*See whether you can do the following* (find the value of $x$ or $y$):

1. $x-3=0$     3. $x+17=42$     5. $x-7=3$
2. $x+5-6=3$     4. $y+21=37$     6. $y+2=1$

If 4 oranges cost 20¢, 1 orange will cost 5¢. We found this by dividing
20 by 4.

Then if $4x=20$ (Divide both sides by 4.)
$x=5$
If $6x=96$ (Divide both sides by 6.)
$x=16$
If $3x=12$ (Divide both sides by 3.)
$x=4$

### EXERCISE 9

*See whether you can do these* (find the value of $x$):

1. $5x=25$     3. $7x=63$     5. $2x=22$
2. $12x=144$     4. $9x=81$     6. $5x=15$

Now let us go a step farther:

$$4x+3=15 \qquad \text{Find } x.$$
$$4x=15-3$$
$$4x=12$$
$$\text{Ans.} \qquad x=3$$

$$12x-3x+7=16 \qquad \text{Find } x.$$
$$9x+7=16$$
$$9x=16-7$$
$$9x=9$$
$$\text{Ans.} \qquad x=1$$

EXERCISE 10

*Find the value of x:*

1. $x-3=14$     3. $4x=x+2$     5. $-6-5x=19$
2. $2x=5-x$     4. $3x+4=x-6$     6. $4x-6=18$

If half a dozen eggs cost 30¢, 1 dozen cost 60¢. We found this by multiplying $30\times2$, or

$$\tfrac{1}{2}\ \text{doz.}=30$$
$$1\ \text{doz.}=30\times2 \quad \text{(Multiply both sides by 2.)}$$
$$1\ \text{doz.}=60$$

In other words:

$$\text{If } \tfrac{1}{2}d=30$$
$$d=30\times2$$
$$d=60$$

$$\text{If } \tfrac{1}{3}x=10 \quad (\tfrac{1}{3}x \text{ is written } \tfrac{x}{3}.)$$
$$x=10\times3 \quad \text{(Multiply both sides by 3.)}$$
$$x=30$$

$$\text{If } \tfrac{x}{7}=4$$
$$x=4\times7 \quad \text{(Multiply both sides by 7.)}$$
$$x=28$$

EXERCISE 11

*Find the value of x:*

1. $\dfrac{x}{3}=14$     3. $\dfrac{x}{14}=17$     5. $\dfrac{x}{10}=31$

2. $\dfrac{2x}{6}=20$     4. $\dfrac{x}{3}=100$     6. $\dfrac{x}{4}=9$

By "solving an equation" is meant finding the value of $x$ (or whatever other letter is taken to represent the unknown).

1. Solve $6x-7=3x+2$.

Collect the $x$'s thus:

$$6x-3x-7=\quad+2$$

$$3x-7=+2$$

Transpose the $-7$ thus:

$$3x\quad=2+7$$

$$3x=9$$
$$x=3$$

Check by substituting 3 for $x$ in the original problem, thus:

$$6x-7=3x+2$$
$$18-7=9+2$$
$$11=11$$

2. Solve $4t+3-t+5=t-10$.

Collect the $t$'s thus:

$$4t+3-t+5-t=\quad-10$$

$$2t+8=-10$$

$$2t\quad=-10\ -8$$

$$2t=-18$$
$$t=-\ 9$$

Check by substituting $-9$ for $t$ in the original problem.

$$4t+3-t+5=t-10$$
$$-36+3+9+5=-9-10$$
$$-19=-19$$

3. Solve $x+2=\dfrac{x}{4}+8$.

First multiply both sides of the equation by 4 to change $\dfrac{x}{4}$ to $x$, thus:

$$4x+8=x+32$$

Next collect the $x$'s on the left side.

$$4x-x+8=\quad+32$$

$$3x+8=+32$$

$$3x\quad=32-8$$

$$3x=24$$
$$x=\;8$$

Check by substituting 8 for $x$ in the original problem.

$$x+2=\dfrac{x}{4}+8$$
$$8+2=\dfrac{8}{4}+8$$
$$8+2=2+8$$
$$10=10$$

4. Solve $-3+2x+2=\dfrac{2x}{4}-2x+6$.

First multiply both sides by 4 in order to change $\dfrac{2x}{4}$ to $2x$ (this is called clearing of fractions).

$$-12+8x+8=2x-8x+24$$

Next collect the $x$'s on the left side, thus:

$$-12+8x+8-2x+8x=24$$
$$-12+14x+8=24$$
$$14x=28$$
$$x=2$$

Check by substituting 2 for $x$ in the original problem.

$$-3+2x+2=\frac{2x}{4}-2x+6$$

$$-3+4+2=\frac{4}{4}-4+6$$

$$3=1-4+6$$

$$3=3$$

EXERCISE 12

*Find the value of x:*

1. $4x-2=3x+2$     3. $6x-3-3x=21$     5. $x+3-2x=2$
2. $3x-20=8x+25$     4. $5x-7+2x=49$     6. $2x+x-4=8$

## APPLICATION OF EQUATIONS TO SIMPLE PROBLEMS

Before we apply these equations to problems, it is essential that we understand how to express ourselves algebraically.

For example, express the following algebraically: 3 times a certain number diminished by 5 equals the number increased by 7.

Let $x$ be that certain number. Then 3 times that certain number is $3x$; and 3 times that certain number diminished by 5 is $3x-5$.

Now we are told that this equals the number increased by 7.

Hence $3x-5=x+7$.

EXERCISE 13

*See whether you can write the following algebraically and solve the equations:*

1. Three times a certain number less 25 equals twice the number less 15. What is the number?
2. A certain number is doubled and the result increased by 10. The sum is 14. What is the number?
3. Twice a certain number added to 30 gives the same result as three times the number subtracted from 90. What is the number?

Now let us study a few problems and note carefully how we go about solving them.

## PROBLEMS

The sum of three numbers is 22. The first number is 5 less than the second number, and the third number is 3 more than twice the second number. What are the numbers?

We note, first of all, that the sum of the three numbers is 22, but we do not know any of the numbers. We do know, however, that the first and third numbers both bear a definite relationship to the second number, as they are less and greater, respectively. Therefore, if we let $x$ equal the second number, we can express the problem algebraically.

So we start by letting $x =$ the second number.

Then the first number is 5 less than $x$, or $x$—5; and the third number is 3 more than twice $x$, or $2x+3$.

We know all these together $= 22$.

Therefore

$$\underbrace{x-5}_{\text{1st no.}} + \underbrace{x}_{\text{2nd no.}} + \underbrace{2x+3}_{\text{3rd no.}} = \underset{\text{Total}}{22}$$

$$x+x+2x=22+5-3$$
$$4x=24$$
$$x=6 \quad \text{(second number)}$$
$$x-5=1 \quad \text{(first number)}$$
$$2x+3=15 \quad \text{(third number)}$$
$$\overline{22}=\text{total}$$

A man can afford to spend $160 a week for office help. If the stenographer gets $20 a week and the bookkeeper gets ¾ as much as the salesman, how much does he pay each?

We note that there are three people to be paid. We are told that the stenographer gets $20 a week. Therefore it is only a question of finding how much the salesman and the bookkeeper get. Inasmuch as the bookkeeper gets ¾ as much as the salesman, it follows that $x$ should be made to equal the salesman's salary, and $\frac{3}{4}x$ the bookkeeper's, or $\frac{3x}{4}$. Therefore:

$$\underset{\text{salesman}}{x} \quad + \quad \underset{\text{bookkeeper}}{\frac{3x}{4}} \quad + \quad \underset{\text{stenographer}}{20} \quad = \quad \underset{\text{total}}{\$160}$$

Multiplying by 4 to clear the fraction:
$$4x+3x+80=640$$
$$7x=560$$
$$x=80 \quad \text{(salesman's salary)}$$
$$\frac{3x}{4}=60 \quad \text{(bookkeeper's salary)}$$

You can see at once that $80+60+20$ (the stenographer's salary) equals 160, or the total.

*See whether you can do the following problems:*

1. An uncle who is twice as old as his nephew is also twelve years older than his nephew. Find the age of each.
2. There are two numbers such that the larger is twice the smaller. If twelve is added to the larger, it will be six times as large as the smaller. Find the numbers.
3. A man is one year older than his wife; the age of their son is one-third that of his mother. Their combined ages are 64 years. How old is each?

## PARENTHESES

Suppose you order at a lunch counter a glass of milk and a piece of cake. You are served

$$milk + cake$$

If you know something about baking, you will realize that the cake is made up of flour and butter and sugar and eggs and milk. What you really eat is

$$milk + (flour + butter + sugar + eggs + milk)$$

All the ingredients in the parentheses, taken together, are called cake.

Numbers are like this cake; they can be separated into any number of ingredients. Thus: $4 = (5-1)$, $6 = (2+4)$, $18 = (12+6)$, etc. Of course, these same numbers could be separated differently; for example, $18 = (9+9)$ or $(10+8)$, etc.

When we write $7+3$, we could just as well write it:

$$7+(4-1) \text{ or } 7+(2+1) \text{ or } 7+(6-3), \text{ etc.}$$

All the numbers in parentheses are equal to 3. And if we remove the parentheses in each case, we shall always get the same result, namely, 10. Thus:

$$7+(4-1)=7+4-1=10$$
$$7+(2+1)=7+2+1=10$$
$$7+(6-3)=7+6-3=10$$

You will notice that in each case we *added* the two numbers in the parentheses to 7. You will remember that when we studied subtraction the rule was to change the sign and add. Now, if we *subtract* the numbers in the parentheses from 7 instead of adding them, it becomes **necessary to** change the signs of those numbers and add them. Thus:

$$7-(4-1)=7-4+1=4^*$$
$$7-(2+1)=7-2-1=4$$
$$7-(6-3)=7-6+3=4$$

*Note that the $4-1$ becomes $-4+1$.

We removed the parenthesis, but this time we changed the sign of the numbers in the parenthesis, and so we have the RULE: *Whenever we remove a parenthesis with a minus sign in front of it, we change the signs of all the numbers or letters inside the parenthesis. Whenever we remove a parenthesis with a plus sign in front of it, we do not change the signs of the numbers or letters inside the parenthesis.*

Note the following examples:

$$6+(8-2+6)=6+8-2+6=18$$
$$6-(8-2+6)=6-8+2-6=-6$$
$$4-(-2-3+6)=4+2+3-6=3$$
$$a+(b-c+d)=a+b-c+d$$
$$x-(-y+z+2)=x+y-z-2$$

EXERCISE 15

*See whether you can do the following:*

1. $8+(3-1)=?$
2. $9-(4+6-3)=?$
3. $17-(5-2+6)=?$
4. $x+(2x+3y-z)=?$
5. $x-(2a-b+3c-d)=?$
6. $x-(a+2x-3a+2)=?$

# MULTIPLICATION

We have seen that

$$a+a+a+a=4a$$

The number 4 is called the *coefficient* of $a$, and is written to the left of the letter. The coefficient before a letter tells us how many of that letter we have added together. Thus, $7x$ is a short way of expressing the sum $x+x+x+x+x+x+x$.

We have also seen that

$$a \cdot a \cdot a \cdot a = a^4$$

The number 4 in this case is called the *exponent* of $a$, and is written to the right of, and slightly above the letter. Thus, $x^7$ is a short way of expressing the product $x \cdot x \cdot x \cdot x \cdot x \cdot x \cdot x$. The coefficient and exponents are examples of what we meant by algebra shorthand mentioned at the beginning of this section. Note that, in $3n^4$, 3 is the coefficient and 4 the exponent, while $3n^4$ itself is a shorthand notation for

$$n \cdot n \cdot n \cdot n + n \cdot n \cdot n \cdot n + n \cdot n \cdot n \cdot n$$

Note how the following may be simplified:

1. $a \cdot a \cdot a + a \cdot a \cdot a = a^3 + a^3 = 2a^3$
2. $x \cdot x \cdot x \cdot x \cdot x + x \cdot x \cdot x \cdot x \cdot x + x \cdot x \cdot x \cdot x \cdot x = x^5 + x^5 + x^5 = 3x^5$
3. $b \cdot b + b \cdot b + b \cdot b + b \cdot b + b \cdot b + b \cdot b + b \cdot b = b^2 + b^2 + b^2 + b^2 + b^2 + b^2 + b^2$
   $= 7b^2$

And the reverse:

4. $5x^3 = 5 \cdot x \cdot x \cdot x$
5. $3b^5 = 3 \cdot b \cdot b \cdot b \cdot b \cdot b$
6. $4n^2 = 4 \cdot n \cdot n$

Note these examples:

$$5x^3 \quad \text{5 is the coefficient; 3 is the exponent.}$$
$$6a^2 \quad \text{6 is the coefficient; 2 is the exponent.}$$
$$8b^4 \quad \text{8 is the coefficient; 4 is the exponent.}$$

Let us study this a little more closely. When just the letter appears without any exponent, like $a$, it really means $a^1$. For example, $a \times a$ is the same as $a^1 \times a^1$, which equals $a^2$, thus

$$a \times a = a^2$$
$$a \times a \times a = a^3$$
$$a \times a \times a \times a = a^4$$
$$a \times a \times a \times a \times a = a^5$$

Then $a^2 \times a^3 = (a \times a) \times (a \times a \times a) = a^5$.

Notice that we *add* the exponents of $a^2$ and $a^3$ instead of multiplying them.

$$a^2 \times a^3 = a^{2+3} = a^5$$

In the same way:

$$a^4 \times a^3 = a^{4+3} = a^7$$
$$x^2 \times x^4 = x^{2+4} = x^6$$
$$b^4 \times b^4 = b^{4+4} = b^8$$
$$a^{12} \times a^6 = a^{12+6} = a^{18}$$

This holds true for any number of letters. Thus:

$$a^4b \times a^2b^2 = a^6b^3$$
$$a^5b \times a^2b^3 = a^7b^4$$
$$a^2 \times a^3b \times a^4b = a^9b^2$$

You will notice that we *added* all the exponents for each letter and wrote the sum in the answer.

EXERCISE 16

*See whether you can multiply these* (remember to *add* the exponents):

1. $b^4 \times b^8 = ?$     3. $x^4 \times x^2 = ?$     5. $a^4b^3 \times ab = ?$
2. $a^3 \times a^7 = ?$     4. $a^3b \times a^2b^2 = ?$     6. $bd^2 \times b^3d^3 = ?$

If we have coefficients as well as exponents, we *multiply these coefficients* and *add the exponents*. Thus:

$$4a^2 \times 3a^4 = 12a^6$$

We multiplied the coefficients 4 and 3, and got 12. We added the exponents 2 and 4, and got 6.

$$5b^4 \times 3b^5 = 15b^9$$

We multiplied the coefficients 5 and 3, and got 15. We added the exponents 4 and 5, and got 9.

This holds true for any number of letters:

$$5ab \times 6a^2 = 30a^3b$$
$$6a^2b^2 \times 4a^3b^4 = 24a^5b^6$$
$$10a^3b^2c^4 \times 3a^4b^3c^2 = 30a^7b^5c^6$$
$$7x^4y^2z \times 4x^3y^3z^2 = 28x^7y^5z^3$$
$$4a^2b^3c^2 \times 8a^3c = 32a^5b^3c^3$$

EXERCISE 17

*See whether you can do these* (remember to *multiply* the coefficients and *add* the exponents):

1. $3b^2 \times 4b^4 = ?$     3. $7a^2 \times 4ab = ?$     5. $6x^2y^2z^2 \times 4x^4y^3z^5 = ?$
2. $5a^2 \times 6a^4 = ?$     4. $8bc^2 \times 3b^3c^4 = ?$     6. $15a^3b^2c^4 \times 2bc = ?$

Remember our rule for multiplying unlike signs: like signs $+$, unlike signs $-$.

7. $8a^3b \times -3a^2b = ?$           9. $5x^3y \times -10x^5y^2 = ?$
8. $-4ad \times -3a^2d^3 = ?$        10. $x^2 \times x^3y \times x^4y^2 = ?$

118

So far we have learned to multiply single terms, or *monomials*. Now suppose we have to multiply polynomials. How do we go about it? You will remember that a polynomial was defined as an expression of two or more terms, like $2x+3y$, or $3a^2+4b^2$, or $6x^3+3y^3-2z^2$.

Let us see how we would multiply these:

Multiply $4x^2-3x+2$ by $5x$.

We arrange the problem as follows:

$$\begin{array}{r} 4x^2-3x+2 \\ 5x \\ \hline \end{array}$$

and multiply each term of the trinomial by the monomial $5x$ as if there were three separate examples, thus:

$$\begin{array}{ccc}
4x^2 & -3x & +2 \\
\times\ 5x & \times\ 5x & \times\ 5x \\
\hline
20x^3 & -15x^2 & +10x
\end{array}$$

We write the complete example as follows:

$$\begin{array}{r} 4x^2-3x+2 \\ 5x \\ \hline 20x^3-15x^2+10x \end{array}$$

Note these examples:

$$\begin{array}{r} 6x^3-4x^2+3x \\ 2x \\ \hline 12x^4-8x^3+6x^2 \quad \text{Ans.} \end{array}$$

$$\begin{array}{r} 14a^2+2b^2-3ac \\ 2c \\ \hline 28a^2c+4b^2c-6ac^2 \quad \text{Ans.} \end{array}$$

$$\begin{array}{r} 3a^2b^3d+5a^3b^2d^2 \\ 4a^2bd \\ \hline 12a^4b^4d^2+20a^5b^3d^3 \quad \text{Ans.} \end{array}$$

$$\begin{array}{r} 15a^3b^2c-3a^2b^3c+12ab^4c^2 \\ -5a^2b^2c \\ \hline -75a^5b^4c^2+15a^4b^5c^2-60a^3b^6c^3 \end{array}$$

EXERCISE 18

*Multiply:*

1. $x+2b-cd$ by $2b$.
2. $x+3xy+2y$ by $2y$.
3. $4x^2-5x+2$ by $x^2$.
4. $10a+3b-4ac$ by $4a^2bc$.
5. $4a^2b-6bc+3c$ by $3ab$.
6. $2b^2+ab+a^3$ by $4ab^2$

We now know how to multiply a polynomial by a monomial. We shall next learn how to multiply one polynomial by another.

In arithmetic we say

$$5\times14=70$$

In algebra we do this another way and get the same result. Thus:

$$5\times14=5\times(10+4)=50+20=70$$

(We have multiplied the 10 by 5, then the 4 by 5, and added these results.)

For example:

$$6\times18 \text{ can be expressed: } 6(10+8)=\ 60+48=108$$
$$7\times10 \text{ can be expressed: } 7(\ 8+2)=\ 56+14=\ 70$$
$$8\times14 \text{ can be expressed: } 8(16-2)=128-16=112$$
$$12\times\ 6 \text{ can be expressed: } 12(10-4)=120-48=\ 72$$

### EXERCISE 19

*See whether you can do these* (remember to multiply both numbers in the parentheses separately by the number outside the parentheses and add the results):

1. $3(8+2)=?$
2. $7(14-3)=?$
3. $5(8-5)=?$
4. $4(10+2)=?$
5. $6(8-3)=?$
6. $4(10+3)=?$
7. $5(7+2)=?$
8. $2(9+4)=?$
9. $-1(6+7)=?$

The same rule is followed in multiplying letters. In multiplying an expression in parentheses by a letter, multiply each term in the parentheses separately by that letter, and add the results:

$a(b+c)=ab+ac$ We multiplied $b$ by $a$ and $c$ by $a$, and added.

$a(b-c)=ab-ac$ We multiplied $b$ by $a$ and $c$ by $a$, and added.

$a(a+b)=a^2+ab$ We multiplied $a$ by $a$ and $b$ by $a$, and added.

$a^2b(a^3+b^2)=a^5b+a^2b^3$ We multiplied $a^3$ by $a^2b$ and $b^2$ by $a^2b$, and added.

$a^2bc^3(a^2+3b^3+c)=a^4bc^3+3a^2b^4c^3+a^2bc^4$ We multiplied each term in the parentheses by $a^2bc^3$, and added.

*See whether you can do these:*

1. $x(x-y)=?$
2. $2x(x+3y)=?$
3. $3a^2(a+3b^2)=?$
4. $4a^3(a^2+3b+c)=?$

5. $ab(a^2+2ab)=?$
6. $2a^2(a^3+2a^4)=?$
7. $5ab^2(ab^2-3a^2b^3)=?$
8. $10a^3b^2(ab^3-4a^2b^2)=?$

Now let us multiply polynomials by one another. Let us apply the same simple principle to this, and we shall see that it is just as simple as ordinary multiplication.

$$(3x+2)\ (4x-7)=?$$

We write the example as shown below, thus:

$$3x+2$$
$$\underline{4x-7}$$

and multiply just as if we had two separate examples, as follows:

$$
\begin{array}{cc}
3x+2 & \qquad\qquad 3x+2 \\
4x & \qquad\qquad -7 \\
\hline
12x^2+8x & \qquad\qquad -21x-14
\end{array}
$$

On adding the two results, we find

$$12x^2+\ 8x$$
$$\underline{\qquad -21x-14}$$
$$12x^2-13x-14$$

In practice, the complete example looks like this:

$$
\begin{array}{c}
3x\ +\ 2 \\
\underline{4x\ -\ 7} \\
12x^2+\ 8x \\
\underline{\qquad -21x-14} \\
12x^2-13x-14
\end{array}
$$

You will see that we have multiplied each term in the upper line by each term in the lower line (first by $4x$ and then by $-7$), and then added the results.

This can be made clearer if we do it with actual numbers. If we wish to multiply 25 by 15, we can separate them as follows: $(20+5)$ $(10+5)$. Now, multiplying these polynomials, we get:

$$
\begin{array}{r}
20+\ 5 \\
10+\ 5 \\
\hline
200+\ 50 \\
+100+25 \\
\hline
200+150+25=375
\end{array}
$$

*Examples:*

1.     $(5x^2+3x)$  $(2x^2+4x)$

$$
\begin{array}{r}
5x^2+\ 3x \\
2x^2+\ 4x \\
\hline
10x^4+\ 6x^3 \\
+20x^3+12x^2 \\
\hline
10x^4+26x^3+12x^2
\end{array}
$$

2.     $(3a+2b)$  $(4a-3b)$

$$
\begin{array}{r}
3a\ +2b \\
4a\ -3b \\
\hline
12a^2+8ab \\
-9ab-6b^2 \\
\hline
12a^2-\ ab-6b^2
\end{array}
$$

3.     $(2x^2-3x+5)$  $(2x-1)$

$$
\begin{array}{r}
2x^2-3x\ +\ 5 \\
2x\ -\ 1 \\
\hline
4x^3-6x^2+10x \\
-2x^2+\ 3x-5 \\
\hline
4x^3-8x^2+13x-5
\end{array}
$$

EXERCISE 21

*See whether you can do these:*

1.  $(2x^2-8x)(x^2+2x)$

2.  $(a^2+3ab)(a^3+2ab)$

3.  $(2x^2-3x-8)(2x-4)$

4.  $(3m^2-2m+7)(2m^2-3m)$

5.  $(3x^2+5x-2)(3x^2-2x)$

6.  $(x^3+2x^2+x)(x-4)$

IMPORTANT SPECIAL PRODUCTS

There are three special kinds of products in algebra which are very important. These special products should be learned and memorized, as

they will be extremely useful later on in our work. The first one is the
square of a binomial.

$$\text{I.} \qquad\qquad (a+b)^2 = a^2 + 2ab + b^2$$

This can be demonstrated in two ways. The first is ordinary multiplication:

$$
\begin{array}{l}
a + b \\
a + b \\
\hline
a^2 + \phantom{2}ab \\
\phantom{a^2 +} + ab + b^2 \\
\hline
a^2 + 2ab + b^2
\end{array}
$$

The second is to take two units of length, $a$ and $b$,

$$a$$
$$b$$

and lay them off on a straight line:

Then the length of this line is $a+b$. If we make a square of this (draw
a square with each side equal to $a+b$), we can divide this square into 4

parts. The first part (I) is a square with $a$ on each side, and its area is therefore $a^2$. The next part (II) has $b$ for one side and $a$ for the other; therefore its area is $ab$. The third part (III) has $a$ for one side and $b$ for the other; therefore its area is also $ab$. The last part (IV) is a small square with $b$ on each side, and therefore its area is $b^2$. We can easily see, then, that

$$(a+b)^2 = a^2 + 2ab + b^2$$

It is essential for you to memorize this rule: *The square of the sum of two terms is equal to the square of the first term, plus twice the product of the first term by the second term, plus the square of the second term.*

The second product is

II. $$\qquad (a-b)^2 = a^2 - 2ab + b^2$$

This can be seen from multiplication:

$$
\begin{array}{r}
a - b \\
a - b \\
\hline
a^2 - ab \phantom{+b^2} \\
- ab + b^2 \\
\hline
a^2 - 2ab + b^2
\end{array}
$$

It is essential for you to memorize this rule also: *The square of the difference of two terms is equal to the square of the first term, minus twice the product of the first term by the second term, plus the square of the second term.*

Now that we have learned these rules, let us apply them to a few examples:

$$(12)^2 = 144$$

Writing this as $(10+2)^2$, we get:

$$
\begin{aligned}
(10+2)^2 &= 10^2 + 2(10\times 2) + 2^2 \\
&= 100 + 2(20) + 4 \\
&= 100 + 40 + 4 \\
&= 144
\end{aligned}
$$

Find the square of 24.

$$
\begin{aligned}
(24)^2 = (20+4)^2 = 20^2 &+ 2(20\times 4) + 4^2 \\
&= 400 + 2(80) + 16 \\
&= 400 + 160 + 16 \\
&= 576
\end{aligned}
$$

This result can also be obtained by means of the *second product* $(a-b)^2$ merely by letting $24=30-6$:

$$(24)^2=(30-6)^2=30^2-2(30\times6)+6^2$$
$$=900-2(180)+36$$
$$=900-360+36$$
$$=576$$

You will note that in the first example we let $24=20+4$ and applied the formula:

$$(a+b)^2=a^2+2ab+b^2$$

letting $a=20$ and $b=4$. In the second example we let $24=30-6$ and applied the formula:

$$(a-b)^2=a^2-2ab+b^2$$

letting $a=30$ and $b=6$. We always found $(24)^2=576$.

Of course, we could let 24 equal the sum or difference of any two numbers we choose. For example:

$$(24)^2+(18+6)^2=18^2+2(18\times6)+6^2$$
$$=324+2(108)+36$$
$$=324+216+36$$
$$=576$$

No matter what two numbers make up 24, we can readily see that by applying the formula:

$$(a+b)^2=a^2+2ab+b^2$$

or

$$(a-b)^2=a^2-2ab+b^2$$

we *always* get the same result: 576.

Let us study the following:

$$(x+1)^2=x^2+2x+1$$
$$(4+x)^2=16+8x+x^2$$
$$(x-2t)^2=x^2-4tx+4t^2$$
$$(7x-y)^2=49x^2-14xy+y^2$$
$$11^2=(8+3)^2=64+48+9=121$$
$$8^2=(7+1)^2=49+14+1=64$$
$$6^2=(10-4)^2=100-80+16=36$$

*Now see whether you can do these:*

1. $(14)^2=(10+4)^2=?$    4. $(x+y)^2=?$    6. $(5-2y)^2=?$
2. $(22)^2=(20+2)^2=?$    5. $(2x-3y)^2=?$    7. $(3a-y)^2=?$
3. $(48)^2=(50-2)^2=?$

The third important product is called "the sum and difference of two terms" and is written:

III.
$$(a+b)\ (a-b)=a^2-b^2$$

This can be done by multiplication:

$$
\begin{array}{l}
a-b \\
a+b \\
\hline
a^2-ab \\
\quad +ab-b^2 \\
\hline
a^2 \qquad -b^2
\end{array}
$$

(The $+ab$ and $-ab$ cancel each other.)

It is essential to memorize this rule: *The product of the sum and difference of two terms equals the difference of their squares.*

$$(x+y)\ (x-y)=x^2-y^2$$
$$(c+d)\ (c-d)=c^2-d^2$$

Let us apply this to a few examples:

1.
$$22\times18=?$$
Let $22=20+2$ (the same as $a+b$)
Let $18=20-2$ (the same as $a-b$)
Then $22\times18=(20+2)\ (20-2)=20^2-2^2$
$$=400-4$$
$$=396$$

2.
$$31\times29=?$$
Let $31=30+1$
Let $29=30-1$
Then $31\times29=(30+1)\ (30-1)=30^2-1^2$
$$=900-1$$
$$=899$$

3.
$$52\times40=(46+6)\ (46-6)=46^2-6^2$$
$$=2116-36$$
$$=2080$$

4.
$$17\times7=(12+5)\ (12-5)=12^2-5^2$$
$$=144-25$$
$$=119$$

5.
$$(x+2y)\ (x-2y)=x^2-4y^2$$

6.
$$(3a+b)\ (3a-b)=9a^2-b^2$$

EXERCISE 23

*See whether you can do these:*

1. $21\times15=?$    3. $30\times20=?$         5. $(3x+2y)\ (3x-2y)=?$
2. $27\times17=?$    4. $(a+2b)\ (a-2b)=?$

# DIVISION

When we multiplied two letters with exponents and coefficients, we *added* the exponents of like letters and *multiplied* the coefficients. In division it is *exactly the reverse*. When we divide two letters with exponents and coefficients, we *subtract* the exponents of like letters and *divide* the coefficients. Thus

$$\frac{8c^3}{4c^2}=2c^{3-2}=2c$$

We divided the coefficient 8 by 4, and got 2.
We subtracted the exponent 2 from 3, and got 1.

$$\frac{16a^6}{4a^2}=4a^{6-2}=4a^4$$

We divided the coefficient 16 by 4, and got 4.
We subtracted the exponent 2 from 6, and got 4.

$$\frac{12x^{10}}{4x^2}=3x^{10-2}=3x^8$$

We divided the coefficient 12 by 4, and got 3.
We subtracted the exponent 2 from 10, and got 8.

$$\frac{15a^3b^6}{3ab}=5a^{3-1}b^{6-1}=5a^2b^5$$

127

We divided the coefficient 15 by 3, and got 5.

We subtracted the exponents 1 from 3, and 1 from 6, and got 2 and 5.

$$\frac{6c^2d^3}{3c^2d}=2d^2$$

We divided the coefficient 6 by 3, and got 2.

We noted that we had $c^2$ divided by $c^2$, which is 1. We subtracted the exponent 1 from 3, and got 2.

Note that $\frac{c}{c}=1$. Dividing a letter with an exponent by the same letter with the same exponent is always 1.

EXERCISE 24

*See whether you can do these* (remember to divide the coefficients and subtract exponents):

1. $\dfrac{6x^6}{3x^4}=?$   3. $\dfrac{10a^4b^2c^4}{5a^2bc^2}=?$

2. $\dfrac{18a^3b^2}{6a^2b^2}=?$   4. $\dfrac{21a^7b^4}{7a^4b}=?$

The rule of signs is the same in division as it is in multiplication, namely:

$$+ \text{ divided by } + = +$$
$$+ \text{ divided by } - = -$$
$$- \text{ divided by } + = -$$
$$- \text{ divided by } - = +$$

or, like signs $+$, unlike signs $-$. Thus:

$$\frac{+14a^3b^2}{-2ab}=-7a^2b$$

$$\frac{-6x^4y^3}{+3x^2y}=-2x^2y^2$$

$$\frac{-8x^3y^2}{-4xy}=2x^2y$$

We saw in multiplication that when we multiplied a polynomial by a single term, we multiplied each term in the polynomial by that single

128

term. In division we do the same thing, except that we divide each term. For example:

$$\frac{9x^4-12x^3+21x^2}{3x^2}=3x^2-4x+7$$

We divided the $9x^4$ first and got $\frac{9x^4}{3x^2}=3x^2$.

Then we divided the $-12x^3$ and got $\frac{-12x^3}{3x^2}=-4x$.

And lastly we divided the $21x^2$ and got $\frac{21x^2}{3x^2}=+7$.

Examples:

$$\frac{25x^2y^2+30xy^4}{-5xy}=5xy-6y^3 \qquad \text{(Remember that } \tfrac{x}{x}=1.)$$

$$\frac{ab+ad}{a}=b+d \qquad \text{(Remember that } \tfrac{a}{a}=1.)$$

$$\frac{9x-18x^3}{3x}=3-6x^2$$

$$\frac{6a^2+8a-12a^4}{2a}=3a+4-6a^3$$

EXERCISE 25

*See whether you can do these:*

1. $\dfrac{14np^2-28n^2p^3}{7np}=?$

2. $\dfrac{16a^4b^5-24a^5b^6-32a^6b^7}{8a^2b^3}=?$

3. $\dfrac{49xy-63x^2y^3+7xy^2}{7xy}=?$

4. $\dfrac{18a^2x-6a^3x^2+36a^4x^3}{6ax}=?$

Dividing one polynomial by another polynomial is similar to long division in arithmetic. In arithmetic, long division is commonly arranged as follows:

$$
\begin{array}{r}
\phantom{\text{Divisor } 32 \,|\,}\ 2048 \quad \text{Quotient}\\
\text{Divisor } \underline{32\ |}\ \overline{65536} \quad \text{Dividend}\\
\underline{64}\phantom{536}\\
153\phantom{36}\\
\underline{128}\phantom{36}\\
\underline{256}\phantom{6}\\
256\phantom{6}\\
\end{array}
$$

129

The same arrangement is followed in algebra. Compare carefully each step in the following examples in algebra with the corresponding step of the example in arithmetic.

*Example:* Divide $2x^2-10x+12$ by $x-2$.
*Solution:*

$$
\begin{array}{r}
2x - 6 \qquad \text{Quotient} \\
\text{Divisor} \quad x-2 \enclose{longdiv}{2x^2-10x+12} \quad \text{Dividend} \\
2x^2- 4x \\
\hline
- 6x+12 \\
- 6x+12 \\
\hline
\end{array}
$$

*Example:* Divide $n^2+n-6$ by $n-2$.
*Solution:*

$$
\begin{array}{r}
n+3 \quad \text{Quotient} \\
\text{Divisor} \quad n-2 \enclose{longdiv}{n^2+ n-6} \quad \text{Dividend} \\
n^2-2n \\
\hline
3n-6 \\
3n-6 \\
\hline
\end{array}
$$

*Example:* Divide $x^3-6x^2+11x-6$ by $x-3$.
*Solution:*

$$
\begin{array}{r}
x^2-3x +2 \qquad \text{Quotient} \\
\text{Divisor} \quad x-3 \enclose{longdiv}{x^3-6x^2+11x-6} \quad \text{Dividend} \\
x^3-3x^2 \\
\hline
-3x^2+11x \\
-3x^2+ 9x \\
\hline
+ 2x-6 \\
+ 2x-6 \\
\hline
\end{array}
$$

You will notice that in all these examples we started by dividing the first term of the divisor into the first term of the dividend, and placing the result above the line (getting the first term of the quotient). We multiplied the divisor by this result, and placed the answer under the corresponding term of the dividend. We then subtracted, and in the subtraction we were careful to change the signs and add. The new result we then treated like the original dividend. The operation is then repeated until the problem is completed, each new term of the quotient being placed next to the previous one.

*See whether you can do these problems in division:*

Divide:

1. $a^2-6a+8$ by $a-4$.
2. $4p^2-8np+3n^2$ by $2p-3n$.
3. $n^3-n^2-12n$ by $n+3$.
4. $18a^2+45a^3+18a^4$ by $3a^2+6a$

# FACTORING

Factoring, like division, is the reverse of multiplication. In multiplication we multiplied two numbers together and obtained a product. In factoring we take that product and break it up into the two numbers.

In multiplication we say: $2\times5=10$.

In factoring we say: 10 can be "broken up" into two *factors:* 2 and 5.

Any numbers which, when multiplied together, will give a certain number, are called *factors* of that certain number.

We learned that when we multiply a binomial by a single term we get

$$a(b+c-d)=ab+ac-ad$$

That is, we multiply each letter separately in the parentheses by the single letter outside the parentheses.

Now we can say that $ab+ac-ad$ can be broken up or factored into $a(b+c-d)$, because we knew that when we multiplied $a(b+c-d)$ we got $ab+ac-ad$. In other words, $(a)$ is one factor and $(b+c-d)$ is another factor.

Now suppose we are given an expression with several terms, and are asked to break it up or factor it. How do we go about it? For example, find the factors of $4a^2b^2-32ab$.

First we notice that $ab$ is contained in both terms. We also notice that 4 will go into both terms evenly (it will go into the first term once, and into the second term eight times). We therefore know that $4ab$ will go into both terms evenly. $4ab$, then, is one factor, and whatever remains by dividing $4ab$ into $4a^2b^2-32ab$ will be the other factor. Hence we divide:

$$\frac{4a^2b^2-32ab}{4ab}=ab-8$$

The two factors are $4ab$ and $(ab-8)$

$$\text{or } 4ab(ab-8)=4a^2b^2-32ab$$

Whenever we factor a polynomial, we always look to see whether there is a common term which is contained in all the terms of the polynomial. If there is one, we then divide the polynomial by this common term and put the result in a parenthesis.

This process of picking out the common term is extremely simple. We do it all the time whenever we talk. Instead of saying, for example, "Mr. Jones owns a boat and Mr. Jones owns a car and Mr. Jones owns a radio and Mr. Jones owns a house," we simply say that "Mr. Jones owns (a boat, and a car, and a radio, and a house)."

The factors of:

$$ax+ay+ab=a(x+y+b)$$
$$5ax+10a^2x^2+30a^3x^2=5ax(1+2ax+6a^2x)$$
$$6a^2+8a-12a^4=2a(3a+4-6a^3)$$

EXERCISE 27

*See whether you can factor these:*

1. $3ax-15a^2x=?$
2. $12b^3y+8b^2y^2-4by=?$
3. $ay-abc-aby=?$
4. $3c^2-12c-18c^4=?$
5. $5ad+10a^2d^2-15a^3d=?$

Now suppose you came across the following sentence. How would you make it simpler and shorter?

Mrs. $a$ has a cat and Mrs. $a$ has a dog and Mrs. $b$ has a cat and Mrs. $b$ has a dog.

Naturally you would write it first this way:

Mrs. a has (a cat and dog)<br>and Mrs. b has (a cat and dog).

Then you would write it

(Mrs. a and Mrs. b) have (a cat and dog).

If the cat and dog are abbreviated to $c$ and $d$, we get:

$$ac+ad+bc+bd \quad \text{(1st sentence)}$$
$$a(c+d)+b(c+d) \quad \text{(2nd sentence)}$$
$$(a+b)(c+d) \quad \text{(last sentence)}$$

Note these examples:

$$3(a-b)+c(a-b)=(3+c)(a-b)$$
$$x(a+b)+y(a+b)=(x+y)(a+b)$$

$$4a(2x-7)-3(2x-7)=(4a-3)(2x-7)$$
$$2m+bm+2z+bz=(2+b)m+(2+b)z=(2+b)(m+z)$$
$$3ax-6bx-ay+2by=3x(a-2b)-y(a-2b)=(3x-y)(a-2b)$$
$$ac-ax+bx-bc=a(c-x)-b(c-x)=(a-b)(c-x)$$

EXERCISE 28

*See whether you can do these:*

1. $4(x+2y)+a(x+2y)=?$

2. $a(x^2+2)+b(x^2+2)=?$

3. $ax+ay+bx+by=?$

4. $4by+7by+8ax+3ax=?$

We have already seen that:

$$(a+b)^2=a^2+2ab+b^2$$
$$(a-b)^2=a^2-2ab+b^2$$
$$(a+b)(a-b)=a^2-b^2$$

We memorized these formulæ and understand them thoroughly. Now let us put them in the language of factoring, and say

The factors of $a^2+2ab+b^2$ are $(a+b)(a+b)$

The factors of $a^2-2ab+b^2$ are $(a-b)(a-b)$

The factors of $a^2-b^2$ are $(a+b)(a-b)$

We will use these three typical formulæ a great deal in factoring. The first or second formula will apply to any expression that is the sum or the difference of two squares. All we need do in order to determine whether a given expression *is* the sum or difference of two squares is to take the square root of the first term, add to it or subtract it from the square root of the last term, and multiply this by itself (square it). If the result is the given expression, that expression is a perfect square. For example:

Is $x^2+4x+4$ a perfect square?

The square root of $x^2$ is $x$.

The square root of 4 is 2.

$$(x+2)^2=x^2+4x+4$$
Ans. *Yes.*

The factors are $(x+2)^2$.

Factor the following:

$$a^2+12a+36=(a+6)^2$$
$$(a+6)^2=a^2+12a+36$$

You will note that the middle term is always twice the product of the square root of the first and the square root of the second terms. If it is not twice this product, the expression is *not* a perfect square. Thus:

$$9c^2+12c+4$$

The middle term is $12c$.
The square root of the first term is $3c$.
The square root of the last term is $2$.

$$2\times3c=6c, \text{ and } twice\ 6c \text{ is } 12c.$$

Therefore $9c^2+12c+4$ is a perfect square with factors:

$$(3c+2)(3c+2)$$

If this expression were:

$$9c^2+8c+4$$

the middle term, $8c$, would *not* be twice the first and last term; hence it would *not* be a perfect square.

Find what is necessary to make these expressions perfect squares:

$$a^2+?+b^2$$

The $\sqrt{a^2}=a$; the $\sqrt{b^2}=b$. Twice $ab=2ab$.
Therefore $a^2+2ab+b^2$.

$$x^2+?+25$$

$\sqrt{x^2}=x$; $\sqrt{25}=5$. Twice $5x=10x$.
Therefore $x^2+10x+25$.

$$1+?+16t^2$$

$\sqrt{1}=1$; $\sqrt{16t^2}=4t$. Twice $4t=8t$.
Therefore $1+8t+16t^2$.

The first thing to do, then, when factoring a trinomial (three-term expression), is to find out whether or not it is a perfect square. If it is, apply the formula:

$$a^2+2ab+b^2=(a+b)^2$$

or if the middle term is preceded by a minus sign:

$$a^2-2ab+b^2=(a-b)^2$$

Factor the following:

$$9x^2+6x+1$$

The $\sqrt{9x^2}=3x$; the $\sqrt{1}=1$.

$9x^2+6x+1$, being a perfect square, is of the form $a^2+2ab+b^2$, whose factors are $(a+b)^2$ or $(a+b)(a+b)$. Hence the factors of $9x^2+6x+1$ are $(3x+1)^2$ or $(3x+1)(3x+1)$.

EXERCISE 29

*See whether you can factor the following* (remember $a^2+2ab+b^2=(a+b)^2$; $a^2-2ab+b^2=(a-b)^2$)

1. $x^2+4x+4=?$
2. $a^2+6a+9=?$
3. $y^2-10y+25=?$
4. $b^2-14b+49=?$

The third formula in the group which we learned is

$$a^2-b^2=(a+b)(a-b)$$

Let us apply this to factoring the difference of two squares. Thus:

$$a^2-x^2=(a+x)(a-x)$$
$$x^2-1=(x+1)(x-1)$$
$$16-t^2=(4+t)(4-t)$$
$$4x^2-9=(2x+3)(2x-3)$$

Whenever you see the difference of two squares, apply the formula:

$$a^2-b^2=(a+b)(a-b)$$

For example:

$$x^4-81=(x^2+9)(x^2-9)$$

But $x^2-9$ is also the difference of two squares, or

$$x^2-9=(x+3)(x-3)$$

Therefore $x^4-81=(x^2+9)(x+3)(x-3)$

If $a=2$, $b=5$, $c=4$, $x=3$, $y=\frac{1}{2}$, find the numerical value of the following expressions:

**1.** $5c$

**2.** $4x$

**3.** $2by$

**4.** $4a^2$

**5.** $5b^2$

**6.** $6abcx$

**7.** $3a^2b^2c^2$

**8.** $4(b+x^2)$

**9.** $2a(cy+bc)$

**10.** $4y+3b$

**11.** $8ac+5ax$

**12.** $2(a^2+b^2+x)$

**13.** $\sqrt{c}$

**14.** $\sqrt{x^2}$

**15.** $\sqrt[3]{2c}$

**16.** $\sqrt[3]{b^3}$

**17.** $a\sqrt{b^2}$

**18.** $(a+c)\sqrt{10ab}$

**19.** $c(b-a)$

**20.** $(c+x)^2$

**21.** $a^2-y^2$

**22.** $\dfrac{c}{a}+\dfrac{b}{y}$

**23.** $\dfrac{1}{a}+\dfrac{1}{c}$

**24.** $\dfrac{1}{x}+\dfrac{1}{y}$

**25.** $4bc-3ax$

**26.** $2c^2-x^2$

**27.** $x^2+y^2$

**28.** $(x+y)^2$

**29.** $(x+y)^3$

**30.** $(x-y)^2$

---



**1.** $7a$
$5a$
$4a$
$3a$

**2.** $16bx$
$12bx$
$8bx$

**3.** $-5abc$
$-8abc$
$-10abc$

**4.** $-2a^2x$
$-9a^2x$
$-4a^2x$

**5.** $+25by$
$+18by$
$-12by$

**6.** $-16xy$
$-14xy$
$+15xy$

**7.** $3b$
$-5b$
$8b$

**8.** $-\ mn$
$5mn$
$-12mn$

**9.** $-15ax^2$
$-18ax^2$
$22ax^2$
$12ax^2$

**10.** $11b^2y$
$-6b^2y$
$-7b^2y$
$4b^2y$

**11.** $6ab$
$5ab$
$-8ab$
$-13ab$

**12.** $-14bc^2$
$6bc^2$
$-18bc^2$
$9bc^2$

**13.** $4a-6c$
$-5a-5c$
$-8a+4c$

**14.** $-7x+4y$
$-9x-6y$
$5x+7y$

**15.** $8b+3d$
$-3b-5d$
$-12b-10d$

**16.** $-5m-6n$
$-9m+5n$
$m-4n$

---



**1.** Subtract $12ax$ from $18ax$

**2.** Subtract $14b^2y^2$ from $-5b^2y^2$

**3.** Subtract $-16a^2b^2$ from $-22a^2b^2$

**4.** Subtract $-10mn$ from $8mn$

**5.** Subtract $-36x^2y^2$ from $-24x^2y^2$

**6.** Subtract $21ac$ from $-9ac$

**7.** Subtract $7ay$ from $3ay$

**8.** Subtract $-15abc$ from $-18abc$

**9.** Subtract $-24xy$ from $32xy$

**10.** Subtract $9ac^2$ from $-6ac^2$

**11.** Subtract $48z+14y$ from $36z-12y$

**12.** Subtract $-30abc-10bx$ from $20abc-18bx$

**13.** Subtract $8a+9b$ from $6a+4b$

**14.** From $-21x-25y$ take $33x+28y$

**15.** From $14x+16y$ take $-7x-8y$

EXERCISE 33

1. $12+(5+2)$
2. $12+(5-2)$
3. $12-(5+2)$
4. $12-(5-2)$
5. $a+(b+a)$

6. $a+(b-2a)$
7. $a-(b-2a)$
8. $4a+3(b-a)$
9. $5a-2(a-b)$
10. $9-(2-4)$

11. $10-(6+3)$
12. $(3a-3b)-(b+c)$
13. $8ab-(2ab-2a^2)$
14. $a-[-(-a)]$
15. $a+[b-(a-b)]$

---

Perform the following multiplications:

EXERCISE 34

1. $a\times a$
2. $c^2\times c$
3. $a^2\times a^4$
4. $2a^2\times 3a^3$
5. $(-5b)\times(-3b^2)$
6. $(-b^2)\times(-b^3)$
7. $4a\times(-3a^2)$
8. $(-3c)\times(8c^3)$
9. $2a\times 3a^2\times 5a$
10. $(6a^2)\times(-4a)\times(3a)$

11. $(-x^2)\times(-3x)\times(-2x^3)$
12. $2ab(a+b+c)$
13. $3a^2c(2a-3b-c)$
14. $-5a(2x^2-2y^2)$
15. $(3a-4b)(5a-6b)$
16. $(a+b)(a-b)$
17. $(2a+3b)(4a+5b)$
18. $(8a-2b)(2b+4a)$
19. $(2x+3y)(2x-3y)$
20. $(2x+3y)(2x+3y)$

---

Perform the following divisions:

EXERCISE 35

1. $18x^3\div 6x$
2. $24x^4y^3\div 3x^2y^2$
3. $-16x^3y^4\div(-8xy)$
4. $-12abc\div(-2ab)$
5. $32a^2x^3\div(-4a^2x)$
6. $27b^5c^4\div(-9bc)$
7. $-36x^3y^3\div 4xy^2$
8. $-40a^3d^3\div 5a^2d$
9. $(24a^2b^2+18a^3b^3)\div 2ab$
10. $(16a^3x^2-12a^2x^3)\div 4ax$
11. $(21b^4y^5+18b^5y^6)\div(-3b^2y^2)$
12. $(14a^4y^4-7a^2y^2)\div(-7ay)$

13. $(x^2+5x+6)\div(x+2)$
14. $(x^2-8x+15)\div(x-3)$
15. $(x^2-y^2)\div(x+y)$
16. $(a^2+2ab+b^2)\div(a+b)$
17. $(x^2-2xy+y^2)\div(x-y)$
18. $\dfrac{48m^7n^7p}{-6mp}$
19. $\dfrac{-14a^2b^3c^4}{-14a^2b^3c^4}$
20. $\dfrac{-12xy^3}{-12y^3}$

---

Solve the following equations:

EXERCISE 36

1. $5x=10+4x$
2. $12x-4=7x+6$
3. $3x+3=18$
4. $4x-5=3x+2$
5. $ax=b$
6. $ax+b=c$
7. $ax+b=cx+d$
8. $6(x+2)=5(x+4)$
9. $4(x-2)=2(x+6)$

10. $\dfrac{3x}{b}=a-c$
11. $\dfrac{5x}{a}=b+c$
12. $3x^2+3=15$
13. $2x^2-12=x^2+24$
14. If $C=2\pi R$, solve for $R$.
15. $V=lwh$; solve for $h$.
16. $N=PD$; solve for $D$.

# PLANE GEOMETRY

# PLANE GEOMETRY

## WHAT PLANE GEOMETRY IS

WE ALL HAVE first-hand experience with the objects whose properties are studied in geometry. For instance, we know that a block of wood, a stone, and a chunk of coal are solid figures. *Solid* geometry is the study of the properties of solid figures.

The boundary of a solid figure is a *surface*. For example, the surface of a ball is what we call the outside of the ball. The surface of a cube consists of the six faces. The surface of a cylinder like a tin can consists of the top, the bottom, and the rounded part joining them.

Not all surfaces are boundaries of solids. The flat surface called a *plane,* for example, is not the boundary, by itself, of any solid. The study of figures drawn on a plane is called *plane geometry,* and such figures are called *plane figures.* They are made up of points and lines. The figure made up of three points joined by three lines is called a *triangle.* The

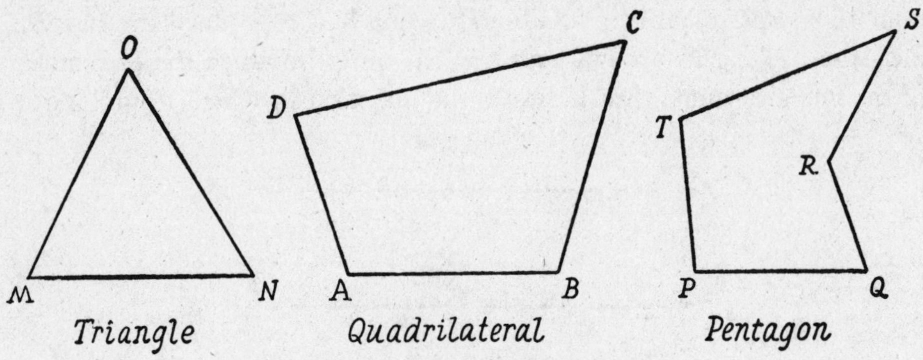


DIAGRAM I. Types of plane figures.

figure made up of four points joined by four lines is called a *quadrilateral.* In the same way, five points joined by five lines form a *pentagon,* etc. All these figures have one general name—they are called *polygons.* The prefix "poly" means many; the suffix "gon" means side.

In speaking of plane figures, we usually label each point with a different letter of the alphabet, using capital letters, and read these letters in succession. For instance, the quadrilateral on the previous page is read as ABCD, the pentagon is PQRST, etc.

## LINES

A *line* is the path of a moving point. The simplest line is a straight line. The best example of a straight line is a string stretched taut between two points, like *AB*.

There are several kinds of lines. A *curved* line is one of which no part is straight, as *CD*.

A *broken* line is composed of a number of straight lines, as *EF*.

We refer to or identify a line in plane geometry by naming its extremities (between which it runs), as *AB* in the first diagram, *CD* in the second diagram, and *EF* in the last diagram (above).

To "produce" a line means to prolong it. For instance, to produce the line *AB* means to prolong it through point *B*. To produce the line *BA* means to prolong it through point *A*. The order in which the extremities of the line are named thus indicates the direction in which to prolong it.

To bisect a line means to divide it into two equal parts, thus:

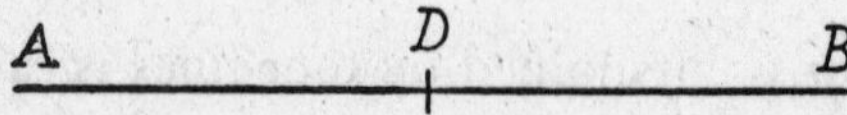

The point *D* bisects the line *AB*. It divides the line *AB* into two equal parts: *AD* and *DB*.

## ANGLES

If a straight line, *OA*, rotates about one of its points, *O*, until it reaches any position, such as *OB*, the amount of this rotation is called an *angle*.

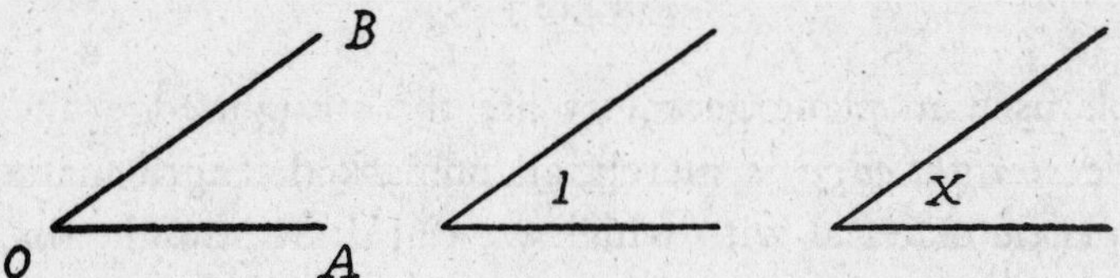

The angle in the figure shown above is designated by *AOB*.

The vertex letter (*O*) of an angle should always be read between the other letters. Frequently a number or letter is placed inside the angle, in which case it is read "angle 1" or "angle x," as in the figures above.

When the straight line *OA* rotates about *O*, the point *A* travels along a path called a circle. Every angle determines part of a circle. A complete rotation of line *OA* about *O* produces a complete circle. We say that the angle and the circle contains 360 degrees (written 360°). A half-circle or semi-circle contains 180°; a quarter-circle contains 90°.

The angle that marks off a quarter-circle is called a *right angle*. A right angle, then, contains 90°.

Any angle less than a right angle is called an acute angle. An acute angle, therefore, always contains less than 90°. Any angle greater than a right angle and less than a straight angle is called an *obtuse angle*. An obtuse angle, therefore, always contains more than 90° and less than 180°.

A *straight angle* is a straight line (180° or half a circle).

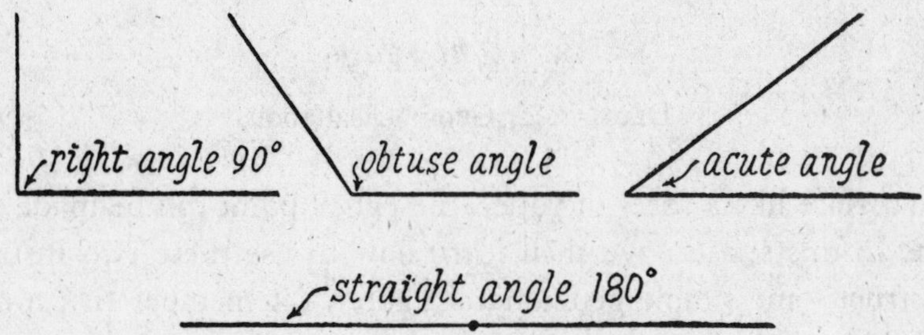


It is easily seen, then, that a circle contains two straight angles or four right angles.

Angles are measured in degrees, minutes, and seconds. (The size of an angle has nothing to do with the length of its sides.) There are 60 seconds in a minute, and 60 minutes in a degree. The second is indicated by two short strokes (″), the minute by one short stroke (′), the degree by a small circle (°). Thus, 61 degrees, 21 minutes, and 14 seconds is written: 61° 21′ 14″.

## CONSTRUCTING WITH GEOMETRICAL TOOLS

The tools used in plane geometry are the straight-edge and the compasses. The *straight-edge* is merely an unmarked length made of wood, metal, or plastic material with which we can draw straight lines. A ruler is not a straight-edge, because it has markings on it, but we can use it as a straight-edge by disregarding the markings. The *compasses* are made by joining two bars at one end of each bar. The other end of one bar has a sharp point, while the other end of the other has a pencil point or pen-point attached. If the compasses are opened, and the sharp end stuck into

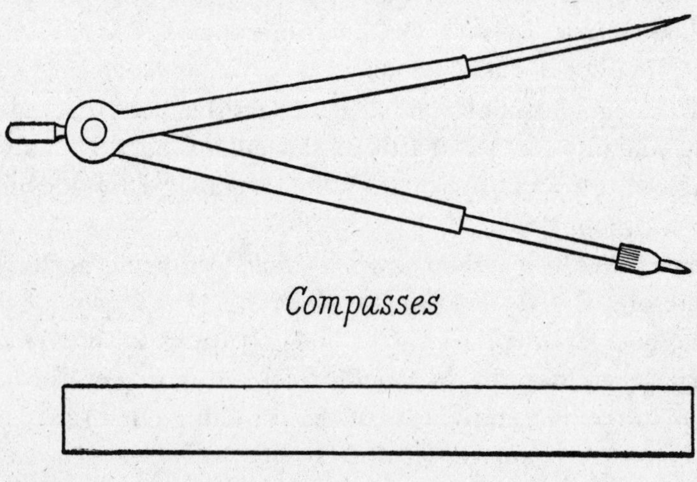

*Compasses*

*Straight - edge*

DIAGRAM 2. Geometrical tools.

a plane surface like a sheet of paper, the pencil point can be made to draw a circle. In this section, we shall learn how to use these two instruments to construct some simple geometrical figures. (Remember that a *compass* is used by navigators to determine direction, while *compasses* are used to draw circles.)

We shall first use the straight-edge and compasses to bisect a line. Suppose that we have been given the line *AB* to bisect. We open the compasses so that the two points are at a distance greater than half the length of line *AB*. Placing the sharp point of the compasses on the end *A* of the line *AB,* we allow the writing point to travel, making an arc of about 120°. Without changing the angle between the legs of the compasses, place the sharp point on the end *B* of the line *AB* and draw a second arc cutting the first. If the directions are carefully followed, the two arcs drawn will cut each other at two points (labeled *X* and *Y* in the figure). With the

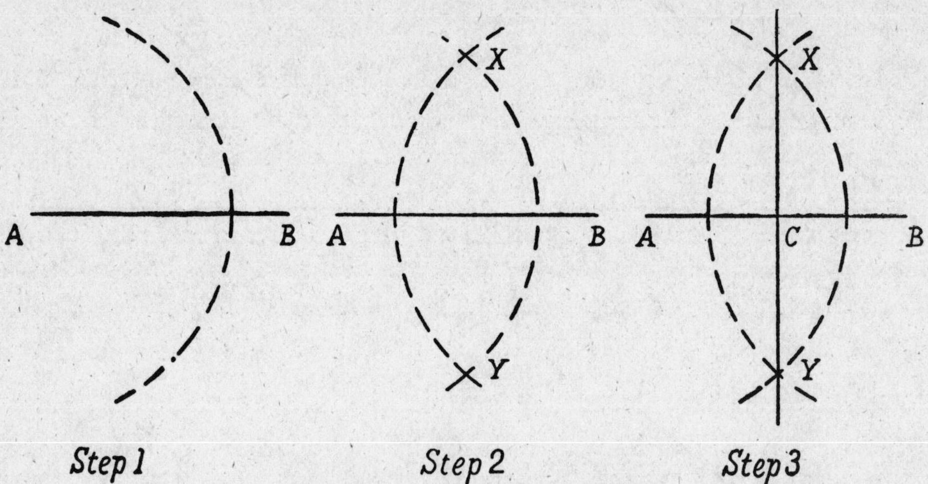


DIAGRAM 3. Bisecting a line.

straight-edge, draw a line joining points *X* and *Y*. This line will bisect line *AB* and be perpendicular to it as well. In fact, we have constructed the perpendicular bisector of line *AB.*

We shall next use our instruments to bisect an angle. Suppose that we have been given the angle *AOB* to bisect. We open the compasses to any convenient angle, and place the sharp point on the vertex *O* of the angle. We then allow the writing point to travel, making an arc long enough to cut both sides of the angle. Suppose side *OA* is cut at point *X* and side *OB* is cut at point *Y*. Without altering the angle between the legs of the compasses, we then place it with the sharp point of *X* and draw an arc lying inside the angle. Still keeping the legs of the compasses in the same position, place the sharp point at *Y* and draw a second arc cutting the first arc, say at point *P*. With the straight-edge, draw a line joining points *O* and *P*. The line *OP* will bisect the angle *AOB.*

Since the method given above for bisecting an angle can be used for angles of any size, it will work for the special case when the angle given is a straight angle. There is one slight change which must be made, however. Before drawing the arcs with centers at *X* and *Y*, we must open the legs of the compasses somewhat wider than when drawing the arc with center *O*. Let us go through with the complete construction in this case.

We start with the straight angle *AOB*. With the legs of the compasses opened to any angle, we draw the arc *XY* as before. Next we open the legs of the compasses more and then draw the arcs with centers *X* and *Y*, meeting at point *P*. Finally, we draw line *OP*.

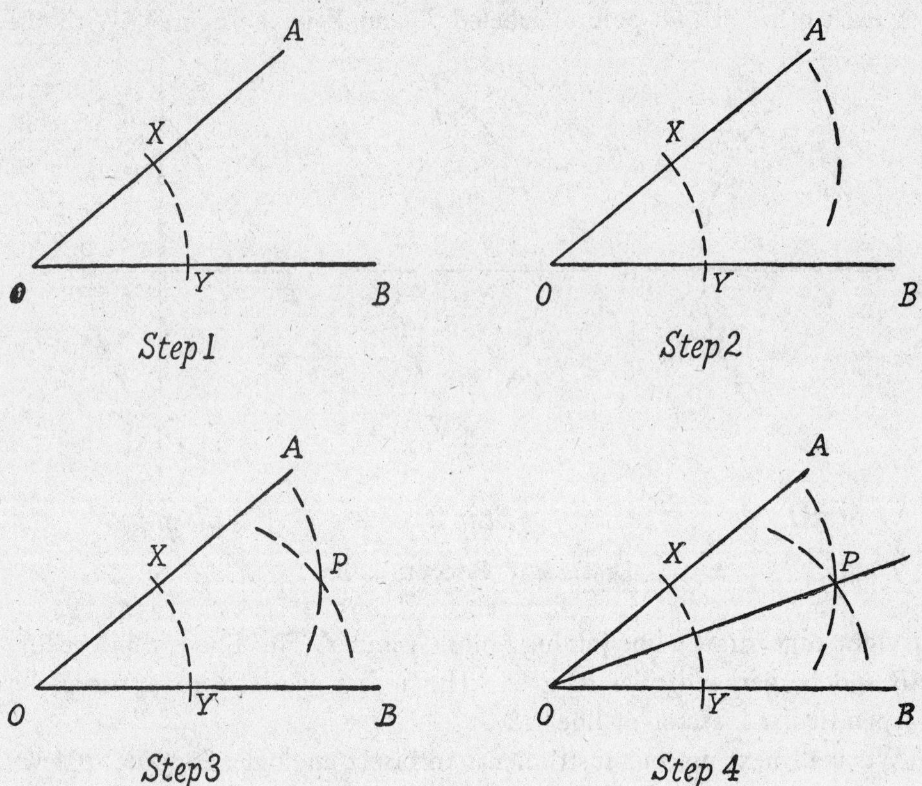

DIAGRAM 4. Bisecting an angle.

Since a straight angle has 180°, and since we have bisected angle *AOB*, it follows that angle *AOP* and angle *POB* are both equal to 90°. In other words, line *OP* is perpendicular to line *AB* at point *O*. In this construction, therefore, we do three things at once—we bisect a straight angle,

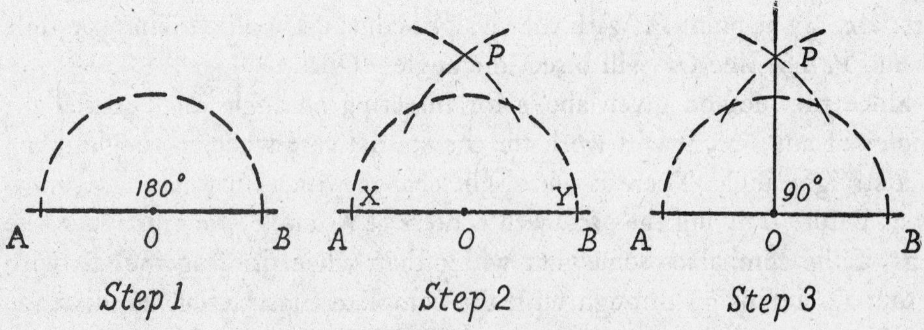

DIAGRAM 5. Bisecting a straight angle.

we construct an angle of 90°, and we construct a perpendicular at a point on a line. Remember this construction and use it whenever you are asked to do any one of the three.

The last construction described in this section is used when one wishes to draw a line perpendicular to a given line from a point not on that line. The method is very simple, and we shall describe it briefly. Suppose we

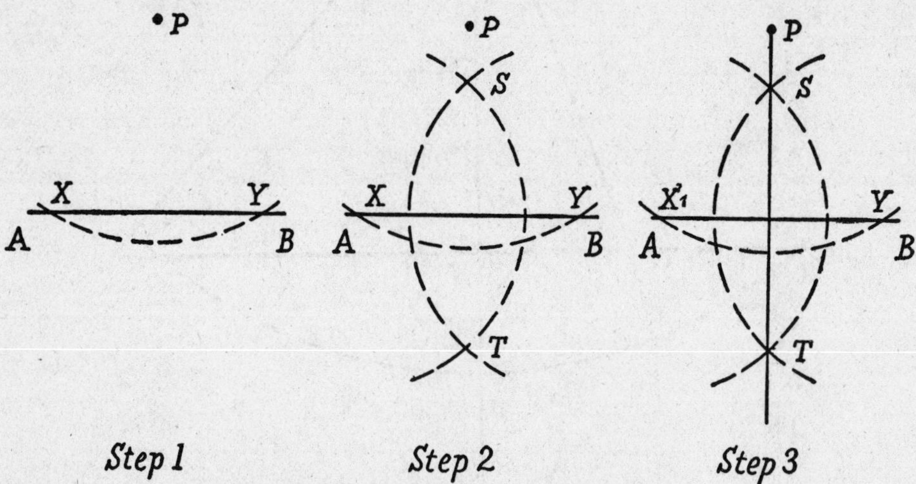


DIAGRAM 6. Dropping a perpendicular.

have been asked to construct a line from point $P$ which shall be perpendicular to line $AB$. First, open the compasses so that the distance between the sharp point and the writing point is greater than the distance from point $P$ to line $AB$. Place the sharp point on $P$ and draw an arc $XY$ cutting line $AB$ at the two points $X$ and $Y$. Finally, bisect line $XY$ as described in the first construction. The perpendicular bisector you construct will pass through point $P$ and will, consequently, be perpendicular to line $AB$.

Since the perpendicular will pass through the three points $P$, $S$, and $T$, and since all you need is two points to draw a line, you can simplify the construction by leaving out either all the arcs which lie above the line $AB$ or all the arcs which lie below $AB$. Again, you may find it necessary to extend line $AB$ either to the left or to the right in order to find the points $X$ and $Y$. This can very easily be done and presents no great problem.

A line which starts from one vertex of a triangle and is perpendicular to the side opposite is called an *altitude*. The construction of an altitude is an example of construction of a perpendicular to a line from a point not on it. In the diagram, you can trace the steps and see how the altitude can be constructed.

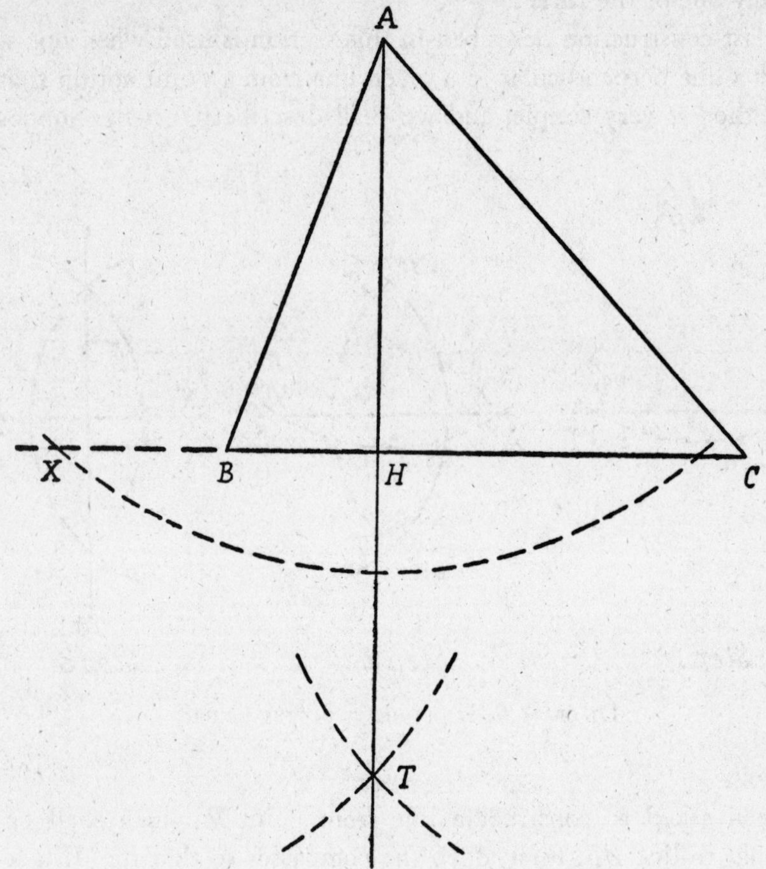

DIAGRAM 7. Constructing an altitude.

**EXERCISE 1**

1. Construct an angle of 45°.
2. Draw a triangle and construct the three perpendicular bisectors of the sides.
3. Draw a triangle and construct the three angle bisectors.
4. Draw an angle and divide it into four equal parts.
5. Draw any line and divide it into four equal parts. **Check by measuring** each part.
6. Draw a triangle and construct the three altitudes.

## GENERAL TERMS NEEDED

Two angles are *complementary* if their sum is a right angle. Thus, Angle 1 is complementary to Angle 2 (below) because Angle 1 plus Angle 2 equals a right angle (90°).

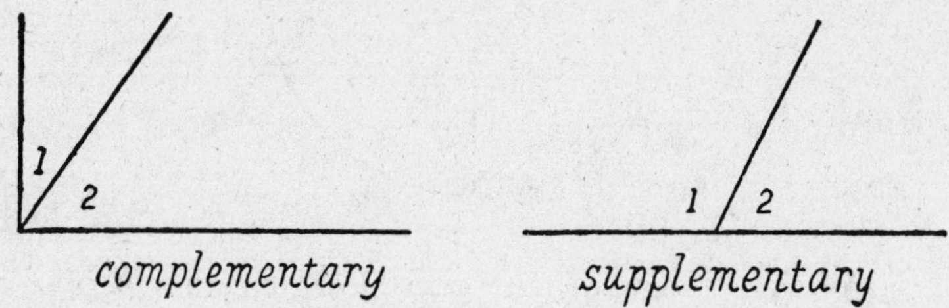

complementary          supplementary

Two angles are *supplementary* if their sum is a straight angle (a straight line). Thus, Angle 1 is supplementary to Angle 2 in the right hand drawing shown above.

Two angles that have a common side and a common vertex are called *adjacent* angles. Thus, Angle 1 is adjacent to Angle 2 because they both have a common vertex and a common side (the middle line).

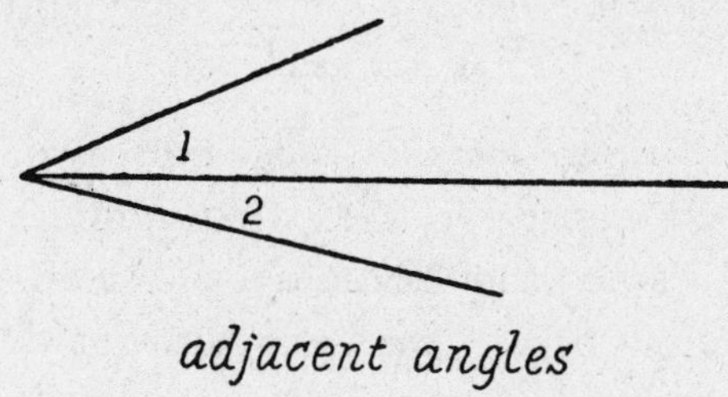

adjacent angles

Two angles are *vertical* if, when they are placed apex to apex, their sides are mutually continuous (see diagram below). Two intersecting straight lines always form four vertical angles. Thus, Angle 1 and Angle 2 are vertical angles; Angle 3 and Angle 4 are vertical angles (below).

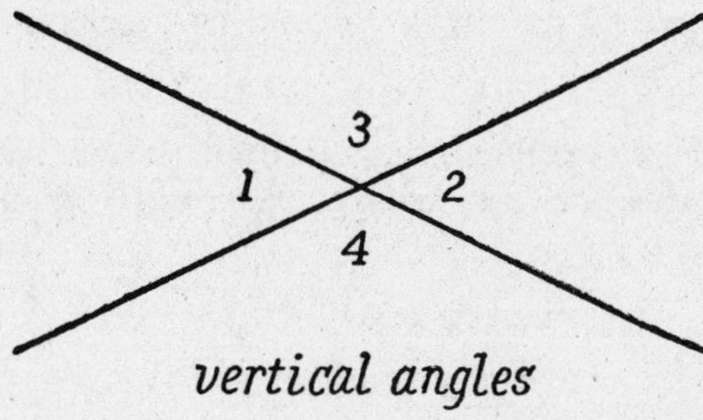

vertical angles

Two lines are *perpendicular* if they meet at right angles. "Perpendicular" always means "at right angles." A perpendicular angle measures 90°.

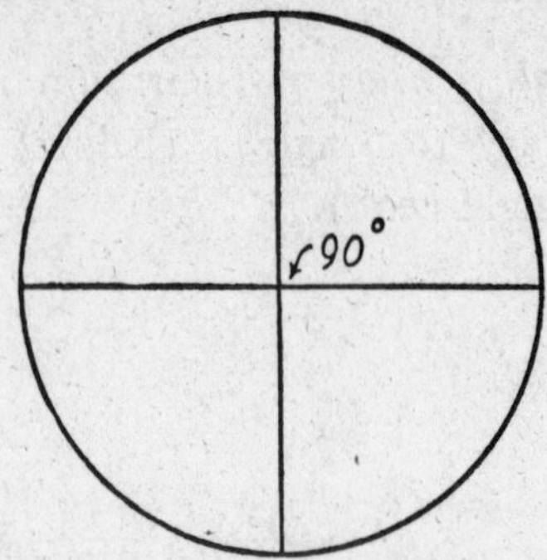


A *proposition* is a statement the truth of which is to be demonstrated or proved. Geometry consists of a number of propositions. Each proposition starts off with a hypothesis and a statement of what is to be proved. The hypothesis is really the conditional part of the proposition—it is what is given to you. The proof is a statement of what you are to prove.

A *theorem* is essentially the same as a proposition. A *corollary* is a theorem easily derived from another theorem. A *postulate* is a purely geometric axiom.

## AXIOMS

An *axiom* is a self-evident fact. There is no necessity to prove an axiom. For instance, "We all must eat to live" is an axiom. There is no necessity to prove it; it just is a fact and is admitted by everybody. Another axiom is: "No two bodies can occupy the same space at the same time." That is just pure common sense.

There are a few important axioms which we must learn and memorize. They are as follows:

1. *Things equal to the same thing, or to equal things, are equal to each other.*

2. *If equals are added to equals, the sums are equal.*

3. *If equals are subtracted from equals, the remainders are equal.*

4. *If equals are multiplied by equals, the products are equal. (Hence, doubles of equals are equal.)*

5. *If equals are divided by equals, the quotients are equal. (Hence, halves of equals are equal.)*

6. *The whole is equal to the sum of all its parts.*

7. *The whole is greater than any of its parts.*

8. *A quantity may be substituted for an equal one in an equation or in an inequality. (Called "substitution.")*

9. *One straight line, and only one, can be drawn through two points. Two points therefore determine a straight line.*

10. *A straight line is the shortest distance between two points.*

11. *All straight angles are equal; similarly, halves of straight angles are equal—therefore all right angles are equal.*

12. *Two intersecting straight lines cannot both be parallel to a third straight line.*

13. *A geometric figure may be moved from one position to another without change of form or size.*

14. *Two straight lines can intersect in only one point.*

## SYMBOLS AND ABBREVIATIONS

For convenience in writing the precepts and propositions of geometry, a number of symbols and abbreviations are used. Instead of writing "triangle," "angle," etc., every time, we use the equivalent symbol given in the following table:

| | | | |
|---|---|---|---|
| $+$ | plus or added to. | $\parallel$s | parallels. |
| $-$ | minus or diminished by. | $\sim$ | is similar to, or similar. |
| $=$ | equals, or is equivalent to. | $\angle$ | angle. |
| $\cong$ | congruent. | $\angle$s | angles. |
| $\neq$ | is not equal to. | $\triangle$ | triangle. |
| $>$ | is greater than. | $\triangle$s | triangles. |
| $<$ | is less than. | $\square$ | parallelogram. |
| $\therefore$ | therefore, or hence. | $\square$s | parallelograms. |
| $\perp$ | perpendicular, or is perpendicular to. | $\odot$ | circle. |
| | | $\odot$s | circles. |
| $\perp$s | perpendiculars. | $\frown$ | arc, as $\overset{\frown}{AB}$, arc $AB$. |
| $\parallel$ | parallel, or is parallel to. | | |

| | | | |
|---|---|---|---|
| ax. | axiom. | iden. | identity. |
| circum. | circumference. | int. | interior. |
| comp. | complement. | isos. | isosceles. |
| cor. | corollary. | rt. | right. |
| corr. | corresponding. | st. | straight. |
| def. | definition. | sub. | substitution. |
| ext. | exterior. | sup. | supplementary, or supplement. |
| hy. | hypotenuse. | | |
| hyp. | hypothesis. | | |

## TRIANGLES

A triangle is a three-sided figure. We classify triangles according to sides or according to angles.

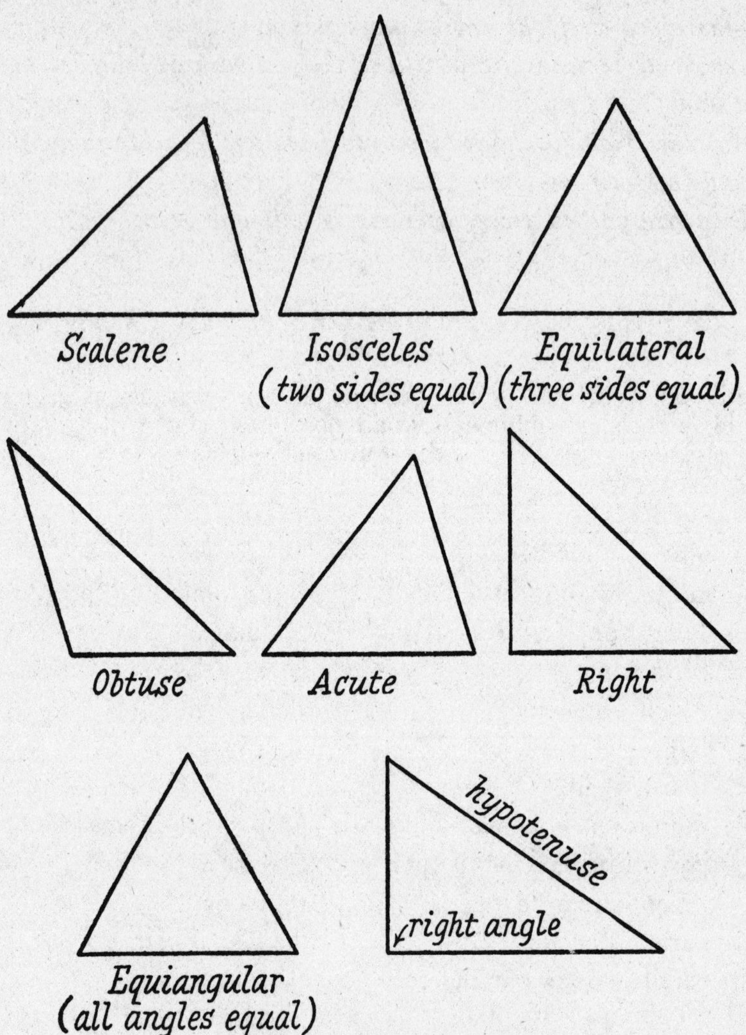


DIAGRAM 8. Kinds of triangles.

If we consider the sides of triangles, there are three kinds, namely, (1) the *scalene* triangle, which is a triangle whose three sides are all of different lengths; (2) the *isosceles* triangle, which has two equal sides; (3) the *equilateral* triangle, which has all three sides equal.

If we classify triangles with respect to angles, we have three kinds, namely, (1) an *obtuse* triangle, in which one angle is an obtuse angle (greater than 90°); (2) an *acute* triangle, in which all angles are acute (less than 90°); (3) a *right* triangle, of which one angle is a right angle.

The *base* of a triangle is the side on which the triangle appears to rest. The other sides are sometimes called arms or legs. The *vertex angle* of a triangle is the angle opposite the base. The side opposite the right angle in a right triangle is called the *hypotenuse.* The *altitude* of a triangle is the length of a line drawn from the vertex angle to the base and perpendicular to it. The sum of the angles of a triangle is always equal to 180°.

There are three classifications of triangles, namely, *congruent* triangles, *similar* triangles, and *equivalent* triangles.

When we say that two triangles are *congruent,* we mean that they will coincide exactly if one is superimposed on the other. In congruent triangles all sides and angles of one triangle equal all corresponding sides and angles of the other triangle. For example, triangles *ABC* and *A'B'C'* are congruent because the side *AB* of triangle *ABC* equals the side *A'B'* of triangle *A'B'C'*, and the sides *BC* and *AC* of triangle *ABC equal the sides B'C'* and *A'C'* of triangle *A'B'C'*.

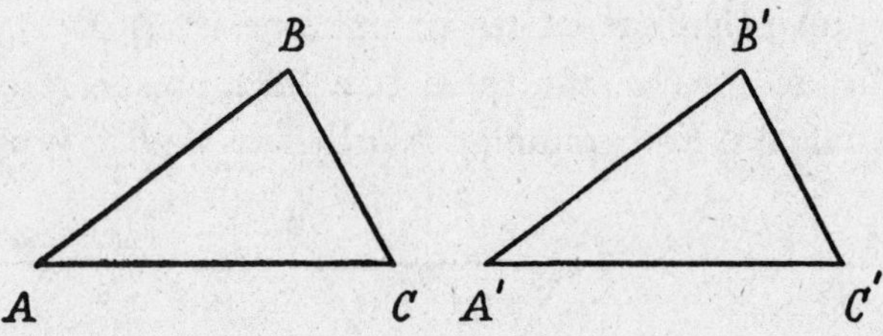


The angles *A, B,* and *C* of triangle *ABC* are equal, respectively, to the angles *A', B',* and *C'* of triangle *A'B'C'*.

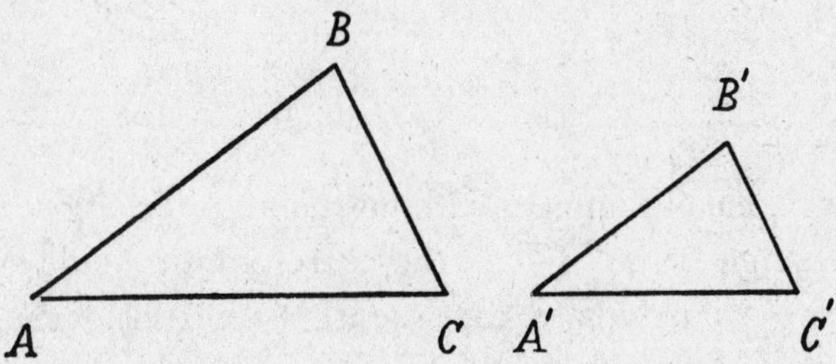


By two *similar* triangles we mean two triangles whose angles are equal and whose sides are proportional. Similar triangles are not necessarily congruent triangles. One triangle may be larger or smaller than the other, but the angles of one must be equal to the corresponding angles of the other. In the diagram, triangle *ABC* is similar to triangle *A'B'C'* because angle *A* equals angle *A'*, and angle *B* equals angle *B'*, and angle *C* equals angle *C'*.

By *equivalent* triangles we mean triangles whose areas are equal. These triangles are not necessarily congruent or similar, but their areas must be

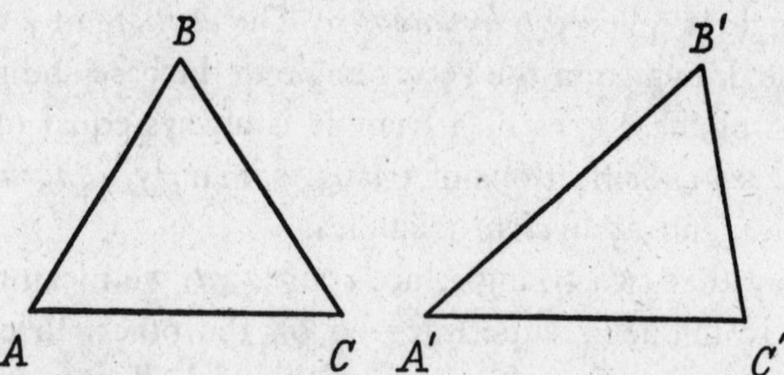

equal. The accompanying diagram shows two equivalent triangles. The area of triangle *ABC* equals the area of triangle *A'B'C'*.

## CONGRUENT TRIANGLES

In order to prove that the length of one line is equal to the length of some other line, we prove that these two lines are corresponding sides of congruent triangles. For example, to prove that *AB* is equal to *CD*, we

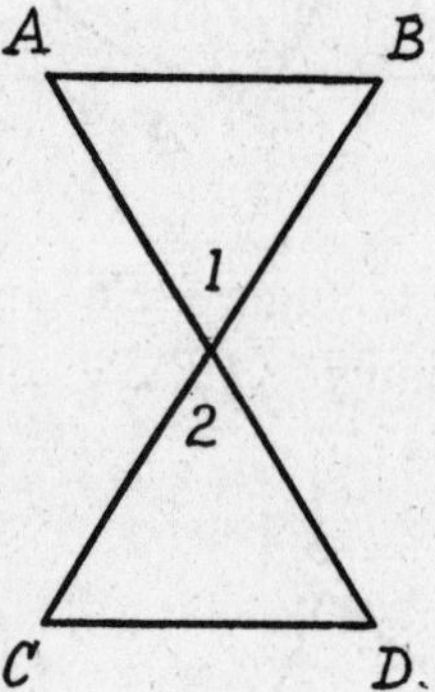

must first prove that Triangle 1 is congruent to Triangle 2 because *AB* is a side of Triangle 1 and *CD* is the corresponding side of Triangle 2, and if these two triangles are congruent, the corresponding sides must be equal. To prove that one angle is equal (in degrees) to another angle, we must prove that they are both corresponding angles of congruent triangles. Thus, in the diagram above, if we want to prove angle *B* equal to angle *C*, we must prove Triangle 1 congruent to Triangle 2, for if these two triangles are congruent, the corresponding angles are equal.

## The Method of Geometry

All propositions and problems in geometry are done in the following regular way:

1. *Draw the diagram and write the proposition over it or next to it.*

2. *State the things which you know about the diagram—things which have been given to you. This is called the hypothesis. We shall write it "given."*

3. *State what you must prove or find out.*

4. *Give the proof. Write your statements to the left and the reason for these statements to the right.*

### Proposition I

*Vertical angles are equal.*

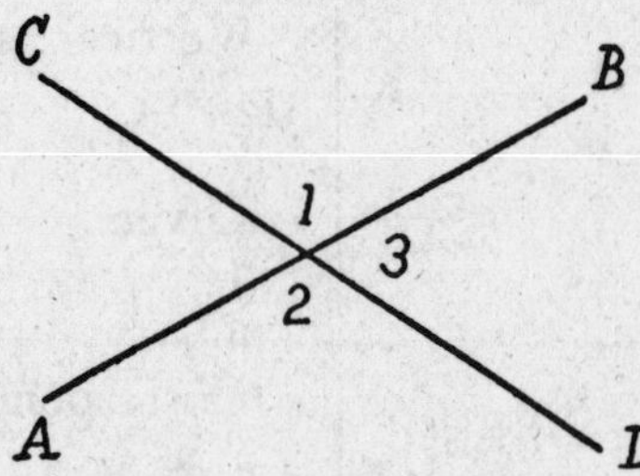


GIVEN   $AB$ and $CD$ are straight lines which intersect to form angles 1 and 2.

TO PROVE   $\angle 1 = \angle 2.$

#### PROOF

| STATEMENTS | REASONS |
|---|---|
| $\angle 1 + \angle 3 = 180°$ | $\angle 1 + \angle 3$ forms a straight angle. |
| $\angle 2 + \angle 3 = 180°$ | $\angle 2 + \angle 3$ forms a straight angle. |
| $\therefore \angle 1 = \angle 2.$ | Axiom 1. |

To our list of axioms and postulates, we now add two which are extremely important:

15. *Two triangles are congruent if two angles and the included side of one are equal to two angles and the included side of the other. (In symbols, the △ are ≅ by a.s.a.)*

16. *Two triangles are congruent if two sides and the included angle of one are equal to two sides and the included angle of the other. (In symbols, the △ are ≅ by s.a.s.)*

With these postulates, we are now able to solve a great number of problems. Let us first see some sample problems worked out so that we can become accustomed to the method of proof.

## PROBLEM 1

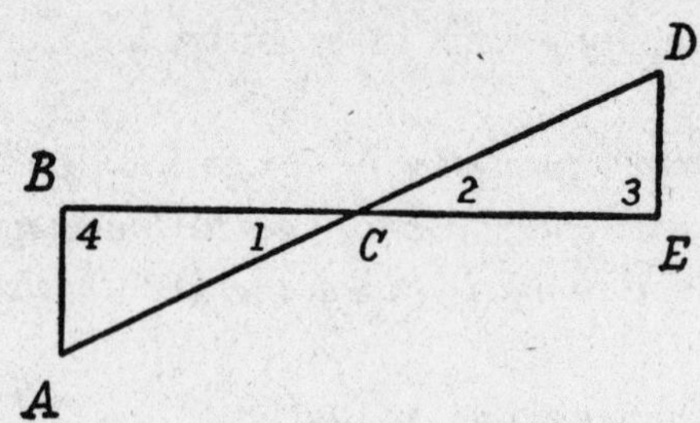


GIVEN   *C* is the midpoint of line *BE* and $\angle 3$ and $\angle 4$ are right $\angle$.

TO PROVE                    $AB=DE,\ AC=CD.$

### PROOF

| STATEMENTS | REASONS |
|---|---|
| $\angle 1 = \angle 2.$ | Vertical $\angle$ are equal (Proposition I). |
| $BC=CE.$ $\}$ $\angle 3 = \angle 4.$ | Given. |
| $\therefore \triangle BAC \cong \triangle CDE.$ | a.s.a. |
| $\therefore AB=DE.$ $\}$ $AC=CD.$ | Corresponding parts of equal $\triangle$ are =. |

## PROBLEM 2

GIVEN   $\triangle ABC$ is isosceles, $\angle 1 = \angle 2.$

TO PROVE          $\angle 3 = \angle 4,\ AD=DC.$

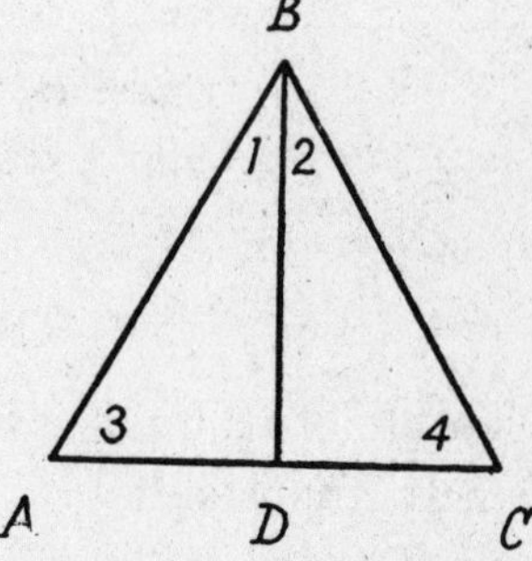


### PROOF

| STATEMENTS | REASONS |
|---|---|
| $AB=BC.$ | Given. *ABC* is an isos. $\triangle$. |
| $\angle 1 = \angle 2.$ | Given. |
| $BD=BD.$ | Identity. |
| $\therefore \triangle ABD \cong \triangle CBD.$ | s.a.s. |
| $\therefore AD=DC.$ $\}$ $\angle 3 = \angle 4.$ | Corresponding parts of $\cong$ $\triangle$ are equal. |

## PROBLEM 3

GIVEN $\angle 1 = \angle 2$, $AB = BC$.
TO PROVE $AD = DC$, $\angle 3 = \angle 4$.

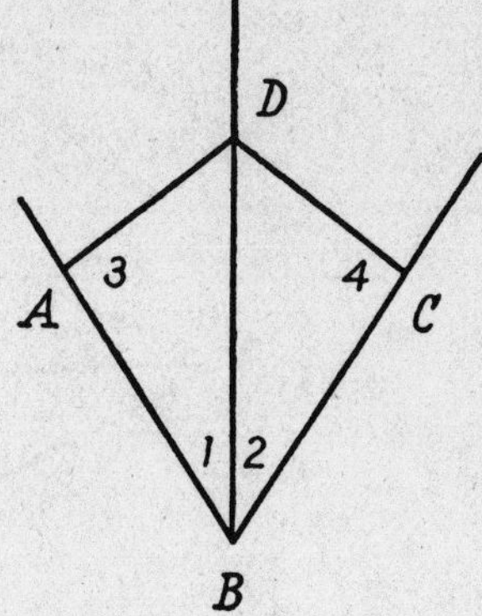

## PROBLEM 4

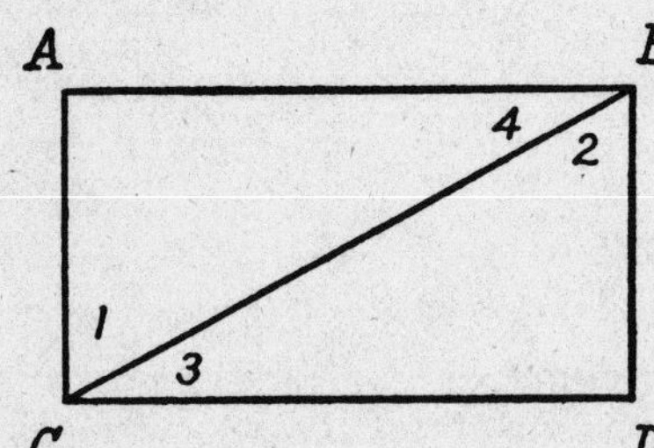

GIVEN $\angle 1 = \angle 2$, $\angle 3 = \angle 4$.
TO PROVE $AB = CD$, $AC = BD$.

## PROBLEM 5

GIVEN $\angle B = \angle C$, $\angle 1 = \angle 2$.
TO PROVE $BE = DC$.

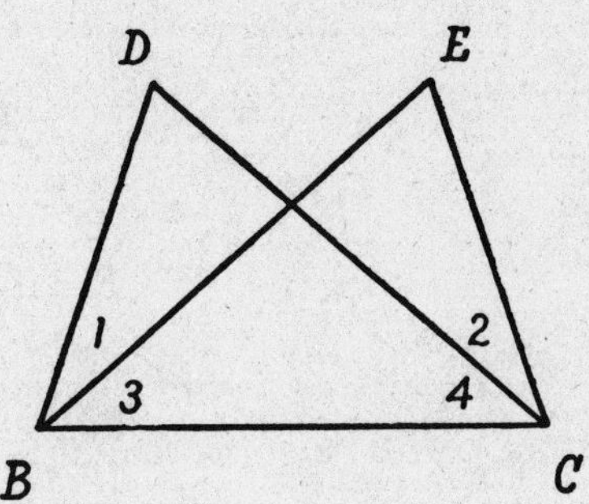

## PROBLEM 6

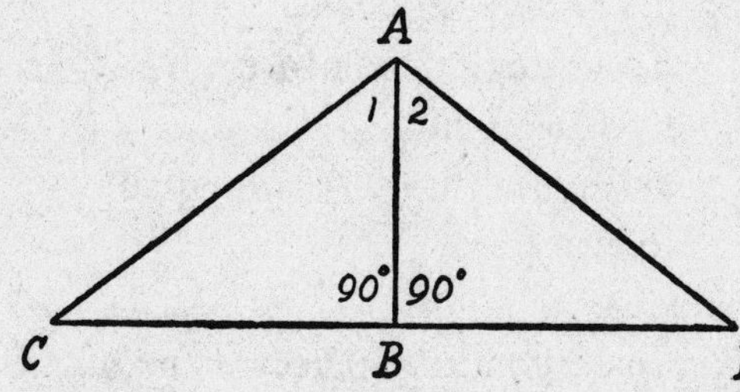

GIVEN $AB \perp CD$, $\angle 1 = \angle 2$.
TO PROVE $AC = AD$.

## Problem 7

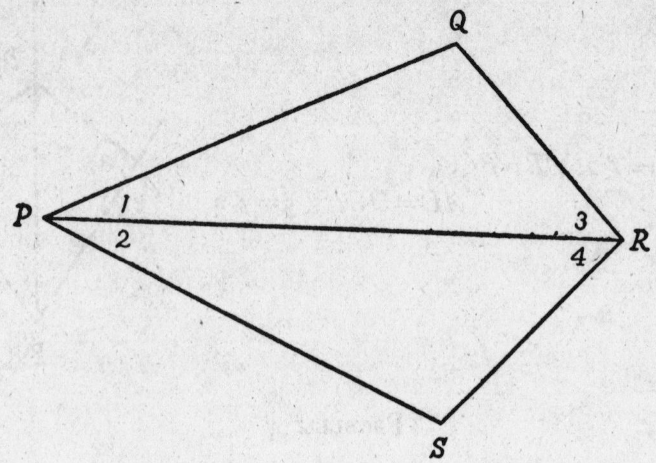

GIVEN $\angle 1 = \angle 2,\ \angle 3 = \angle 4.$

TO PROVE $\angle Q = \angle S$

## Proposition II

*The base angles of an isosceles triangle are equal.*

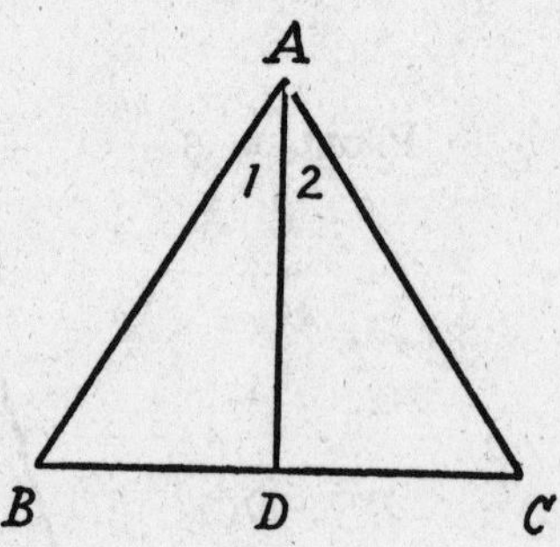

GIVEN $ABC$ is an isosceles $\triangle$.

TO PROVE $\angle B = \angle C.$

### PROOF

| STATEMENTS | REASONS |
|---|---|
| Draw $AD$ so that it bisects $\angle A$. | Every angle has a bisector. |
| Then $\angle 1 = \angle 2.$ | By bisection. |
| $AB = AC.$ | Sides of an isos. $\triangle$ are equal. |
| $AD = AD.$ | Identity. |
| $\therefore \triangle ABD \cong \triangle ADC.$ | s.a.s. |
| $\therefore \angle B = \angle C$ | Corresponding parts of $\cong$ $\triangle$. |

COROLLARY. *An equilateral triangle is equiangular.*

This is given as a corollary because it follows easily from the main theorem on isosceles triangles. The proof, in written form, is as follows:

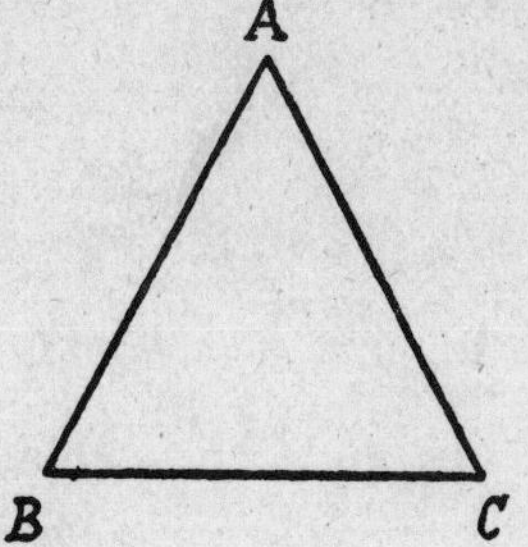


GIVEN   $\triangle ABC$, $AB=BC=CA$.

TO PROVE   $A=\angle B=\angle C.$

PROOF

| STATEMENTS | REASONS |
| --- | --- |
| $AB=BC.$ | Given. |
| $BC=CA.$ | Given. |
| $\angle B=\angle C.$ <br> $\angle C=\angle A.$ | Base angles of an isosceles $\triangle$ are equal. |
| $\angle A=\angle B=\angle C.$ | Axiom 1. |

A theorem which is easily derived from another theorem is called a *corollary,* and stated without proof. Here are more corollaries of the theorem on isosceles triangles:

COROLLARY. *The bisector of the vertex angle of an isosceles triangle divides it into two congruent triangles.*

COROLLARY. *The bisector of the vertex angle of an isosceles triangle bisects the base.*

COROLLARY. *The bisector of the vertex angle of an isosceles triangle is perpendicular to the base.*

The following problems all are solved by using the theorem on isosceles triangles:

PROBLEM 8

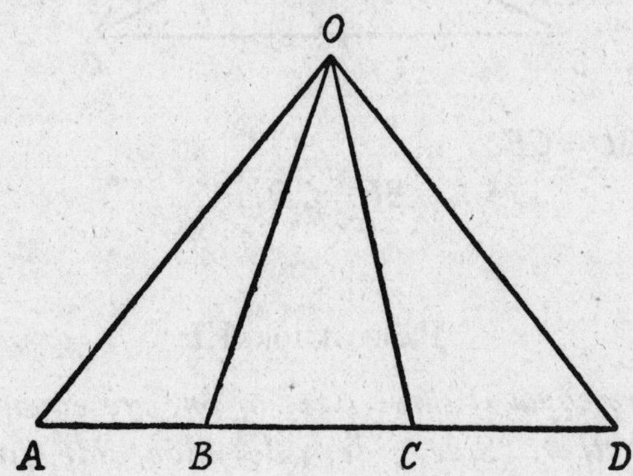

GIVEN $OA=OD, AB=CD.$

TO PROVE $\qquad OB=OC.$

PROBLEM 9

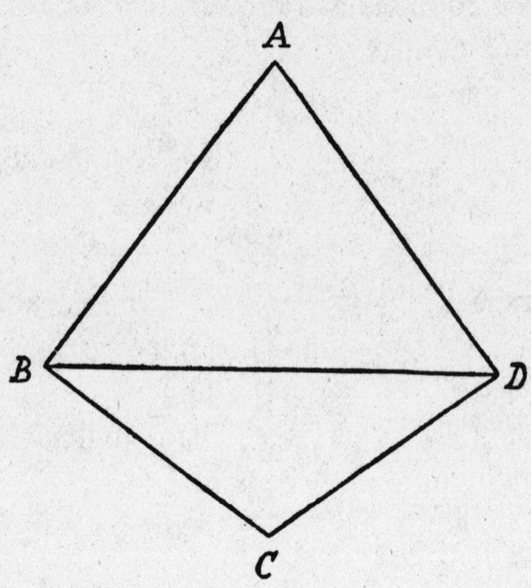

GIVEN $AB=AD, BC=CD.$

TO PROVE $\qquad \angle ABC = \angle ADC.$

PROBLEM 10

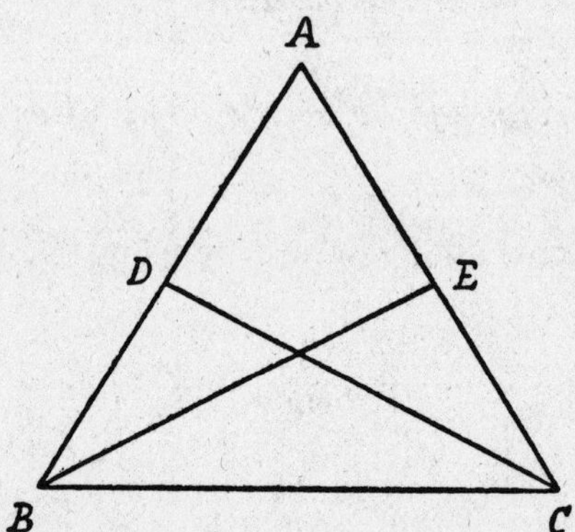

GIVEN $AB=AC, BD=CE.$

TO PROVE $\qquad BE=CD.$

## PROPOSITION III

*Two triangles are equal if three sides of one are equal, respectively, to three sides of the other. (Side, side, side=side, side, side—s.s.s.=s.s.s.)*

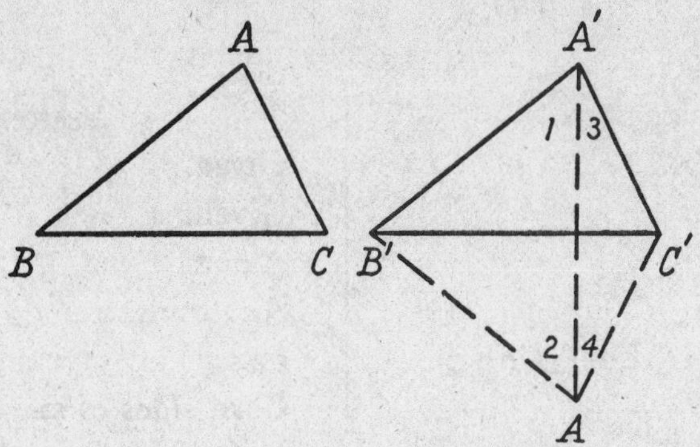

GIVEN  △ABC and A'B'C', with AB=A'B', BC=B'C', AC=A'C'.
TO PROVE  $\triangle ABC \cong \triangle A'B'C'$

**PROOF**

| STATEMENTS | REASONS |
|---|---|
| Place $\triangle ABC$ so that $BC$ shall coincide with $B'C'$ and $A$ and $A'$ lie on opposite sides of $B'C'$. | { Axiom 13. <br> { $BC=B'C'$, given. |
| Draw $AA'$. | Axiom 9. |
| $\triangle AB'A'$ is isosceles. | $AB=A'B'$, by hyp. |
| $\therefore \angle 1 = \angle 2$. | Proposition II. |
| $\triangle AC'A'$ is isosceles. | $AC=A'C'$, by hyp. |
| $\therefore \angle 3 = \angle 4$. | Proposition II. |
| $\therefore \angle 1 + \angle 3 = \angle 2 + \angle 4$. | Axiom 2. |
| Or $\angle A = \angle A'$. | Substitution. |
| $\therefore \triangle AB'C' \cong \triangle A'B'C'$. | s.a.s. |
| i.e. $\triangle ABC = A'B'C'$. | |

We have now learned that the base angles of an isosceles triangle are equal and that when three sides of one triangle are respectively equal to three sides of another triangle, the two triangles are equal.

Let us now apply these new propositions to some problems:

PROBLEM II

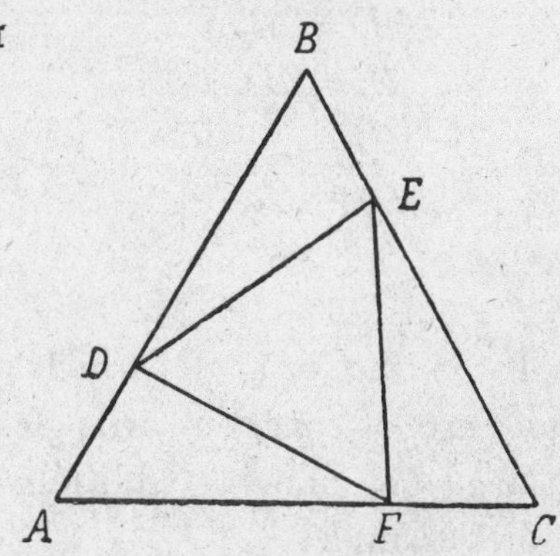

GIVEN  $AB=BC=CA$.
$AD=BE=CF$.
TO PROVE  $\triangle DEF$ is equilater

### PROOF

| STATEMENTS | REASONS |
|---|---|
| $AB=BC=CA.$ | Given. |
| $AD=BE=CF.$ | Given. |
| $BD=CE=FA.$ | Axiom 3. |
| $\angle A=\angle B=\angle C.$ | An equilateral $\triangle$ is equiangular. |
| $\triangle ADF\cong\triangle DBE\cong\triangle CFE$ | s.a.s. |
| $DE=EF=FD$ | Corr. sides of $\cong$ ⧊ are equal. |
| $\triangle DEF$ is equilateral. | Def. of equilateral $\triangle$. |

### PROBLEM 12

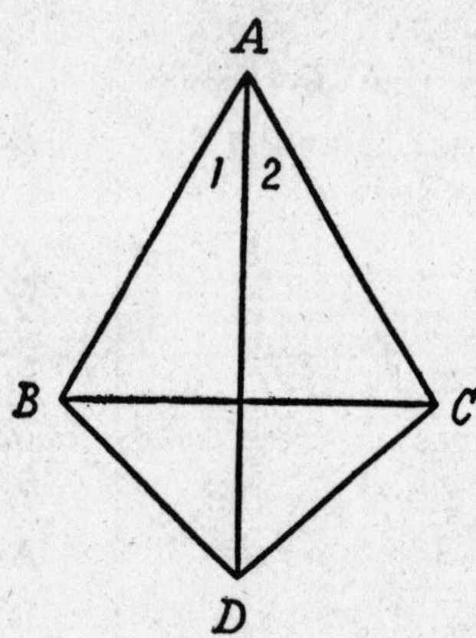


GIVEN   $ABC$ and $BDC$ are two isosceles ⧊ on the same base $BC$.

TO PROVE   $\angle 1=\angle 2.$

### PROOF

| STATEMENTS | REASONS |
|---|---|
| $AB=AC.$ | |
| $BD=DC.$ | Hyp. |
| $AD=AD.$ | Identity. |
| $\therefore \triangle ABD\cong\triangle ACD.$ | s.s.s. |
| $\therefore \angle 1=\angle 2.$ | Corresponding parts of $\cong$ ⧊ are equal. |

If the lines or angles which we wish to prove equal to one another are not parts of congruent triangles, we try to make them parts of congruent triangles by drawing additional lines.

For example:

PROBLEM 13

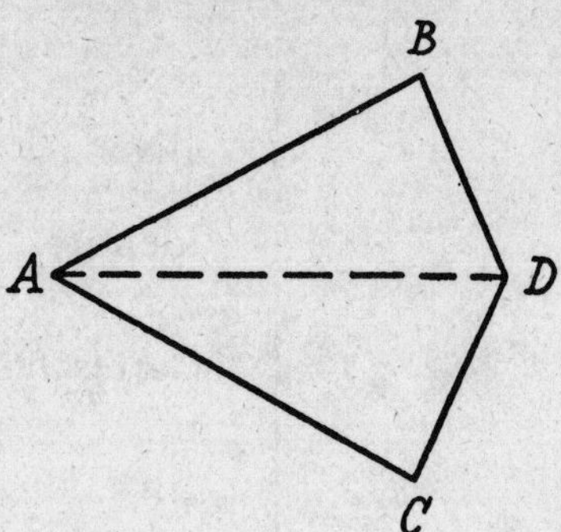

GIVEN $AB=AC$, $BD=DC$.

TO PROVE $\angle B = \angle C$

PROOF

| STATEMENTS | REASONS |
|---|---|
| Draw line $AD$. | Axiom 9. |
| Then, in triangles $ABD$ and $ACD$: | |
| $AB=AC.$ $\Big\}$ $BD=DC.$ | Given. |
| $AD=AD.$ | Identity. |
| $\therefore \triangle ABD \cong \triangle ACD.$ | s.s.s. |
| $\therefore \angle B = \angle C.$ | Corresponding parts of $\cong$ $\triangle$ are equal. |

If we cannot prove the required pair of triangles $\cong$, we prove the congruence of another pair of triangles whose corresponding parts will enable us to prove the equality of the required pair. In the following we do this very thing:

PROBLEM 14

GIVEN $AB=CD$, $AC=BD$, $\angle 1 = \angle 2$.

TO PROVE $CE=BF$.

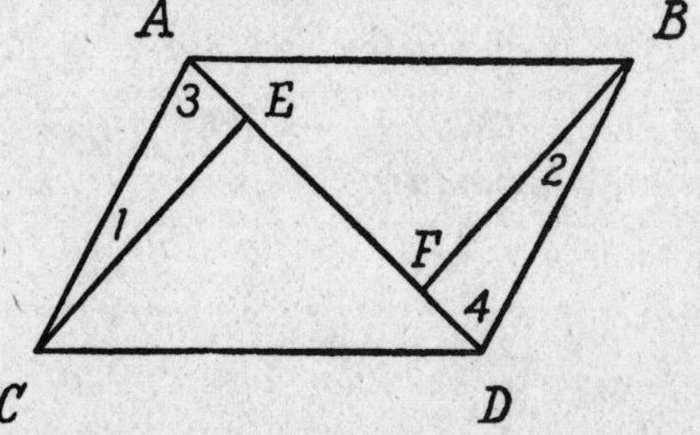

$CE$ and $BF$ are parts of triangles $AEC$ and $BDF$. In order to prove these two triangles congruent, we must first prove that $\triangle ACD \cong \triangle ABD$, because we can then prove $\angle 3$ equal to $\angle 4$ and hence have two angles and a side of $\triangle AEC$ equal to two angles and a side of $\angle BFD$.

163

**PROOF**

| STATEMENTS | REASONS |
|---|---|
| $AC=BD.$ <br> $AB=CD.$ | Given. |
| $AD=AD.$ | Identity. |
| $\therefore \triangle ACD \cong \triangle ABD.$ | s.s.s. |
| Then $\angle 3 = \angle 4$ | Corresponding parts of $\cong$ ⟁ are equal. |
| and $\angle 1 = \angle 2$ | Given. |
| and $AC=BD.$ | Given. |
| $\therefore \triangle AEC \cong \triangle BDF.$ | a.s.a. |
| $\therefore CE=BF.$ | Corresponding parts of $\cong$ ⟁ are equal. |

Now let us review what we have learned, and see whether we can summarize it so as to know, once and for all, how to go about proving lines and angles equal to one another.

In order to prove lines and angles equal, we must

*First: Pick out two triangles which contain these lines and angles, and prove these two triangles congruent by one of the three methods:*

1. $a.s.a.=a.s.a.$
2. $s.a.s.=s.a.s.$
3. $s.s.s.=s.s.s.$

*The method used will depend entirely on the hypothesis. If you are given two angles and can pick out a common side, use method 1; if you are given two sides and can find two corresponding angles equal, use method 2; if you are given two sides and can find a common side, use method 3.*

*Second: If the lines and angles whose equality we wish to prove are not parts of congruent triangles or parts of triangles which we can prove congruent, make them parts of triangles which we can prove congruent merely by adding a line or two.*

*Third: If it is impossible to prove the congruence of the two triangles whose sides contain the lines we wish to prove equal, prove the congruence of some other pair or pairs of triangles whose corresponding parts will help to prove the congruence of the first triangles.*

Now see whether you can do these:

## PROBLEM 15

GIVEN   $ABC$ is an isosceles $\triangle$, $BD=BE$.
TO PROVE                     $FE=FD$.

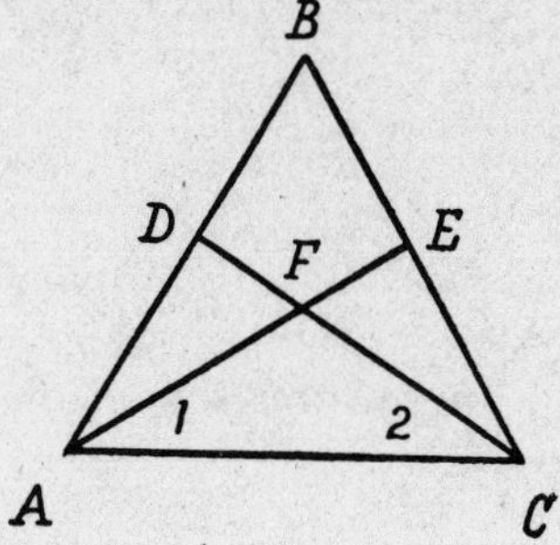

## PROBLEM 16

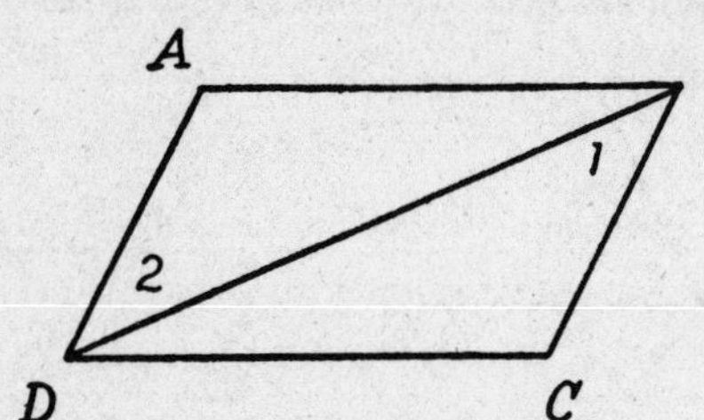

GIVEN   $BC=AD$, $\angle 1 = \angle 2$.
TO PROVE                     $BA=CD$.

## PARALLEL LINES

When one line intersects two or more lines, it is called a transversal. The angles formed by these lines and the transversal are named as follows:

5, 6, 7, and 8 are *exterior* angles.
1, 2, 3, 4 are *interior* angles.
5 and 8 } are *alternate exterior*
6 and 7 }  angles.
1 and 4 } are *alternate interior*
2 and 3 }  angles.
3 and 7 }
8 and 4 } are called *correspond-*
5 and 1 }  *ing* angles.
6 and 2 }

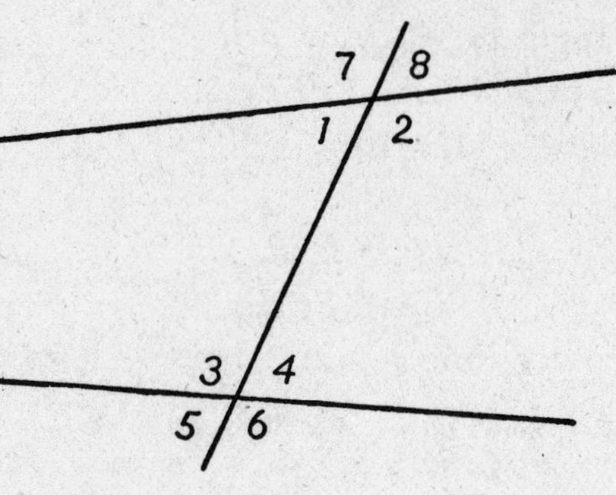

Parallel lines are lines which never meet, no matter how far they may be produced. The most familiar example of parallel lines is a car track. When two parallel lines are crossed by a transversal, we have eight angles formed, the names of which are given above.

*Two intersecting straight lines cannot both be parallel to a third straight line.* This is a postulate; we will refer to it hereafter as Axiom 17.

COROLLARY. *Two straight lines parallel to a third line are parallel to each other.*

### PROPOSITION IV

*An exterior angle of a triangle is greater than either remote interior angle.*

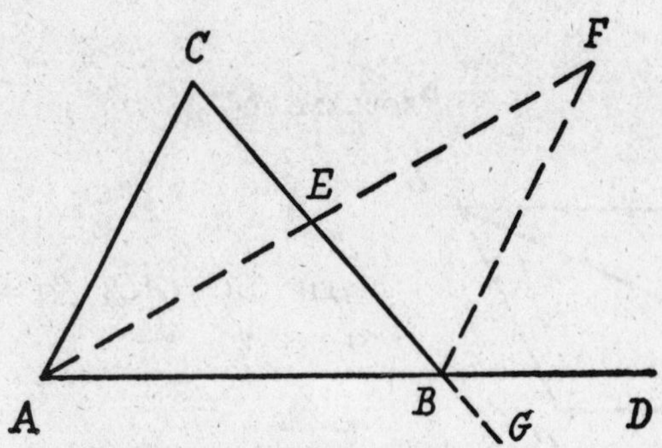

GIVEN    $\triangle ABC$ and the ext. $\angle CBD$.

TO PROVE                 $\angle CBD > \angle C$ or $\angle A$.

**PROOF**

| STATEMENTS | REASONS |
|---|---|
| Let $E$ be the mid-point of $BC$. Draw $AE$ and produce it its own length to $F$. Draw $FB$. | |
| In $\triangle ACE$ and $FBE$, | |
| $AE = EF$. | |
| $EC = BE$. | Construction. |
| $\angle CEA = \angle FEB$. | Vertical $\angle$ are equal. |
| $\triangle ACE \cong \triangle FBE$. | s.a.s. |
| $\angle EBF = \angle C$. | Corresponding parts of $\cong$ $\triangle$ are equal. |
| $\angle CBD > \angle EBF$. | Axiom 7. |
| $\therefore \angle CBD > \angle C$. | Substitution. |

NOTE: By joining the mid-point of $AB$ to $C$, etc., it follows that $\angle ABG > \angle A$, $\angle ABG = \angle CBD$.

$$\therefore \angle CBD > \angle A.$$

## Proposition V

*Two lines are parallel if a transversal to these lines makes a pair of
alternate interior angles equal.*

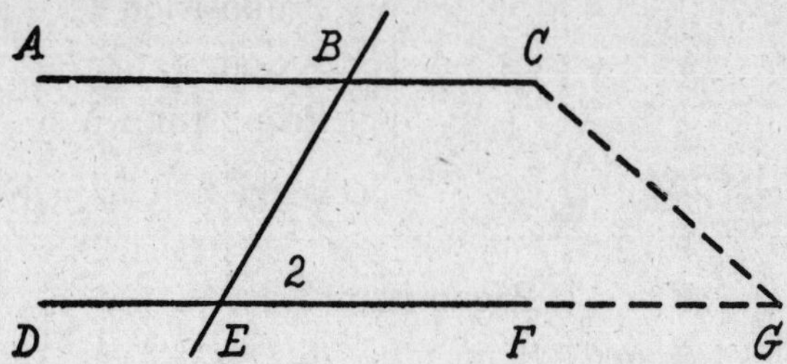

**GIVEN** $AC$ and $DF$ are crossed by a transversal in $B$ and $E$ so that $\angle 1 = \angle 2$.

**TO PROVE** $AC \parallel DF$.

**PROOF**

| STATEMENTS | REASONS |
|---|---|
| $AC$ and $DF$ either meet or are parallel. | Two lines in a plane are $\parallel$ or intersect. |
| Suppose they are not parallel and consequently they meet in some point $G$ (on $DF$ produced). | |
| Then $\angle A'BE$ is the exterior angle of $\triangle BEG$. | Def. of exterior angle. |
| $\therefore \angle A'BE$, or $\angle 1$, is greater than $\angle 2$. | Proposition IV. |
| But $\angle 1 = \angle 2$. | Given. |
| $\therefore AC$ and $DF$ cannot meet and are parallel. | If they meet, it contradicts the hypothesis that $\angle 1 = \angle 2$. |

**COROLLARY.** *Two lines are parallel if a transversal to these lines makes
a pair of corresponding angles equal.*

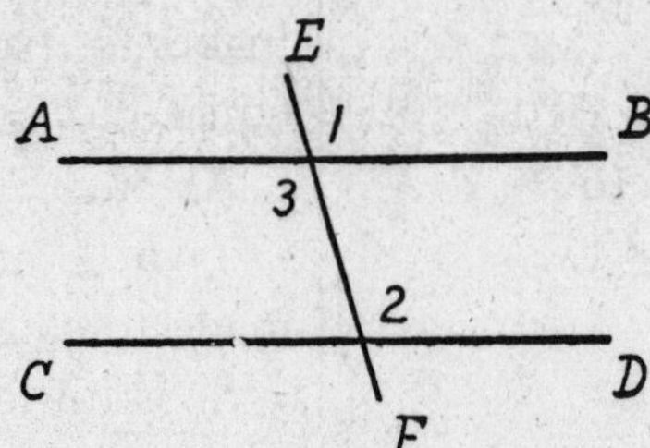

**GIVEN** $AB$ and $CD$, intersected by $EF$ so that $\angle 1 = \angle 2$.

**TO PROVE** $AB \parallel CD$.

PROOF

| STATEMENTS | REASONS |
| --- | --- |
| $\angle 1 = \angle 2$. | Given. |
| $\angle 1 = \angle 3$. | Proposition I. |
| $\angle 2 = \angle 3$. | Axiom 1. |
| $\therefore AB \| CD$. | Proposition V. |

## PROPOSITION VI

*If two lines are parallel, a transversal to these lines makes a pair of alternate interior angles equal.*

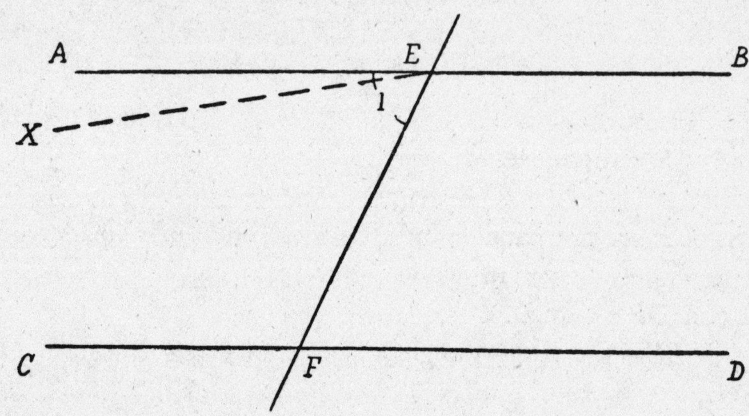


GIVEN  $AB \| CD$  $AB$, $CD$ cut by transversal in $E$ and $F$.

TO PROVE  $\angle 1 = \angle 2$.

PROOF

| STATEMENTS | REASONS |
| --- | --- |
| Construct $XE$ with $\angle XEF = \angle 2$. $XE \| CD$. | Two lines are $\|$ if a transversal makes a pair of alternate angles equal. |
| $XE$ coincides with $AB$. | Axiom 17. |
| $\angle XEF = \angle AEF$ or $\angle 1$. | Two $\angle$ are equal if they can be made to coincide. |
| $\angle 1 = \angle 2$. | Substitution. |

COROLLARY. *If two lines are parallel, a transversal to these lines makes a pair of corresponding angles equal.*

## PARALLEL LINE CONSTRUCTIONS

The last two theorems give us a means of constructing parallel lines by using the straight-edge and compasses. There are at least two ways in which this can be done. We shall discuss both ways. First, however, let us try to construct an angle which will be equal to a given angle.

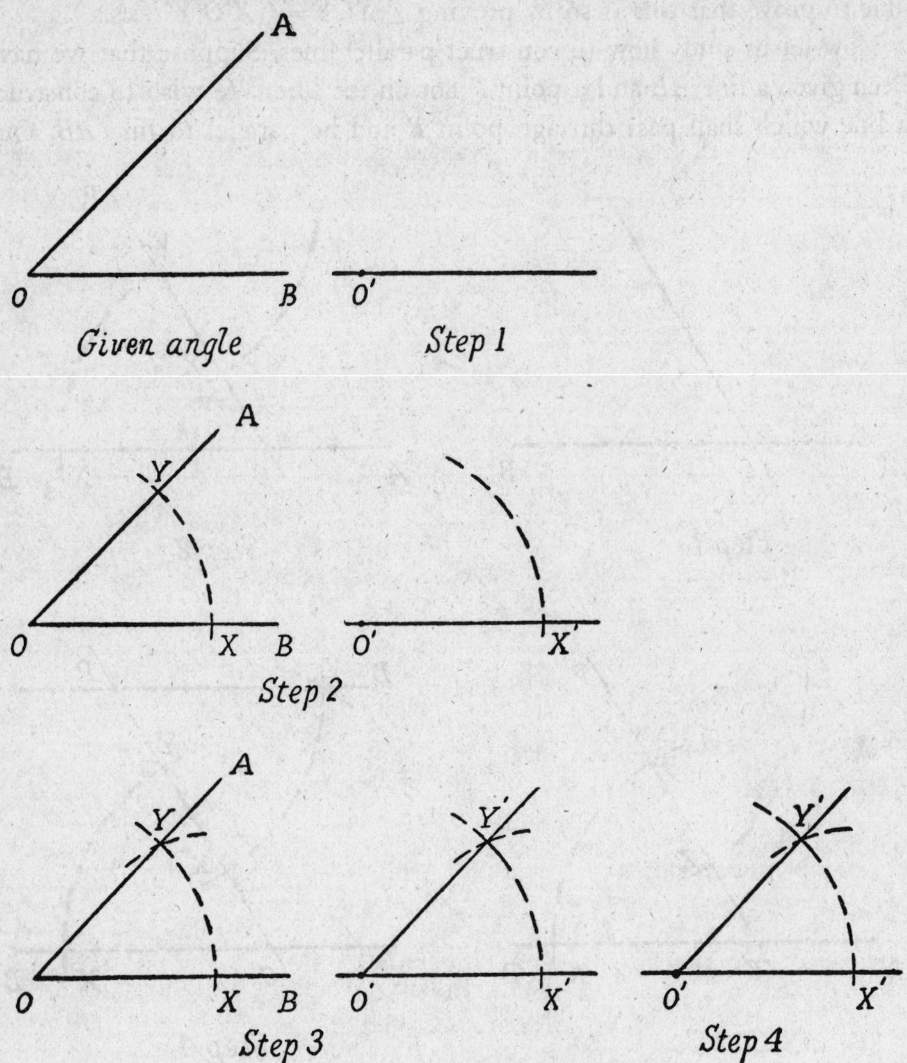


DIAGRAM 9. Constructing an angle equal to a given angle.

Suppose we have been asked to construct an angle equal to angle *AOB* above, and with its vertex at point *O'*. First, we draw any line through point *O'*. This is to be our "working line." We then open the compasses to any angle, place the sharp point at vertex *O,* and with the writing point draw an arc cutting *OA* at *X* and *OB* at *Y*. Without changing the angle between the compasses' legs, we place the sharp point at *O'* and draw an arc cutting the working line at *X'*. Next, we set the compasses so that the sharp point is at *X* and the writing point is at *Y*. Without moving the legs of the compasses, we place the sharp point at *X'* and draw an arc cutting our first arc at *Y'*. Finally, we draw line *O'Y'* with the straight-edge. Angle *Y'O'X'* will equal angle *YOX*. You should be able to prove that this is so by proving $\triangle XOY = \triangle X'O'Y'$ (s.s.s.).

Now let us study how to construct parallel lines. Suppose that we have been given a line *AB* and a point *P* not on the line. We wish to construct a line which shall pass through point *P* and be parallel to line *AB*. Our

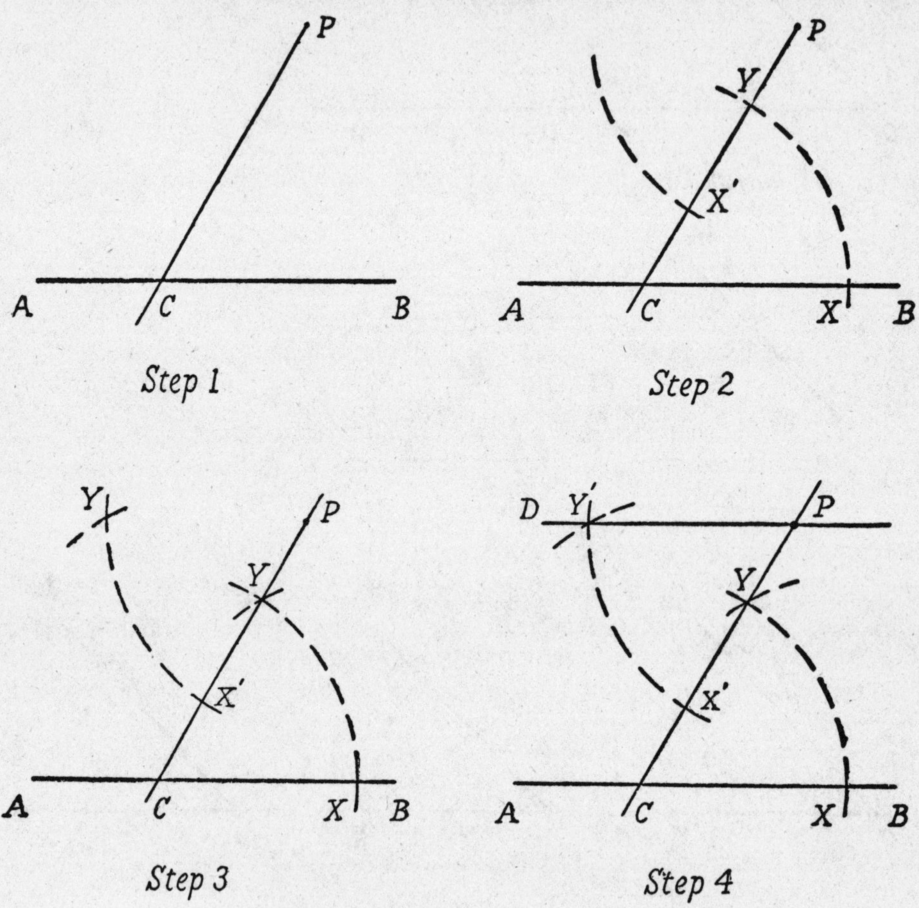


DIAGRAM 10. Constructing a parallel line, method 1.

procedure is as follows: First, we draw any line through point *P* cutting line *AB,* say at point *C*. Next, we construct an angle which is equal to angle *PCB* and also forms alternate interior angles with respect to it. Let this angle be angle *DPC*. Then *DP* will be parallel to line *AB*. The diagrams show the construction fully. Study them to understand the construction.

A second method for constructing a parallel is illustrated below. Again, suppose we have been asked to construct a line passing through point and parallel to line *AB*. First, we construct line *PC* perpendicular to line *AB*

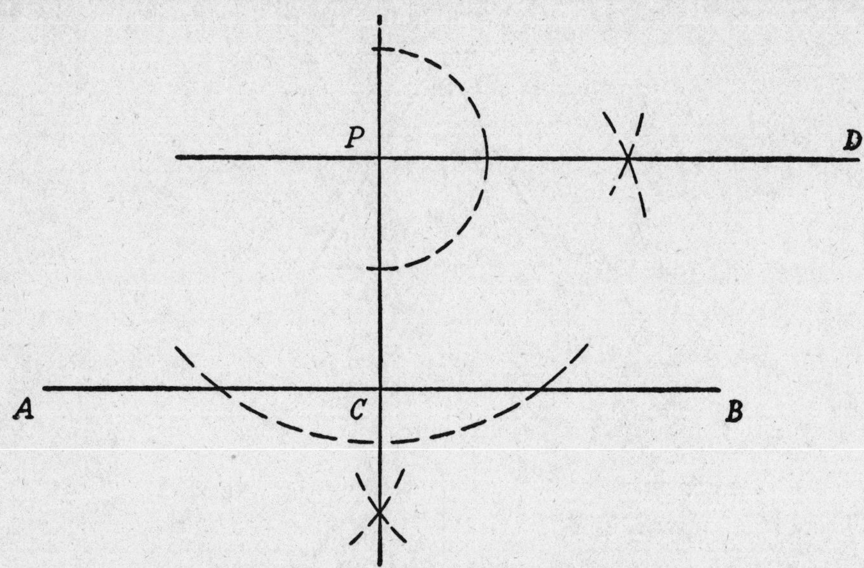

DIAGRAM 11. Constructing a parallel line, method 2.

at *C*. Then we construct line *PD* perpendicular to line *PC* at point *P*. Since angles *DPC* and *PCA* are equal alternate angles, lines *PD* and *AB* must be parallel.

Although either method may be used to construct parallel lines, the first will be found to be somewhat simpler after practice. Now try the following exercises in construction:

1. Draw any triangle, label the vertices with the letters *A, B, C,* and construct a line parallel to side *BC* and passing through point *A*.
2. Draw any triangle as before, and construct an angle *A* which shall be equal to angle *B* and lie outside the triangle. Do the same with angle *C*.
3. Construct a triangle whose angles are equal to those of any triangle *ABC* which you have drawn.
4. Construct any triangle. Then construct another triangle which is congruent to the first, and the sides of which are parallel to those of the first triangle.
5. Draw any six-sided figure. Then construct a five-sided figure, three sides of which shall be parallel to any three sides of the first figure.

### Proposition VII

*The sum of the angles of a triangle is equal to a straight angle (180°).*

GIVEN  $\triangle ABC$.

TO PROVE  $\angle A + \angle B + \angle C =$ a st. $\angle$.

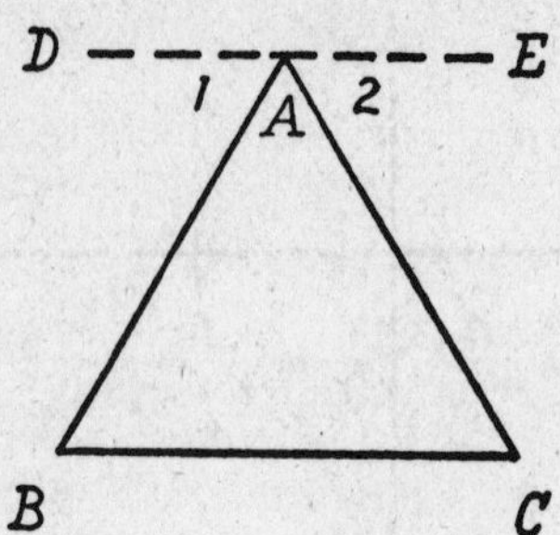

**PROOF**

| STATEMENTS | REASONS |
|---|---|
| Through $A$ draw $DE \parallel BC$. | |
| $\angle 1 = \angle B$. | Prop. VI. |
| $\angle 2 = \angle C$. | Prop. VI. |
| $\angle A + \angle 1 + \angle 2 =$ a st. $\angle$. | Axiom 6. |
| $\therefore \angle A + \angle B + \angle C =$ a st. $\angle$. | Substitution. |

COROLLARY 1. *In a triangle there can be at most one obtuse angle or one right angle.*

COROLLARY 2. *The acute angles of a right triangle are complementary.*

COROLLARY 3. *If two triangles have two angles of the one equal respectively to two angles of the other, the third angles are equal.*

COROLLARY 4. *Two triangles are congruent if two angles and the side opposite one of them are equal respectively to two angles and the corresponding side of the other (s.a.a.=s.a.a.).*

COROLLARY 5. *Each angle of an equiangular triangle is 60°.*

COROLLARY 6. *Two right triangles are congruent if the hypotenuse and an acute angle of one triangle are equal to the hypotenuse and an acute angle of the other triangle.*

COROLLARY 7. *Two right triangles are congruent if an arm and an acute angle of one triangle are equal to an arm and the corresponding acute angle of the other triangle.*

### Converses

If we write two propositions on parallel lines next to each other like this:

| | |
|---|---|
| GIVEN $AB\|CD$. | GIVEN $\angle 1 = \angle 2$. |
| TO PROVE $\angle 1 = \angle 2$ | TO PROVE $AB\|CD$, |

we cannot help but notice a striking difference between them. What is "Given" in one proposition is "To Prove" in the other, and vice versa. Propositions having this form, and, in fact, any two statements having this form are said to be *converses* of each other. Thus, the converse of the statement, "If two triangles are congruent, the corresponding angles are equal" will be, "If the corresponding angles of two triangles are equal, the triangles will be congruent."

The important thing to notice about converse statements is that if one is true, the other need not be true. Thus, the converse of our first theorem on parallel lines is true, but the converse of the statement about the angles of congruent triangles is not true. We cannot, therefore, assume the truth of the converse of a theorem from the truth of the theorem itself. A proof is required.

The converse of our theorem, "The base angles of an isosceles triangle are equal" is "If two angles of a triangle are equal, the triangle is isosceles." To prove this, we make use of the Corollary 4 of the previous theorem.

### Proposition VIII

*If two angles of a triangle are equal, the triangle is isosceles.*

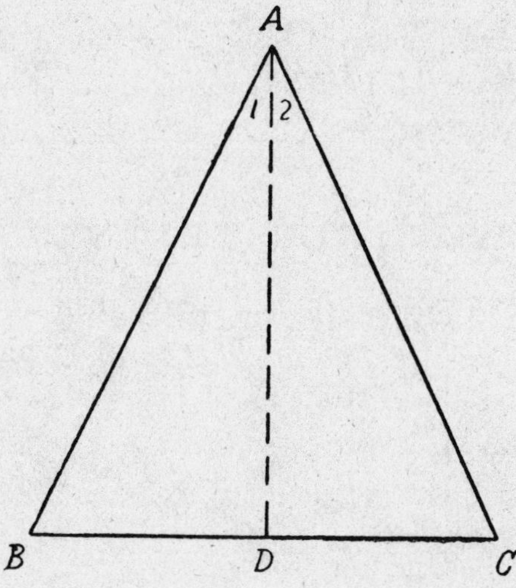

GIVEN   $\triangle ABC$ with $\angle B = \angle C$

TO PROVE   $AB = AC$

**PROOF**

| STATEMENTS | REASONS |
|---|---|
| Construct line $AD$ bisecting angle $A$. | Every angle has a bisector. |
| $\angle 1 = \angle 2$. | Bisection. |
| $\angle B = \angle C$. | Given. |
| $AD = AD$. | Identity. |
| $\triangle ABD = \triangle ACD$. | s.a.a. (Cor. 4, Prop. VII). |
| $AB = AC$. | Corr: sides of $= \triangle$ are equal. |

COROLLARY. *An equiangular triangle is equilateral.*

## THE EQUILATERAL TRIANGLE

Each angle in an equilateral triangle equals 60°.

An equilateral triangle can be divided into two congruent right triangles whose acute angles equal 30°.

Thus $ABC$ is composed of rt. $\triangle$ $ABD$ and $BDC$.

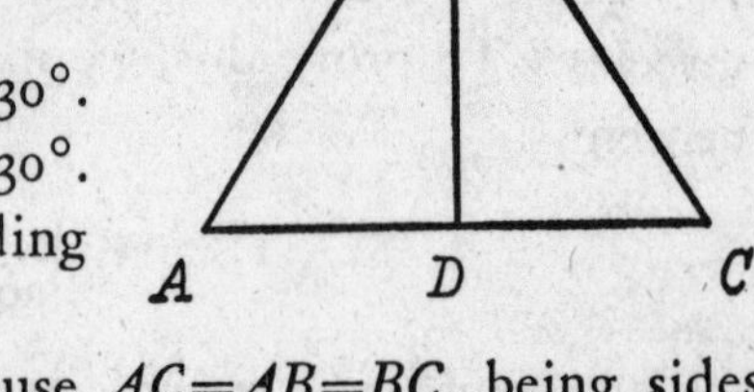

$\angle A = 60°$ and $\angle D = 90°$. Hence $\angle 1 = 30°$.

$\angle C = 60°$ and $\angle D = 90°$. Hence $\angle 2 = 30°$.

$AD = DC$ because they are corresponding parts of congruent triangles.

But $AD + DC = AC$ or $AB$ or $BC$ because $AC = AB = BC$, being sides of an equilateral $\triangle$.

$\therefore AB = AD + DC$.

But since $AD = DC$, $AB = 2AD$.

$\therefore AD = \frac{1}{2}AB$.

## THE RIGHT TRIANGLE

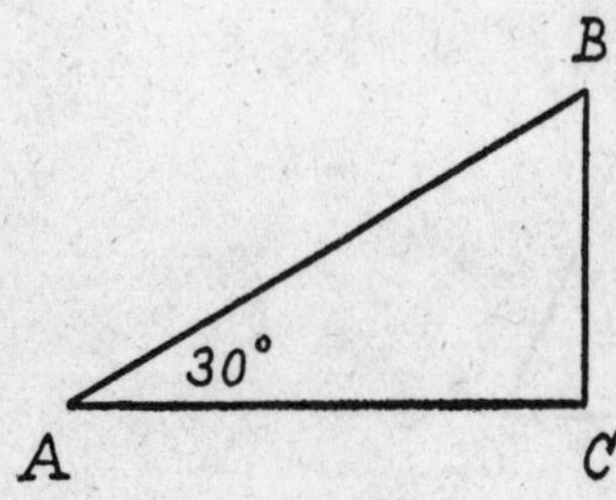

If $\angle A = 30°$, then $\angle B = 60°$ and $AB = 2BC$ or $BC = \frac{1}{2}AB$ (which was just demonstrated).

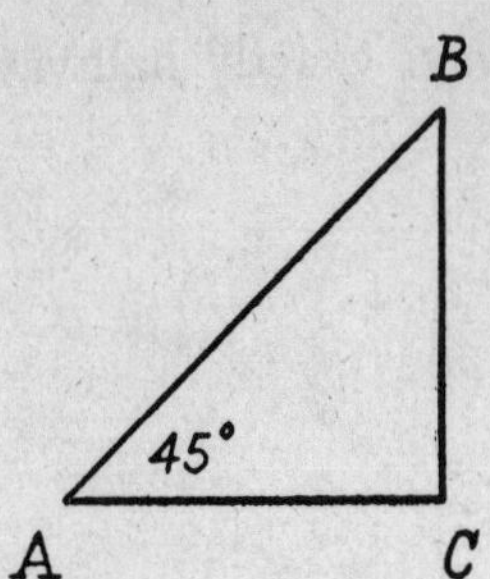

If $\angle A=45°$, then $\angle B=45°$ and $AC=BC$. (This is called an isosceles right triangle.)

Now let us apply what we have learned to some practical problems:

### PROBLEM 17

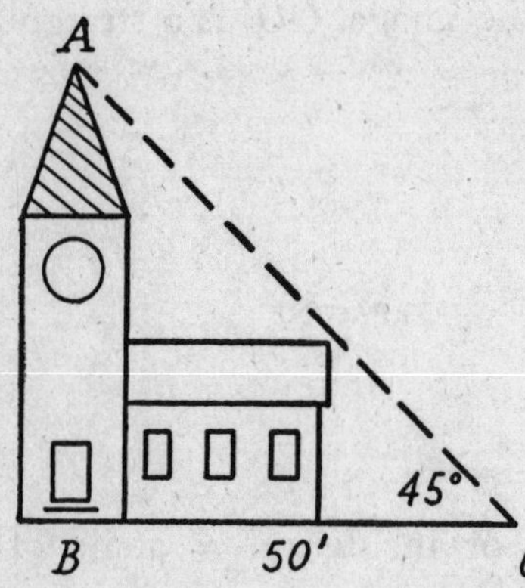

Fifty feet behind a church, the steeple top makes an angle of 45° with the ground. How high is the steeple?

This is an isosceles right triangle one of whose sides is 50 feet. $BC=50'$. Hence $AB$ must be 50 feet.

### PROBLEM 18

The top of a hill is 500′ higher than the bottom, and the angle of inclination of the hill is 30°. How long will it take a car going 50 feet per second to climb the hill?

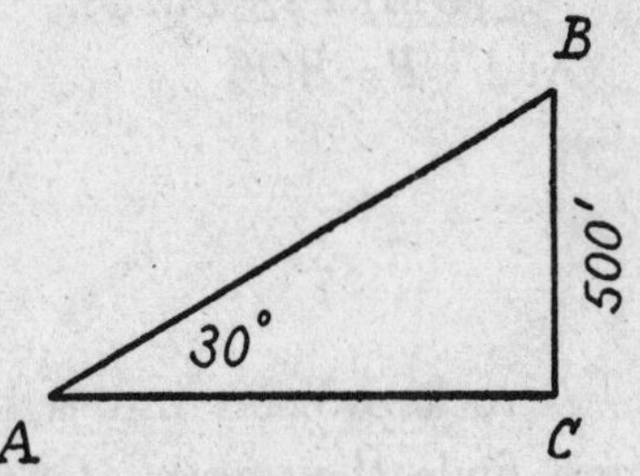

This is a right triangle, $ABC$, whose acute angle, $A$, is 30°. Hence $BC=\frac{1}{2}AB$ (see p. 868). This hill is consequently 1,000 feet long. At 50′ per second, the car will climb the hill in 20 seconds.

### PROBLEM 19

The angle at which light strikes a mirror ($\angle 1$) equals the angle at

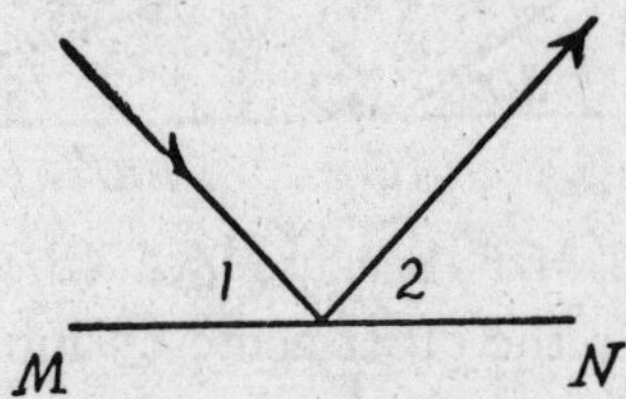

which it is reflected ($\angle 2$). Prove that a mirror is always exactly halfway between image and object.

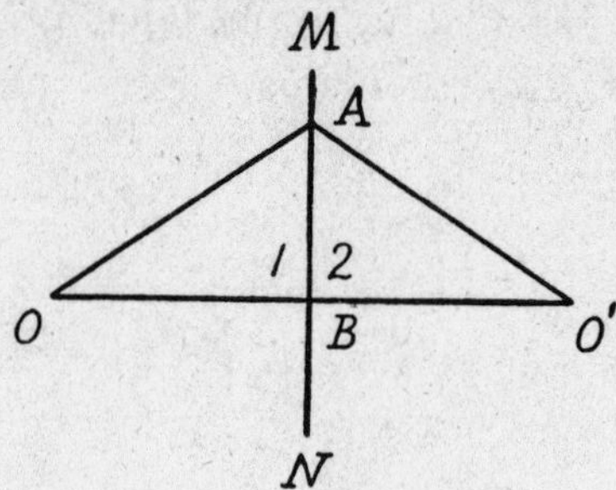

GIVEN   $MN$ is a mirror, $O$ the object, and $O'$ the image. $OO'$ is a straight line $\perp MN$.

TO PROVE   $OB = BO'$.

PROOF

| STATEMENTS | REASONS |
|---|---|
| Draw any line, $OA$, from $O$ to the mirror. | |
| Join $AO'$. | |
| Then $\angle OAB = \angle BAO'$. | Angle of incidence = angle of reflection. |
| $AB = AB$. | Identity. |
| $\angle 1 = \angle 2$. | All right $\angle$ are =. |
| $\therefore \triangle OMB \cong \triangle BMO'$. | a.s.a. |
| And $OB = BO'$. | Corresponding parts of $\cong \triangle$ are equal. |

### PROBLEM 20

A rock projects into a bay. A ship at $C$ sights the top of the rock $A$ and finds the angle $ACB = 30°$. It sails 1000 feet away and, sighting $A$ again, finds the angle to be $15°$. How high is the rock?

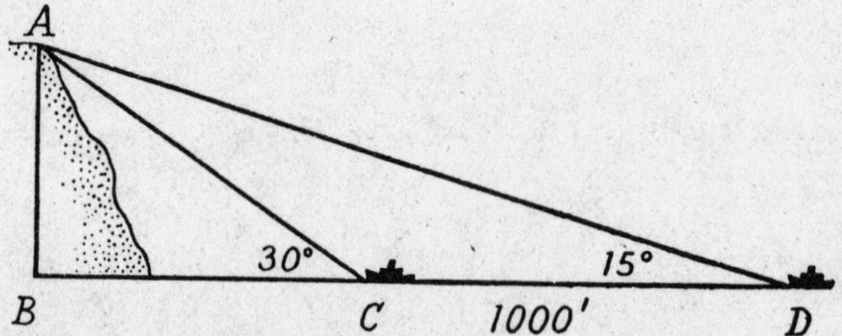


We know that $\angle CAB = 60°$ because $\triangle CAB$ is a rt. $\triangle$ one of whose acute $\angle$ is $30°$ (therefore the other acute $\angle$ must be $60°$).

We know that $\angle BAD$ must be $180°—90°—15°$ because the sum of 3 $\angle$ of a triangle $=180°$; and we know that $\angle ABD$ is a right $\angle$ and $\angle BDA$ is $15°$.

Hence $\angle BAD=(180°—90°)—15°=75°$, $\angle BAC=60°$.

$$\therefore \angle CAD=15° \text{ or } 75°—60°$$

$$\therefore \triangle CAD \text{ is isosceles—base angles are equal.}$$

$$\therefore AC=1000'—\text{sides of an isosceles } \triangle.$$

$\therefore AB=500'$ because in a rt. $\triangle$ with a $30°$ acute $\angle$, the side opposite this acute $\angle$ is equal to one-half the hypotenuse.

PROBLEM 21

The latitude of any point on the earth is found merely by sighting on the North Star (which is directly over the North Pole) and noting the angle between it and the horizon. Prove that this is so.

PROOF

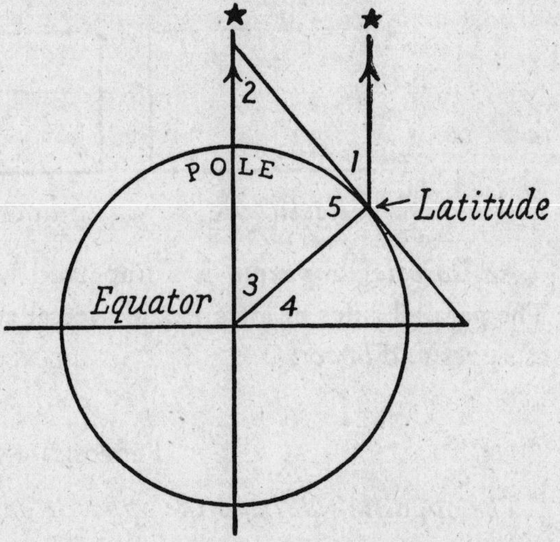


In the diagram, the North Star is shown directly over the Pole. $\angle 4$ is the latitude of the observer. $\angle 5=90°$. $\angle 3+\angle 4 =90°$ because the Pole is $90°$ to the equator. The distance from the earth to the North Star is regarded as infinite; hence the line of sight is parallel to the pole line (or axis of the earth); hence $\angle 1=\angle 2$ (Prop. VI). Then we have:

$$\angle 1=\angle 2.$$
$$\angle 3+\angle 4=90°.$$
$$\angle 3+\angle 2=90°.$$
$$\therefore \angle 4=\angle 2 \text{ (Axiom 1).}$$

$\therefore \angle 4=\angle 1$, or the latitude equals the angle of inclination of the North Star.

# QUADRILATERALS

Any four-sided figure is called a *quadrilateral;* "lateral" means side, "quadri" means four.

There are six types of quadrilaterals, namely, quadrilateral, trapezoid, parallelogram, rectangle, square, rhombus.

A *trapezoid* is a quadrilateral having two, and only two, sides parallel

A *parallelogram* is a quadrilateral having its opposite sides parallel.

A *rectangle* is a parallelogram whose angles are right angles. A *square* is an equilateral rectangle. A *rhombus* is an equilateral parallelogram.

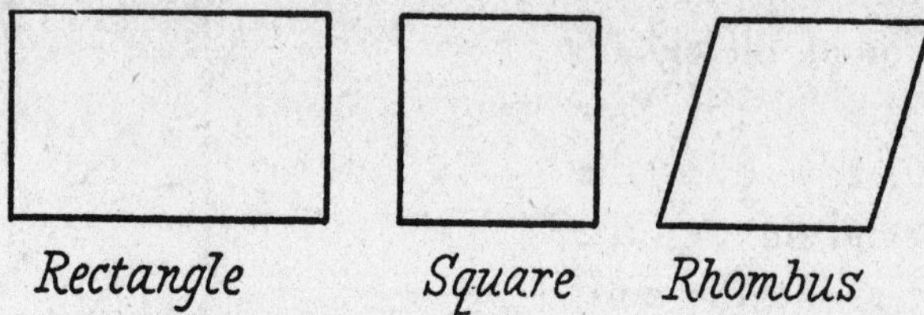


An *isosceles trapezoid* is a trapezoid whose nonparallel sides are equal. The parallel sides of a trapezoid are called its *bases,* and are distinguished as *upper* and *lower*.

PROPOSITION IX

*The opposite sides and the opposite angles of a parallelogram are equal.*

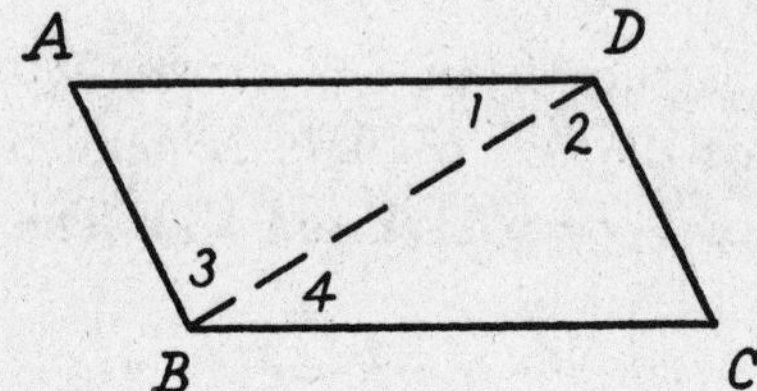


GIVEN  $\square ABCD$.

TO PROVE  $AD = BC$, $AB = CD$, $\angle A = \angle C$, $\angle B = \angle D$.

PROOF

| STATEMENTS | REASONS |
|---|---|
| Draw $BD$. | Two points determine a line. |
| $AD \parallel BC$, $AB \parallel DC$. | The opp. sides of a $\square$ are $\parallel$ (Definition). |
| $\angle 1 = \angle 4$, $\angle 3 = \angle 2$. | Prop. VI. |
| $BD = BD$. | Identity. |

$\triangle ABD \cong \triangle BDC.$  |  a.s.a.

$AD=BC.$  
$AB=CD.$  
$\angle A = \angle C.$  } | Corresponding parts of $\cong$ ⧍ are equal.

In like manner, by drawing $AC$, we can prove $\angle B = \angle D.$ | Steps similar to those above.

COROLLARY 1. *A diagonal divides a parallelogram into two congruent triangles.*

COROLLARY 2. *Parallels included between parallels are equal.*

COROLLARY 3. *Parallel lines are everywhere equidistant.*

### PROPOSITION X

*If three or more parallels intercept equal segments on one transversal, they intercept equal segments on every transversal.*

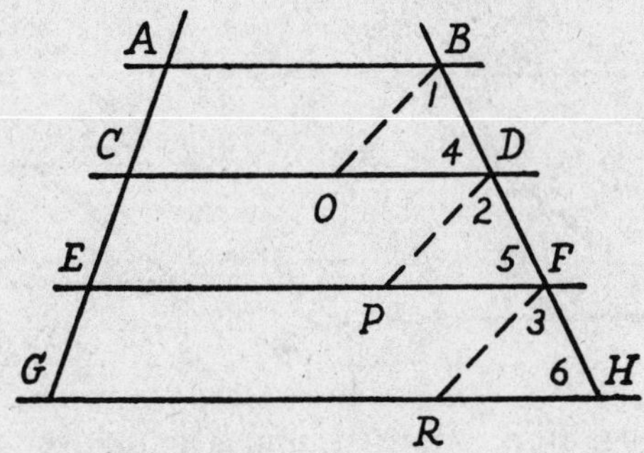


GIVEN $AB\|CD\|EF\|GH$, and $AC=CE=EG.$  
TO PROVE $\qquad BD=DF=FH.$

PROOF

| STATEMENTS | REASONS |
|---|---|
| Draw $BO$, $DP$, and $FR\|AG.$ | A line may be constructed $\|$ to a given line and passing through a given point. |
| $BO\|DP\|FR.$ | Lines $\|$ to the same line are $\|$ to each other. |
| $\angle 1 = \angle 2 = \angle 3.$ }  $\angle 4 = \angle 5 = \angle 6.$ } | Corresponding ⧍ of $\|$ lines are equal. (Cor. Prop. VI.) |
| $BO=AC,\ DP=CE,\ FR=EG.$ | Proposition IX, Corollary 2. |
| $AC=CE=EG.$ | Given. |
| $BO=DP=FR.$ | Axiom 1. |
| $\triangle BOD \cong \triangle DPF \cong \triangle FRH.$ | s.a.a. |
| $\therefore BD=DF=FH.$ | Corresponding sides of $\cong$ ⧍ are equal. |

**Corollary 1.** *The line parallel to one side of a triangle, bisecting another side, bisects the third side.*

**Corollary 2.** *The line that bisects a nonparallel side of a trapezoid and is parallel to the bases bisects the other nonparallel side.*

## SIMILAR TRIANGLES

We have learned how to prove triangles *congruent,* and have been able to apply this knowledge to proving lines and angles *equal.*

Now we shall learn how to prove triangles similar, and we shall see how useful these similar triangles are.

We define similar triangles as two triangles all of whose corresponding angles are equal. We say that if in $\triangle ABC$ and $\triangle A'B'C'$ $\angle A = \angle A'$, $\angle B = \angle B'$, $\angle C = \angle C'$ then $\triangle ABC \sim \triangle A'B'C'$.

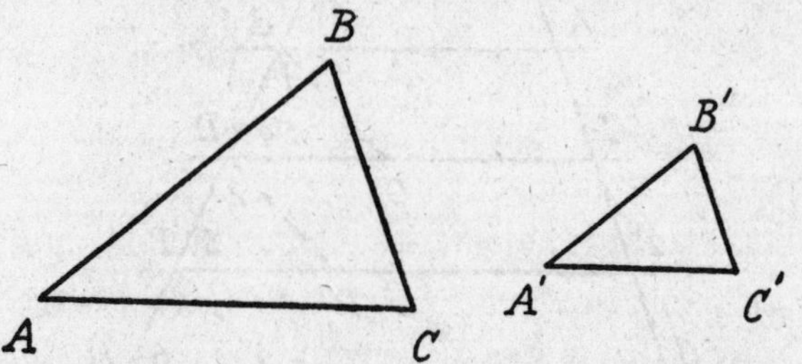

There is something more about triangles which we say is necessary if they are to be similar; that is, that their corresponding sides, instead of being equal (as in the case of congruent triangles), are in proportion. By this we mean that if $\triangle ABC \sim \triangle A'B'C'$, then

$AB$ is to $A'B'$ as $BC$ is to $B'C'$ as $AC$ is to $A'C'$.

We remember from arithmetic that a proportion is a statement of equality of two ratios.

We say $a$ is to $b$ as $c$ is to $d$ is a proportion. This we write as follows:

$$a:b=c:d.$$

We might just as well write it:

$$\frac{a}{b}=\frac{c}{d}$$

for it means the same thing.

A few examples of numerical proportions would be:

$$3:6=4:8;$$
$$5:10=10:20;$$

a cent : a dime = a dime : a dollar.

These three proportions are to be read as follows:

3 is to  6 as  4 is to  8;
5 is to 10 as 10 is to 20;
a cent is to a dime as a dime is to a dollar.

The two dots ( : ) always mean "is to." The equal sign means "as."
These all could be written as equal fractions; thus:

$$\frac{3}{6} = \frac{4}{8}$$

$$\frac{5}{10} = \frac{10}{20}$$

$$\frac{cent}{dime} = \frac{dime}{dollar}.$$

The first and fourth terms of a proportion are called the *extremes;* the second and third, the *means*.

When the means of a proportion are equal, *either* mean is said to be the *mean proportional* between the first and last terms. Thus, in the proportion, $a:b=b:c$, $b$ is the mean proportional between $a$ and $c$.

### PROPOSITION XI

*In any proportion, the product of the means is equal to the product of the extremes.*

GIVEN   $a:b=c:d$.
TO PROVE   $ad=bc$.

**PROOF**

$$\frac{a}{b} = \frac{c}{d} \qquad (\text{GIVEN})$$

Clearing of fractions, *i.e.,* multiplying both members by $bd$,

$$ad=bc. \qquad (\text{Axiom 4.})$$

This important proposition gives us the key to solving propositions. For example:

$$6:8=12:x\text{—Find } x.$$

We simply multiply the *extremes* together and the *means* together and divide one by the other:

$$6x = 96.$$
$$x = 16.$$

CHECK: $6:8 = 12:16.$

$4:x = 16:8.$  **Find *x*.**

$$16x = 32; \; x = 2.$$

CHECK: $4:2 = 16:8.$

$x:10 = 3:5.$  **Find *x*.**

$$5x = 30.$$
$$x = 6.$$

CHECK: $6:10 = 3:5.$

### EXERCISE 2

*See whether you can do these:*

Find *x* in each example:

1. $5:x = 3:6.$
2. $2:7 = 6:x.$
3. $12:3 = x:1.$
4. $x:17 = 4:34.$
5. $10:12 = 20:x.$
6. $6:x = 8:16.$
7. $x:9 = 12:36$
8. $\frac{1}{2}:x = 261:522$
9. $.3:x = 27:270$

### PROPOSITION XII

*If three terms of one proportion are equal to the corresponding terms of a second proportion, then the fourth term of one is equal to the fourth term of the other.*

GIVEN $\quad a:b = c:x \qquad a:b = c:y$

TO PROVE $\qquad x = y$

PROOF

| STATEMENTS | | REASONS |
|---|---|---|
| $a:b=c:x$ | $a:b=c:y$ | Given. |
| $ax=bc$ | $ay=bc$ | Prop. XII. |
| $ax=ay$ | | Axiom 1. |
| $x=y$ | | Axiom 5. |

The propositions on proportions look like and actually are algebraic rules. We connect them with geometry by the following postulate:

AXIOM 18. *A line parallel to one side of a triangle divides the other two sides into segments that are proportional.*

In symbols, if *DE* (in the drawing below) is drawn parallel to side *BC*

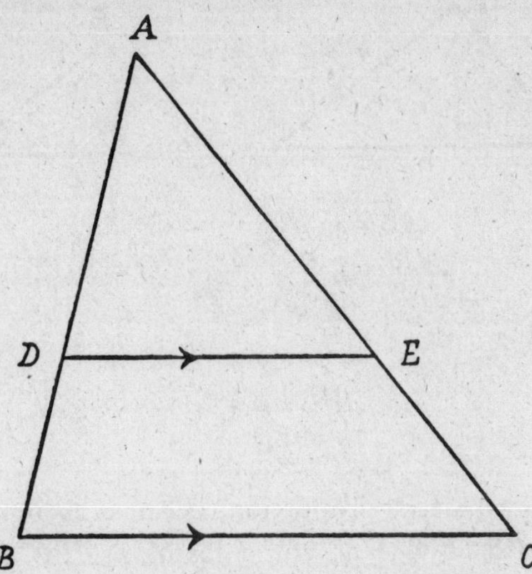

of $\triangle ABC$, then we can write these proportions by Axiom 18:

$$AD:DB=AE:EC \qquad AD:AB=AE:AC \qquad AB:DB=AC:EC$$

For example, suppose that $AD=12$, $DB=8$, $AE=15$. Then, using the first proportion above, we find

$$12:8=15:EC$$
$$12\times EC=120$$
$$EC=10$$



*See whether you can do these (the letters refer to the drawing above):*

1. $AD=10$   $AB=15$   $AE=12$   $AC=?$
2. $AB=20$   $DB=9$   $AC=24$   $CE=?$
3. $AD=8$   $DB=6$   $AC=18$   $AE=?$
4. $AD=16$   $CE=9$   $DB=AE$   $AE=?$
5. $AD=2(DB)$   $AC=30$   $AE=?$

## PROVING TRIANGLES SIMILAR

We have already defined similar triangles as triangles whose corresponding angles are equal and whose corresponding sides are proportional. Now let us see how we can prove triangles similar and how we can make use of these similar triangles.

If two triangles are similar their corresponding sides are proportional. Suppose we have two triangles, *ABC* and *A'B'C'*.

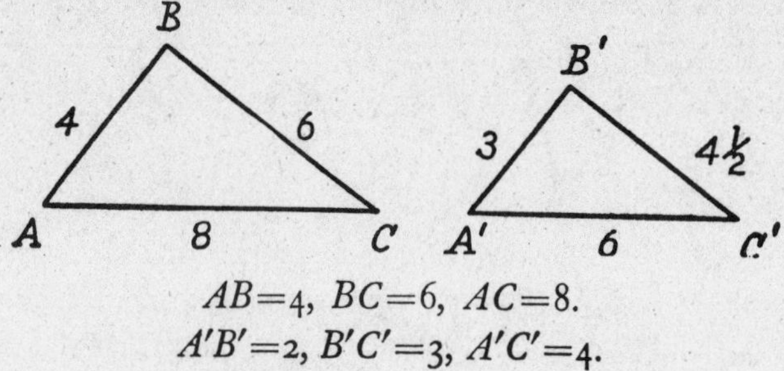

$$AB=4, \quad BC=6, \quad AC=8.$$
$$A'B'=2, \quad B'C'=3, \quad A'C'=4.$$

We say that

$$AB:A'B'=4:2.$$
$$BC:B'C'=6:3.$$

But $4:6=2:3$ is a perfect proportion, because $2\times6=4\times3$ (Prop. XII). Hence $AB:BC=A'B':B'C'$, and the sides of $\triangle ABC$ are proportional to the sides of $\triangle A'B'C'$.

## PROPOSITION XIII

*Two triangles are similar if the three angles of one are equal respectively to the three angles of the other.*

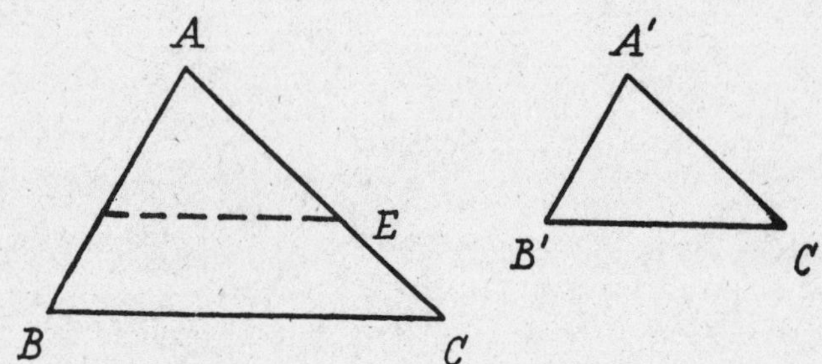

GIVEN in $\triangle$ *ABC* and *A'B'C'*,

$$\angle A=\angle A', \quad \angle B=\angle B', \quad \text{and} \quad \angle C=\angle C'.$$

TO PROVE $\qquad\qquad \triangle ABC \sim \triangle A'B'C'.$

PROOF

| STATEMENTS | REASONS |
|---|---|
| Place $\triangle A'B'C'$ upon $\triangle ABC$, $\angle A'$ on $\angle A$, taking the position $\triangle ADE$. | Axiom 13. |

| | |
|---|---|
| $\angle ADE = \angle B' = \angle B.$ | Given. |
| $DE \parallel BC.$ | If 2 cor. $\angle$ are $=$, lines are $\parallel$. |
| $AB:AD = AC:AE.$ | Axiom 18. |
| $AB:A'B' = AC:A'C'.$ | Sub. |
| By placing $\triangle A'B'C'$ on $\triangle ABC$ so that $\angle B'$ coincides with $\angle B$, we can show that | |
| $AB:A'B' = BC:B'C'.$ | |
| $\therefore \dfrac{AB}{A'B'} = \dfrac{BC}{B'C'} = \dfrac{AC}{A'C'},$ | Steps similar to those preceding. |
| But $\angle A = \angle A'$, $\angle B = \angle B'$, $\angle C = \angle C'.$ | Given. |
| $\therefore \triangle ABC \sim \triangle A'B'C'.$ | Their corresponding $\angle$ are equal. Their corresponding sides are proportional. |

**COROLLARY 1.** *Two triangles are similar if two angles of the one are equal respectively to two angles of the other.*

**COROLLARY 2.** *Two right triangles are similar if an acute angle of the one is equal to an acute angle of the other.*

**COROLLARY 3.** *A line parallel to one side of a triangle cuts off a triangle similar to the given triangle.*

**COROLLARY 4.** *If two triangles are similar to a third triangle, they are similar to each other.*

### PROPOSITION XIV

*Two triangles are similar if an angle of the one is equal to an angle of the other, and the sides including these angles are proportional.*

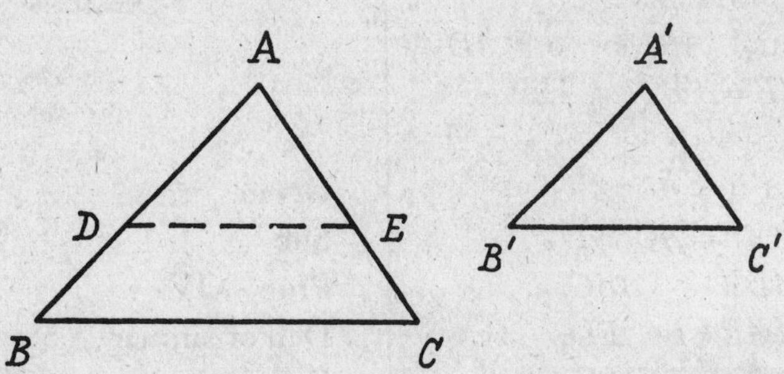


**GIVEN** In $\triangle$ $ABC$ and $A'B'C'$,
$\angle A = \angle A'$, and $AB:A'B' = AC:A'C'.$

**TO PROVE** $\triangle ABC \sim \triangle A'B'C'.$

**PROOF**

| STATEMENTS | REASONS |
|---|---|
| Place $\triangle A'B'C'$ upon $\triangle ABC$ so that $\angle A'$ coincides with $\angle A$ and $\triangle A'B'C'$ takes position $\triangle DAE$. | Axiom 13. Given. Sub. |
| $AB:A'B'=AC:A'C'$ | Converse of Axiom 18. |
| $AB:AD=AC:AE$ | Cor. Prop. V. |
| $DE\|BC$. | |
| $\angle B=\angle ADE$ and $\angle C=\angle DEA$. | Prop. XIII. |
| $\therefore \triangle ABC\sim\triangle ADE$ (or $\triangle A'B'C'$). | |

### Proposition XV

*Two triangles are similar if their corresponding sides are proportional.*

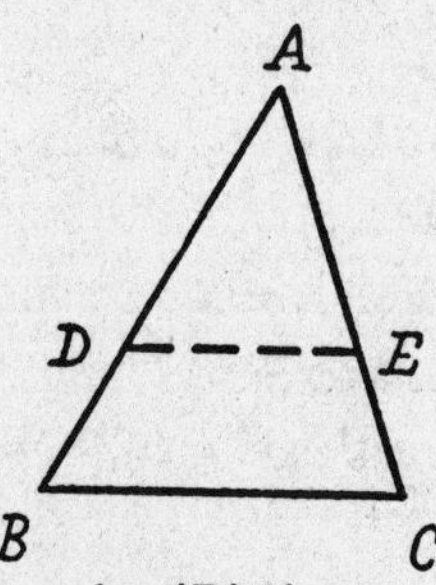 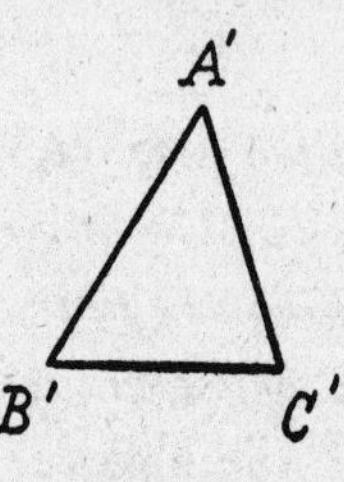

GIVEN   In $\triangle\!\!\!\triangle\ ABC$ and $A'B'C'$,

$$\frac{AB}{A'B'}=\frac{BC}{B'C'}=\frac{AC}{A'C'}$$

TO PROVE   $\triangle ABC\sim\triangle A'B'C'$.

**PROOF**

| STATEMENTS | REASONS |
|---|---|
| On $AC$ and $AB$, lay off $AD=A'C'$ and $AE=A'B'$. | |
| Draw $DE$. | |
| $AB:A'B'=AC:A'C'$. | Given. |
| $AB:AE=AC:AD$. | Sub. |
| $\triangle ADE\sim\triangle ABC$. | Prop. XIV. |
| $AB:AE=BC:ED$. | Def. of similar $\triangle\!\!\!\triangle$. |
| But $AB:A'B'=BC:B'C'$. | Given. |
| $ED=B'C'$. | Prop. XII. |
| $\therefore \triangle A'B'C'\cong\triangle ADE$. | s.s.s. |
| $\therefore \triangle A'B'C'\sim\triangle ABC$. | Sub. |

Now let us summarize what we have learned about similar triangles:

*First:* If three angles of one triangle equal three angles of another triangle, the two triangles are similar.

*Second:* If an angle of one triangle is equal to an angle of another triangle and the sides including the angles are in proportion, the two triangles are similar.

*Third:* If the corresponding sides of two triangles are in proportion to one another, the two triangles are similar.

Just as *congruent triangles* are used to prove lines *equal,* so *similar triangles* are used to prove lines *proportional.* By Proposition XII, we know that if we have three quantities in a proportion given, we can always get the fourth or unknown quantity, because *the product of the means equals the product of the extremes.*

If, therefore, we know three sides of one triangle and only one side of a similar triangle, we can find the other sides of that similar triangle merely by solving the proportion.

Let us study a few examples to illustrate the use and practical application of similar triangles:

### PROBLEM 22

A wall 20 feet high throws a shadow 5 feet long. How long will *your* shadow be if you are 6 feet tall?

Since the sun is inclined at the same angle for both your shadow and the wall's shadow, it follows that the two triangles $ABC$ (the wall and its shadow) wall's shadow, it follows that the two triangles similar. ($\angle A = \angle A'$, $\angle B = \angle B'$ and $\angle C = \angle C'$.

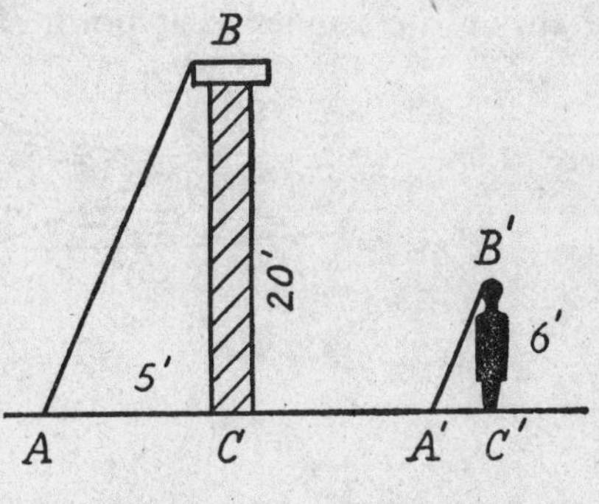


Hence:

$$5':20'=x':6'$$
$$\text{or } 20x=30 \text{ (Prop. XII),}$$
$$x=1.5'.$$

*Answer:* 1½ feet.

### PROBLEM 23

Mount Washington is 6000' high. I hold a foot rule absolutely level and 1 foot away from my eye, and the mountain appears 3" high. How far away am I from the mountain?

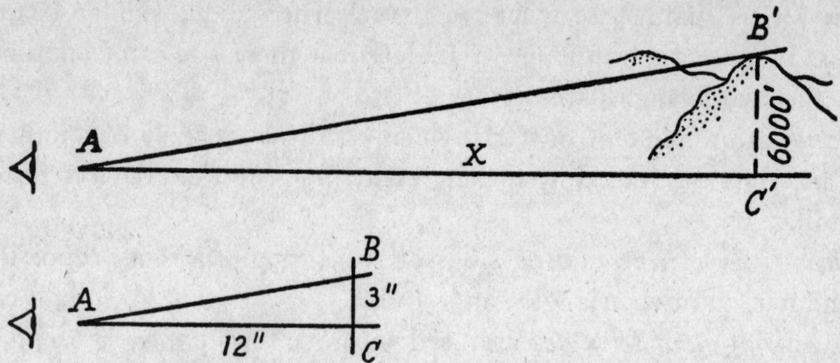



Here we have two similar triangles, *ABC* and *A′B′C′*. In the small triangle *ABC* the rule was held 1 foot away (*AC*) and the mountain measured 3″ (*BC*). In reality the mountain is "*x*" feet away (*A′C′*) and is 6000′ high (*B′C′*). Hence:

$$1' : 3'' = x' : 6000'$$
$$\text{or } 1' : \tfrac{1}{4}' = x' : 6000' - (3'' = \tfrac{1}{4}').$$
$$\tfrac{1}{4}x = 6000'.$$
$$x = 24000' = 4\tfrac{1}{2} \text{ miles.}$$

PROBLEM 24

I want to find the distance across a stream, *AB*. I can't get across, and I am on the same side as point *A*. How do I do it?

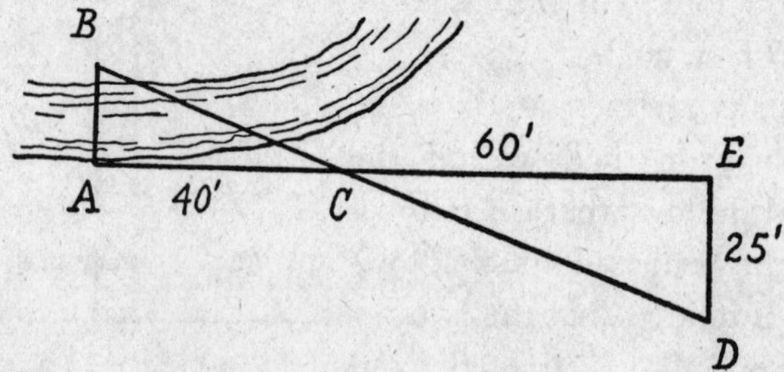



I measure off any distance, *AE*, at right angles to *AB*. This I do by putting a stake at *A* and a stake at *E* and connecting both stakes with a taut string. I measure this distance and find that it is 100 feet. At *E* I turn at right angles and go over to some point, *D,* say, 25 feet. I now line up *B* with *D* and move along this line until I reach the string. This point I call *C.* I now measure *AC* and find it to be 40 feet. Then: $\triangle ABC \sim \triangle CDE$ because $\angle 1 = \angle 2$ (vertical $\angle$) and $\angle A = \angle E$ (right angles).

Then
$$AC : CE = AB : DE$$
$$\text{or } 40 : 60 = AB : 25 - AC = 40', \ CE = 100' - 40' = 60' \text{ and } DE = 25'.$$
$$\therefore 60 AB = 1000.$$
$$AB = 16\tfrac{2}{3}'.$$

## Proposition XVI

*In any right triangle, the altitude on the hypotenuse divides the triangle into two triangles, similar to each other and to the given triangle.*

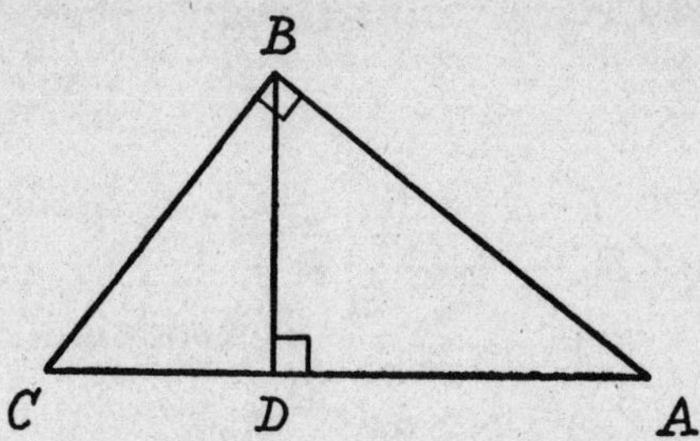

GIVEN in the rt. $\triangle$ $ABC$, $BD$ the $\perp$ to hypotenuse $CA$.

TO PROVE $\qquad\qquad \triangle BCD \sim \triangle ACB \sim \triangle BDA.$

### PROOF

| STATEMENTS | REASONS |
|---|---|
| Each $\triangle$ is a rt. $\triangle$. | |
| In $\triangle$ $ACB$ and $BCD$, $\angle C = \angle C$ | Identity. |
| $\therefore \triangle BCD \sim \triangle ACB.$ | Prop. XV, cor. 2. |
| In $\triangle$ $ACB$ and $BDA$, $\angle A = \angle A.$ | Identity. |
| $\therefore \triangle ACB \sim \triangle BDA.$ | Prop. XIII, cor. 2. |
| $\therefore \triangle BCD \sim \triangle ACB$ | Prop. XIII, cor. 4. |

## Proposition XVII

*In a right triangle, the altitude upon the hypotenuse is the mean proportional between the segments of the hypotenuse, and either arm is the mean proportional between the hypotenuse and the segment adjacent to that arm.*

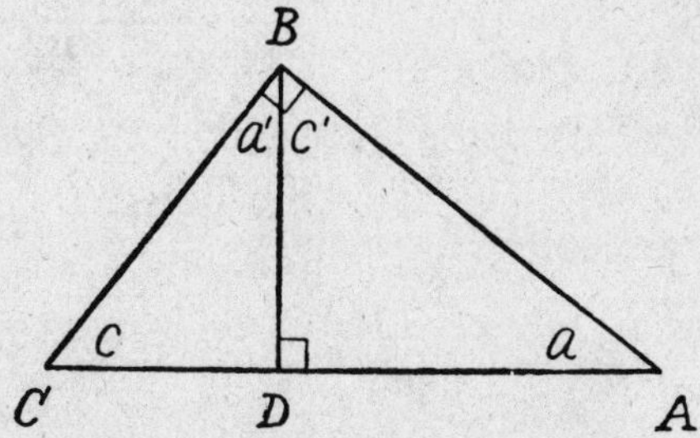

GIVEN in the rt. $\triangle ABC$, $BD$ the altitude upon the hypotenuse $AC$.

TO PROVE

(1) $CD:DB = DB:DA.$

(2) $CA:BA = BA:DA.$

(3) $CA:CB = CB:CD.$

PROOF

| STATEMENTS | REASONS |
|---|---|
| $\triangle ABC \sim \triangle BCD \sim \triangle BDA$. | Prop. XVI. |
| Since $\triangle BCD \sim \triangle BDA$, | |
| $\therefore CD:DB=DB:DA$. | Def. of similar triangles. |
| Since $\triangle ABC \sim \triangle BDA$, | |
| $\therefore CA:BA=BA:DA$. | Def. of similar triangles. |
| Since $\triangle ABC \sim \triangle BCD$, | |
| $\therefore CA:CB=CB:CD$. | Def. of similar triangles. |

Note: $\angle a$ or $\angle A = \angle d'$ and $\angle c$ or $\angle C = \angle c'$.

### Proposition XVIII

*The sum of the squares of the arms of a right triangle is equal to the square of the hypotenuse.*

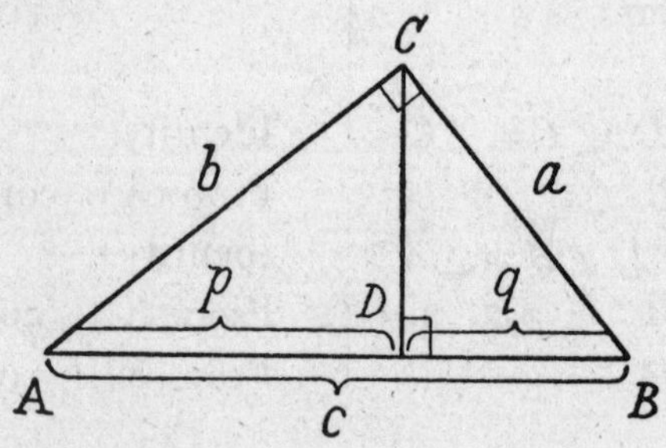

GIVEN $ACB$, a rt. $\triangle$, having its rt. $\angle$ at $C$.

TO PROVE $\qquad\qquad\qquad a^2+b^2=c^2$

PROOF

| STATEMENTS | REASONS |
|---|---|
| Draw $CD \perp AB$, | |
| $\qquad p:b=b:c$. | Prop. XVII. |
| $\qquad \therefore b^2=c \times p$. | |
| Similarly $a^2=c \times q$. | |
| $\qquad a^2+b^2=c \times p+c \times q$ | |
| $\qquad\qquad =c(p+q)$. | |
| $\qquad a^2+b^2=c^2$. | Sub. |

COROLLARY. *The square of either arm of a right triangle is equal to the square of the hypotenuse, diminished by the square of the other arm.*

This proposition is one of the most important in all mathematics. It is known as the *Pythagorean Theorem* because it was first demonstrated by Pythagoras about 500 B.C.

*Now see whether you can use the Pythagorean Theorem to solve these problems. Refer to the table of square roots on page 196 when necessary.*

1. The sides of a right triangle are 6″ and 8″. Find the hypotenuse.

2. A ladder 25 feet long leaning against a wall reaches 24 feet up the wall. How far from the foot of the wall is the foot of the ladder?

3. A gate four feet high and three feet wide has two braces reaching diagonally from corner to corner. How long is each brace?

4. A path runs diagonally across a lot 20 yd. wide and 21 yd. long. How long is the path?

5. What is the length of the longest line you can draw on a sheet of paper 6″ long and 4″ wide?

6. A gable in the form of an isosceles triangle has a width of 24 ft. and a height of 5 ft. How long must the rafters be?

7. The equal sides of an isosceles triangle are 12″ long, and the base is 6″ long. Find the length of the altitude to the base.

8. The sides of a square are 7″ long. How long is the diagonal?

# TRIGONOMETRY

In the diagram below, three similar triangles have been drawn. They

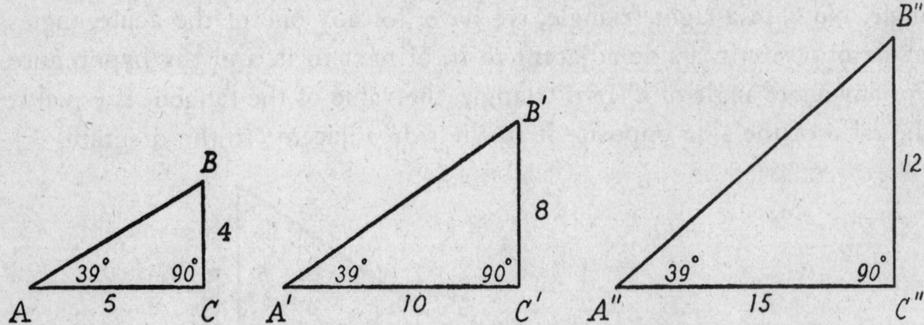


are similar because all have the equal angles of 39° and 90°. It follows that corresponding sides are proportional. For instance,

$$\frac{BC}{AC} = \frac{B'C'}{A'C'} = \frac{B''C''}{A''C''}$$

Now, suppose we were to change the size of angle $A$, leaving angle $C$ equal to 90°, as before. Then $\triangle ABC$ would no longer be similar to the other triangles, and we would have

$$\frac{BC}{AC} \neq \frac{B'C'}{A'C'}$$

Conversely, if we change the length of side *BC* without changing the length of side *AC* or the size of angle *C*, then we would also have

$$\frac{BC}{AC} \neq \frac{B'C'}{A'C'}$$

In other words, the value of the ratio *BC*:*AC* in a right triangle depends on the size of angle *A*, and conversely: to every value of the angle *A* corresponds a different value of the ratio *BC*:*AC*. This ratio is called the *tangent* of angle *A*, and is written "tan *A*." In the diagram below, we see that tan 39° = ⅘ = .8000.

EXERCISE 5

*On page 195, you will find a table which lists the value of the tangent for every angle from 1° to 90°. By referring to it, see whether you can answer the following questions:*

| | | | |
|---|---|---|---|
| 1. | tan 45° = ? | 5. | tan 36° = ? |
| 2. | tan 30° = ? | 6. | tan *A* = .3640    *A* = ? |
| 3. | tan 27° = ? | 7. | tan *x* = .7002    *x* = ? |
| 4. | tan 72° = ? | 8. | tan *θ* = 1.3270    *θ* = ? |

Notice that the tangent of an angle is always referred to as a right triangle. Now, in a right triangle, we have, for any one of the acute angles, a side opposite it, a side adjacent to it, or next to it, and the hypotenuse. For any acute angle of a right triangle, the value of the tangent is equal to the ratio of the side opposite it to the side adjacent; in the diagram,

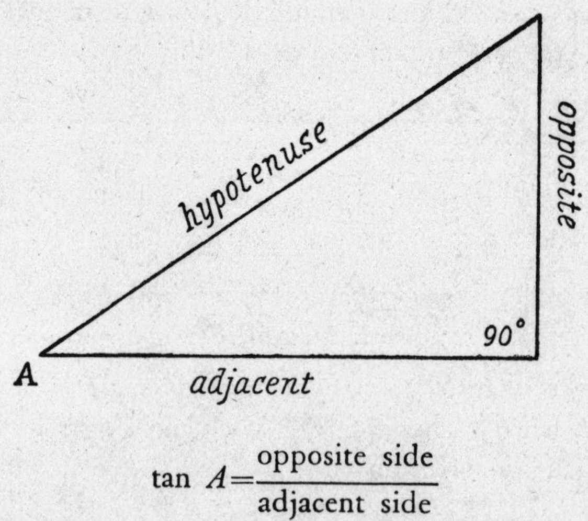


$$\tan A = \frac{\text{opposite side}}{\text{adjacent side}}$$

Now let us see how we can use our new knowledge to solve problems.

## Problem 25

At a distance of 60 feet from the foot of a building, the angle of elevation of the top is found to be 58°. Find the height of the building.

SOLUTION. We first draw a diagram in which side $BC$ represents the building, whose height we call $x$, and $AC$ our distance from it. Then

$$\tan 58° = \frac{BC}{AC} = \frac{x}{60}$$

From the table, we find that tan $58° = 1.6003$. Therefore

$$\frac{x}{60} = 1.6003 \qquad x = 96.0180 \text{ ft.}$$

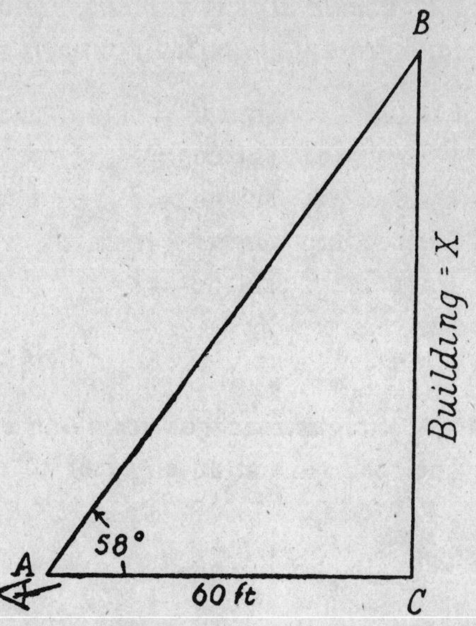


Note that an angle of elevation is an angle measured upward from a horizontal line. An angle of depression is an angle measured downward from a horizontal line.

### EXERCISE 6

*See whether you can solve the following problems:*

1. At a distance of 2000 feet from the base of a cliff, the angle of elevation to the top is found to be 22°. Find the height of the cliff.
2. A man in a lighthouse 80 feet high sees a ship at an angle of depression of 12°. How far from the base of the lighthouse is the ship?
3. When the angle of elevation of the sun is 36°, how long a shadow will a flagpole 80 feet high cast?
4. Find to the nearest degree the angle of elevation of the sun when a stick six feet long casts a shadow whose length is eight feet.

In a right triangle, there are several ratios which we could have chosen instead of the tangent ratio. For example, we could have selected, for any acute angle, the ratio of the side opposite it to the hypotenuse. This ratio also depends on the size of the angle. We call it the sine of the angle and abbreviate it is "sin $A$." In short,

$$\sin A = \frac{\text{opposite side}}{\text{hypotenuse}}$$

### EXERCISE 7

*Our table of trigonometric ratios gives us the value of the sine of every angle from 0° to 90°. By referring to it, see if you can answer these:*

| | | | | |
|---|---|---|---|---|
| 1. | $\sin 30° = ?$ | 6. | $\sin A = .5592$ | $A = ?$ |
| 2. | $\sin 60° = ?$ | 7. | $\sin x = .8090$ | $x = ?$ |
| 3. | $\sin 58° = ?$ | 8. | $\sin \theta = .1908$ | $\theta = ?$ |
| 4. | $\sin 37° = ?$ | 9. | $\sin B = .7660$ | $B = ?$ |
| 5. | $\sin 82° = ?$ | 10. | $\sin A = .0872$ | $A = ?$ |

### PROBLEM 26

A straight road 500 feet long runs from the foot to the top of a hill. The road runs at an angle of 20°. Find the height of the hill.

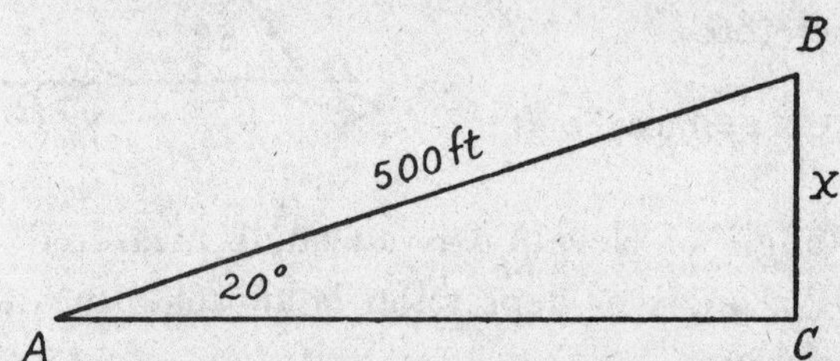


SOLUTION. We draw a diagram with angle $A$ equal to 20°, hypotenuse $AB$ representing 500 feet, and side $BC$ representing the height of the hill.

Then
$$\sin 20° = \frac{BC}{AB} = \frac{x}{500}$$

Referring to the table, we find that $\sin 20° = .3420$. Therefore

$$\frac{x}{500} = .3420 \qquad x = 171 \text{ feet.}$$

### EXERCISE 8

*See whether you can use the sine ratio to solve the following problems.*

1. A tunnel runs into the ground at an angle of 12°. How deep will a shaft be which is driven vertically to meet the tunnel 500 feet from its mouth?
2. How high up a wall will a ladder 24 feet reach if it makes an angle of 82° with the ground?
3. A pole is braced with three guy wires which are 40 feet long each and meet the ground at an angle of 55°. How high up the pole are they fastened?

# NATURAL TRIGONOMETRIC FUNCTIONS

| Angle | Sine | Cosine | Tangent | Angle | Sine | Cosine | Tangent |
|---|---|---|---|---|---|---|---|
| 1° | .0175 | .9998 | .0175 | 46° | .7193 | .6947 | 1.0355 |
| 2° | .0349 | .9994 | .0349 | 47° | .7314 | .6820 | 1.0724 |
| 3° | .0523 | .9986 | .0524 | 48° | .7431 | .6691 | 1.1106 |
| 4° | .0698 | .9976 | .0699 | 49° | .7547 | .6561 | 1.1504 |
| 5° | .0872 | .9962 | .0875 | 50° | .7660 | .6428 | 1.1918 |
| 6° | .1045 | .9945 | .1051 | 51° | .7771 | .6293 | 1.2349 |
| 7° | .1219 | .9925 | .1228 | 52° | .7880 | .6157 | 1.2799 |
| 8° | .1392 | .9903 | .1405 | 53° | .7986 | .6018 | 1.3270 |
| 9° | .1564 | .9877 | .1584 | 54° | .8090 | .5878 | 1.3764 |
| 10° | .1736 | .9848 | .1763 | 55° | .8192 | .5736 | 1.4281 |
| 11° | .1908 | .9816 | .1944 | 56° | .8290 | .5592 | 1.4826 |
| 12° | .2079 | .9781 | .2126 | 57° | .8387 | .5446 | 1.5399 |
| 13° | .2250 | .9744 | .2309 | 58° | .8480 | .5299 | 1.6003 |
| 14° | .2419 | .9703 | .2493 | 59° | .8572 | .5150 | 1.6643 |
| 15° | .2588 | .9659 | .2679 | 60° | .8660 | .5000 | 1.7321 |
| 16° | .2756 | .9613 | .2867 | 61° | .8746 | .4848 | 1.8040 |
| 17° | .2924 | .9563 | .3057 | 62° | .8829 | .4695 | 1.8807 |
| 18° | .3090 | .9511 | .3249 | 63° | .8910 | .4540 | 1.9626 |
| 19° | .3256 | .9455 | .3443 | 64° | .8988 | .4384 | 2.0503 |
| 20° | .3420 | .9397 | .3640 | 65° | .9063 | .4226 | 2.1445 |
| 21° | .3584 | .9336 | .3839 | 66° | .9135 | .4067 | 2.2460 |
| 22° | .3746 | .9272 | .4040 | 67° | .9205 | .3907 | 2.3559 |
| 23° | .3907 | .9205 | .4245 | 68° | .9272 | .3746 | 2.4751 |
| 24° | .4067 | .9135 | .4452 | 69° | .9336 | .3584 | 2.6051 |
| 25° | .4226 | .9063 | .4663 | 70° | .9397 | .3420 | 2.7475 |
| 26° | .4384 | .8988 | .4877 | 71° | .9455 | .3256 | 2.9042 |
| 27° | .4540 | .8910 | .5095 | 72° | .9511 | .3090 | 3.0777 |
| 28° | .4695 | .8829 | .5317 | 73° | .9563 | .2924 | 3.2709 |
| 29° | .4848 | .8746 | .5543 | 74° | .9613 | .2756 | 3.4874 |
| 30° | .5000 | .8660 | .5774 | 75° | .9659 | .2588 | 3.7321 |
| 31° | .5150 | .8572 | .6009 | 76° | .9703 | .2419 | 4.0108 |
| 32° | .5299 | .8480 | .6249 | 77° | .9744 | .2250 | 4.3315 |
| 33° | .5446 | .8387 | .6494 | 78° | .9781 | .2079 | 4.7046 |
| 34° | .5592 | .8290 | .6745 | 79° | .9816 | .1908 | 5.1446 |
| 35° | .5736 | .8192 | .7002 | 80° | .9848 | .1736 | 5.6713 |
| 36° | .5878 | .8090 | .7265 | 81° | .9877 | .1564 | 6.3138 |
| 37° | .6018 | .7986 | .7536 | 82° | .9903 | .1392 | 7.1154 |
| 38° | .6157 | .7880 | .7813 | 83° | .9925 | .1219 | 8.1443 |
| 39° | .6293 | .7771 | .8098 | 84° | .9945 | .1045 | 9.5144 |
| 40° | .6428 | .7660 | .8391 | 85° | .9962 | .0872 | 11.4301 |
| 41° | .6561 | .7547 | .8693 | 86° | .9976 | .0698 | 14.3007 |
| 42° | .6691 | .7431 | .9004 | 87° | .9986 | .0523 | 19.0811 |
| 43° | .6820 | .7314 | .9325 | 88° | .9994 | .0349 | 28.6363 |
| 44° | .6947 | .7193 | .9657 | 89° | .9998 | .0175 | 57.2900 |
| 45° | .7071 | .7071 | 1.0000 | 90° | 1.0000 | .0000 | |

# SQUARE ROOTS OF NUMBERS

| N | 0 | 1 | 2 | 3 | 4 | 5 | 6 | 7 | 8 | 9 |
|---|---|---|---|---|---|---|---|---|---|---|
| 1.0 | 1.000 | 1.005 | 1.010 | 1.015 | 1.020 | 1.025 | 1.030 | 1.034 | 1.039 | 1.044 |
| 1 | 1.049 | 1.054 | 1.058 | 1.063 | 1.068 | 1.072 | 1.077 | 1.082 | 1.086 | 1.091 |
| 2 | 1.095 | 1.100 | 1.105 | 1.109 | 1.114 | 1.118 | 1.122 | 1.127 | 1.131 | 1.136 |
| 3 | 1.140 | 1.145 | 1.149 | 1.153 | 1.158 | 1.162 | 1.166 | 1.170 | 1.175 | 1.179 |
| 4 | 1.183 | 1.187 | 1.192 | 1.196 | 1.200 | 1.204 | 1.208 | 1.212 | 1.217 | 1.221 |
| 1.5 | 1.225 | 1.229 | 1.233 | 1.237 | 1.241 | 1.245 | 1.249 | 1.253 | 1.257 | 1.261 |
| 6 | 1.265 | 1.269 | 1.273 | 1.277 | 1.281 | 1.285 | 1.288 | 1.292 | 1.296 | 1.300 |
| 7 | 1.304 | 1.308 | 1.311 | 1.315 | 1.319 | 1.323 | 1.327 | 1.330 | 1.334 | 1.338 |
| 8 | 1.342 | 1.345 | 1.349 | 1.353 | 1.356 | 1.360 | 1.364 | 1.367 | 1.371 | 1.375 |
| 9 | 1.378 | 1.382 | 1.386 | 1.389 | 1.393 | 1.396 | 1.400 | 1.404 | 1.407 | 1.411 |
| 2.0 | 1.414 | 1.418 | 1.421 | 1.425 | 1.428 | 1.432 | 1.435 | 1.439 | 1.442 | 1.446 |
| 1 | 1.449 | 1.453 | 1.456 | 1.459 | 1.463 | 1.466 | 1.470 | 1.473 | 1.476 | 1.480 |
| 2 | 1.483 | 1.487 | 1.490 | 1.493 | 1.497 | 1.500 | 1.503 | 1.507 | 1.510 | 1.513 |
| 3 | 1.517 | 1.520 | 1.523 | 1.526 | 1.530 | 1.533 | 1.536 | 1.539 | 1.543 | 1.546 |
| 4 | 1.549 | 1.552 | 1.556 | 1.559 | 1.562 | 1.565 | 1.568 | 1.572 | 1.575 | 1.578 |
| 2.5 | 1.581 | 1.584 | 1.587 | 1.591 | 1.594 | 1.597 | 1.600 | 1.603 | 1.606 | 1.609 |
| 6 | 1.612 | 1.616 | 1.619 | 1.622 | 1.625 | 1.628 | 1.631 | 1.634 | 1.637 | 1.640 |
| 7 | 1.643 | 1.646 | 1.649 | 1.652 | 1.655 | 1.658 | 1.661 | 1.664 | 1.667 | 1.670 |
| 8 | 1.673 | 1.676 | 1.679 | 1.682 | 1.685 | 1.688 | 1.691 | 1.694 | 1.697 | 1.700 |
| 9 | 1.703 | 1.706 | 1.709 | 1.712 | 1.715 | 1.718 | 1.720 | 1.723 | 1.726 | 1.729 |
| 3.0 | 1.732 | 1.735 | 1.738 | 1.741 | 1.744 | 1.746 | 1.749 | 1.752 | 1.755 | 1.758 |
| 1 | 1.761 | 1.764 | 1.766 | 1.769 | 1.772 | 1.775 | 1.778 | 1.780 | 1.783 | 1.786 |
| 2 | 1.789 | 1.792 | 1.794 | 1.797 | 1.800 | 1.803 | 1.806 | 1.808 | 1.811 | 1.814 |
| 3 | 1.817 | 1.819 | 1.822 | 1.825 | 1.828 | 1.830 | 1.833 | 1.836 | 1.838 | 1.841 |
| 4 | 1.844 | 1.847 | 1.849 | 1.852 | 1.855 | 1.857 | 1.860 | 1.863 | 1.865 | 1.868 |
| 3.5 | 1.871 | 1.873 | 1.876 | 1.879 | 1.881 | 1.884 | 1.887 | 1.889 | 1.892 | 1.895 |
| 6 | 1.897 | 1.900 | 1.903 | 1.905 | 1.908 | 1.910 | 1.913 | 1.916 | 1.918 | 1.921 |
| 7 | 1.924 | 1.926 | 1.929 | 1.931 | 1.934 | 1.936 | 1.939 | 1.942 | 1.944 | 1.947 |
| 8 | 1.949 | 1.952 | 1.954 | 1.957 | 1.960 | 1.962 | 1.965 | 1.967 | 1.970 | 1.972 |
| 9 | 1.975 | 1.977 | 1.980 | 1.982 | 1.985 | 1.987 | 1.990 | 1.992 | 1.995 | 1.997 |
| 4.0 | 2.000 | 2.002 | 2.005 | 2.007 | 2.010 | 2.012 | 2.015 | 2.017 | 2.020 | 2.022 |
| 1 | 2.025 | 2.027 | 2.030 | 2.032 | 2.035 | 2.037 | 2.040 | 2.042 | 2.045 | 2.047 |
| 2 | 2.049 | 2.052 | 2.054 | 2.057 | 2.059 | 2.062 | 2.064 | 2.066 | 2.069 | 2.071 |
| 3 | 2.074 | 2.076 | 2.078 | 2.081 | 2.083 | 2.086 | 2.088 | 2.090 | 2.093 | 2.095 |
| 4 | 2.098 | 2.100 | 2.102 | 2.105 | 2.107 | 2.110 | 2.112 | 2.114 | 2.117 | 2.119 |
| 4.5 | 2.121 | 2.124 | 2.126 | 2.128 | 2.131 | 2.133 | 2.135 | 2.138 | 2.140 | 2.142 |
| 6 | 2.145 | 2.147 | 2.149 | 2.152 | 2.154 | 2.156 | 2.159 | 2.161 | 2.163 | 2.166 |
| 7 | 2.168 | 2.170 | 2.173 | 2.175 | 2.177 | 2.179 | 2.182 | 2.184 | 2.186 | 2.189 |
| 8 | 2.191 | 2.193 | 2.195 | 2.198 | 2.200 | 2.202 | 2.205 | 2.207 | 2.209 | 2.211 |
| 9 | 2.214 | 2.216 | 2.218 | 2.220 | 2.223 | 2.225 | 2.227 | 2.229 | 2.232 | 2.234 |
| 5.0 | 2.236 | 2.238 | 2.241 | 2.243 | 2.245 | 2.247 | 2.249 | 2.252 | 2.254 | 2.256 |
| 1 | 2.258 | 2.261 | 2.263 | 2.265 | 2.267 | 2.269 | 2.272 | 2.274 | 2.276 | 2.278 |
| 2 | 2.280 | 2.283 | 2.285 | 2.287 | 2.289 | 2.291 | 2.293 | 2.296 | 2.298 | 2.300 |
| 3 | 2.302 | 2.304 | 2.307 | 2.309 | 2.311 | 2.313 | 2.315 | 2.317 | 2.319 | 2.322 |
| 4 | 2.324 | 2.326 | 2.328 | 2.330 | 2.332 | 2.335 | 2.337 | 2.339 | 2.341 | 2.343 |
| 5.5 | 2.345 | 2.347 | 2.349 | 2.352 | 2.354 | 2.356 | 2.358 | 2.360 | 2.362 | 2.364 |
| 6 | 2.366 | 2.369 | 2.371 | 2.373 | 2.375 | 2.377 | 2.379 | 2.381 | 2.383 | 2.385 |
| 7 | 2.387 | 2.390 | 2.392 | 2.394 | 2.396 | 2.398 | 2.400 | 2.402 | 2.404 | 2.406 |
| 8 | 2.408 | 2.410 | 2.412 | 2.415 | 2.417 | 2.419 | 2.421 | 2.423 | 2.425 | 2.427 |
| 9 | 2.429 | 2.431 | 2.433 | 2.435 | 2.437 | 2.439 | 2.441 | 2.443 | 2.445 | 2.447 |
| 6.0 | 2.449 | 2.452 | 2.454 | 2.456 | 2.458 | 2.460 | 2.462 | 2.464 | 2.466 | 2.468 |
| 1 | 2.470 | 2.472 | 2.474 | 2.476 | 2.478 | 2.480 | 2.482 | 2.484 | 2.486 | 2.488 |
| 2 | 2.490 | 2.492 | 2.494 | 2.496 | 2.498 | 2.500 | 2.502 | 2.504 | 2.506 | 2.508 |
| 3 | 2.510 | 2.512 | 2.514 | 2.516 | 2.518 | 2.520 | 2.522 | 2.524 | 2.526 | 2.528 |
| 4 | 2.530 | 2.532 | 2.534 | 2.536 | 2.538 | 2.540 | 2.542 | 2.544 | 2.546 | 2.548 |
| 6.5 | 2.550 | 2.551 | 2.553 | 2.555 | 2.557 | 2.559 | 2.561 | 2.563 | 2.565 | 2.567 |
| 6 | 2.569 | 2.571 | 2.573 | 2.575 | 2.577 | 2.579 | 2.581 | 2.583 | 2.585 | 2.587 |
| 7 | 2.588 | 2.590 | 2.592 | 2.594 | 2.596 | 2.598 | 2.600 | 2.602 | 2.604 | 2.606 |
| 8 | 2.608 | 2.610 | 2.612 | 2.613 | 2.615 | 2.617 | 2.619 | 2.621 | 2.623 | 2.625 |
| 9 | 2.627 | 2.629 | 2.631 | 2.632 | 2.634 | 2.636 | 2.638 | 2.640 | 2.642 | 2.644 |

| N | 0 | 1 | 2 | 3 | 4 | 5 | 6 | 7 | 8 | 9 |
|---|---|---|---|---|---|---|---|---|---|---|
| 7.0 | 2.646 | 2.648 | 2.650 | 2.651 | 2.653 | 2.655 | 2.657 | 2.659 | 2.661 | 2.663 |
| 1 | 2.665 | 2.666 | 2.668 | 2.670 | 2.672 | 2.674 | 2.676 | 2.678 | 2.680 | 2.681 |
| 2 | 2.683 | 2.685 | 2.687 | 2.689 | 2.691 | 2.693 | 2.694 | 2.696 | 2.698 | 2.700 |
| 3 | 2.702 | 2.704 | 2.706 | 2.707 | 2.709 | 2.711 | 2.713 | 2.715 | 2.717 | 2.718 |
| 4 | 2.720 | 2.722 | 2.724 | 2.726 | 2.728 | 2.729 | 2.731 | 2.733 | 2.735 | 2.737 |
| 7.5 | 2.739 | 2.740 | 2.742 | 2.744 | 2.746 | 2.748 | 2.750 | 2.751 | 2.753 | 2.755 |
| 6 | 2.757 | 2.759 | 2.760 | 2.762 | 2.764 | 2.766 | 2.768 | 2.769 | 2.771 | 2.773 |
| 7 | 2.775 | 2.777 | 2.778 | 2.780 | 2.782 | 2.784 | 2.786 | 2.787 | 2.789 | 2.791 |
| 8 | 2.793 | 2.795 | 2.796 | 2.798 | 2.800 | 2.802 | 2.804 | 2.805 | 2.807 | 2.809 |
| 9 | 2.811 | 2.812 | 2.814 | 2.816 | 2.818 | 2.820 | 2.821 | 2.823 | 2.825 | 2.827 |
| 8.0 | 2.828 | 2.830 | 2.832 | 2.834 | 2.835 | 2.837 | 2.839 | 2.841 | 2.843 | 2.844 |
| 1 | 2.846 | 2.848 | 2.850 | 2.851 | 2.853 | 2.855 | 2.857 | 2.858 | 2.860 | 2.862 |
| 2 | 2.864 | 2.865 | 2.867 | 2.869 | 2.871 | 2.872 | 2.874 | 2.876 | 2.877 | 2.879 |
| 3 | 2.881 | 2.883 | 2.884 | 2.886 | 2.888 | 2.890 | 2.891 | 2.893 | 2.895 | 2.897 |
| 4 | 2.898 | 2.900 | 2.902 | 2.903 | 2.905 | 2.907 | 2.909 | 2.910 | 2.912 | 2.914 |
| 8.5 | 2.915 | 2.917 | 2.919 | 2.921 | 2.922 | 2.924 | 2.926 | 2.927 | 2.929 | 2.931 |
| 6 | 2.933 | 2.934 | 2.936 | 2.938 | 2.939 | 2.941 | 2.942 | 2.944 | 2.946 | 2.948 |
| 7 | 2.950 | 2.951 | 2.953 | 2.955 | 2.956 | 2.958 | 2.960 | 2.961 | 2.963 | 2.965 |
| 8 | 2.966 | 2.968 | 2.970 | 2.972 | 2.973 | 2.975 | 2.977 | 2.978 | 2.980 | 2.982 |
| 9 | 2.983 | 2.985 | 2.987 | 2.988 | 2.990 | 2.992 | 2.993 | 2.995 | 2.997 | 2.998 |
| 9.0 | 3.000 | 3.002 | 3.003 | 3.005 | 3.007 | 3.008 | 3.010 | 3.012 | 3.013 | 3.015 |
| 1 | 3.017 | 3.018 | 3.020 | 3.022 | 3.023 | 3.025 | 3.027 | 3.028 | 3.030 | 3.032 |
| 2 | 3.033 | 3.035 | 3.036 | 3.038 | 3.040 | 3.041 | 3.043 | 3.045 | 3.046 | 3.048 |
| 3 | 3.050 | 3.051 | 3.053 | 3.055 | 3.056 | 3.058 | 3.059 | 3.061 | 3.063 | 3.064 |
| 4 | 3.066 | 3.068 | 3.069 | 3.071 | 3.072 | 3.074 | 3.076 | 3.077 | 3.079 | 3.081 |
| 9.5 | 3.082 | 3.084 | 3.085 | 3.087 | 3.089 | 3.090 | 3.092 | 3.094 | 3.095 | 3.097 |
| 6 | 3.098 | 3.100 | 3.102 | 3.103 | 3.105 | 3.106 | 3.108 | 3.110 | 3.111 | 3.113 |
| 7 | 3.114 | 3.116 | 3.118 | 3.119 | 3.121 | 3.122 | 3.124 | 3.126 | 3.127 | 3.129 |
| 8 | 3.130 | 3.132 | 3.134 | 3.135 | 3.137 | 3.138 | 3.140 | 3.142 | 3.143 | 3.145 |
| 9 | 3.146 | 3.148 | 3.150 | 3.151 | 3.153 | 3.154 | 3.156 | 3.158 | 3.159 | 3.161 |
| 10 | 3.162 | 3.178 | 3.194 | 3.209 | 3.225 | 3.240 | 3.256 | 3.271 | 3.286 | 3.302 |
| 1 | 3.317 | 3.332 | 3.347 | 3.362 | 3.376 | 3.391 | 3.406 | 3.421 | 3.435 | 3.450 |
| 2 | 3.464 | 3.479 | 3.493 | 3.507 | 3.521 | 3.536 | 3.550 | 3.564 | 3.578 | 3.592 |
| 3 | 3.606 | 3.619 | 3.633 | 3.647 | 3.661 | 3.674 | 3.688 | 3.701 | 3.715 | 3.728 |
| 4 | 3.742 | 3.755 | 3.768 | 3.782 | 3.795 | 3.808 | 3.821 | 3.834 | 3.847 | 3.860 |
| 15 | 3.873 | 3.886 | 3.899 | 3.912 | 3.924 | 3.937 | 3.950 | 3.962 | 3.975 | 3.987 |
| 6 | 4.000 | 4.012 | 4.025 | 4.037 | 4.050 | 4.062 | 4.074 | 4.087 | 4.099 | 4.111 |
| 7 | 4.123 | 4.135 | 4.147 | 4.159 | 4.171 | 4.183 | 4.195 | 4.207 | 4.219 | 4.231 |
| 8 | 4.243 | 4.254 | 4.266 | 4.278 | 4.290 | 4.301 | 4.313 | 4.324 | 4.336 | 4.347 |
| 9 | 4.359 | 4.370 | 4.382 | 4.393 | 4.405 | 4.416 | 4.427 | 4.438 | 4.450 | 4.461 |
| 20 | 4.472 | 4.483 | 4.494 | 4.506 | 4.517 | 4.528 | 4.539 | 4.550 | 4.561 | 4.572 |
| 1 | 4.583 | 4.593 | 4.604 | 4.615 | 4.626 | 4.637 | 4.648 | 4.658 | 4.669 | 4.680 |
| 2 | 4.690 | 4.701 | 4.712 | 4.722 | 4.733 | 4.743 | 4.754 | 4.764 | 4.775 | 4.785 |
| 3 | 4.796 | 4.806 | 4.817 | 4.827 | 4.837 | 4.848 | 4.858 | 4.868 | 4.879 | 4.889 |
| 4 | 4.899 | 4.909 | 4.919 | 4.930 | 4.940 | 4.950 | 4.960 | 4.970 | 4.980 | 4.990 |
| 25 | 5.000 | 5.010 | 5.020 | 5.030 | 5.040 | 5.050 | 5.060 | 5.070 | 5.079 | 5.089 |
| 6 | 5.099 | 5.109 | 5.119 | 5.128 | 5.138 | 5.148 | 5.158 | 5.167 | 5.177 | 5.187 |
| 7 | 5.196 | 5.206 | 5.215 | 5.225 | 5.235 | 5.244 | 5.254 | 5.263 | 5.273 | 5.282 |
| 8 | 5.292 | 5.301 | 5.310 | 5.320 | 5.329 | 5.339 | 5.348 | 5.357 | 5.367 | 5.376 |
| 9 | 5.385 | 5.394 | 5.404 | 5.413 | 5.422 | 5.431 | 5.441 | 5.450 | 5.459 | 5.468 |
| 30 | 5.477 | 5.486 | 5.495 | 5.505 | 5.514 | 5.523 | 5.532 | 5.541 | 5.550 | 5.559 |
| 1 | 5.568 | 5.577 | 5.586 | 5.595 | 5.604 | 5.612 | 5.621 | 5.630 | 5.639 | 5.648 |
| 2 | 5.657 | 5.666 | 5.675 | 5.683 | 5.692 | 5.701 | 5.710 | 5.718 | 5.727 | 5.736 |
| 3 | 5.745 | 5.753 | 5.762 | 5.771 | 5.779 | 5.788 | 5.797 | 5.805 | 5.814 | 5.822 |
| 4 | 5.831 | 5.840 | 5.848 | 5.857 | 5.865 | 5.874 | 5.882 | 5.891 | 5.899 | 5.908 |
| 35 | 5.916 | 5.925 | 5.933 | 5.941 | 5.950 | 5.958 | 5.967 | 5.975 | 5.983 | 5.992 |
| 6 | 6.000 | 6.008 | 6.017 | 6.025 | 6.033 | 6.042 | 6.050 | 6.058 | 6.066 | 6.075 |
| 7 | 6.083 | 6.091 | 6.099 | 6.107 | 6.116 | 6.124 | 6.132 | 6.140 | 6.148 | 6.156 |
| 8 | 6.164 | 6.173 | 6.181 | 6.189 | 6.197 | 6.205 | 6.213 | 6.221 | 6.229 | 6.237 |
| 9 | 6.245 | 6.253 | 6.261 | 6.269 | 6.277 | 6.285 | 6.293 | 6.301 | 6.309 | 6.317 |

| N | 0 | 1 | 2 | 3 | 4 | 5 | 6 | 7 | 8 | 9 |
|---|---|---|---|---|---|---|---|---|---|---|
| 40 | 6.325 | 6.332 | 6.340 | 6.348 | 6.356 | 6.364 | 6.372 | 6.380 | 6.387 | 6.395 |
| 1 | 6.403 | 6.411 | 6.419 | 6.427 | 6.434 | 6.442 | 6.450 | 6.458 | 6.465 | 6.473 |
| 2 | 6.481 | 6.488 | 6.496 | 6.504 | 6.512 | 6.519 | 6.527 | 6.535 | 6.542 | 6.550 |
| 3 | 6.557 | 6.565 | 6.573 | 6.580 | 6.588 | 6.595 | 6.603 | 6.611 | 6.618 | 6.626 |
| 4 | 6.633 | 6.641 | 6.648 | 6.656 | 6.663 | 6.671 | 6.678 | 6.686 | 6.693 | 6.701 |
| 45 | 6.708 | 6.716 | 6.723 | 6.731 | 6.738 | 6.745 | 6.753 | 6.760 | 6.768 | 6.775 |
| 6 | 6.782 | 6.790 | 6.797 | 6.804 | 6.812 | 6.819 | 6.826 | 6.834 | 6.841 | 6.848 |
| 7 | 6.856 | 6.863 | 6.870 | 6.877 | 6.885 | 6.892 | 6.899 | 6.907 | 6.914 | 6.921 |
| 8 | 6.928 | 6.935 | 6.943 | 6.950 | 6.957 | 6.964 | 6.971 | 6.979 | 6.986 | 6.993 |
| 9 | 7.000 | 7.007 | 7.014 | 7.021 | 7.029 | 7.036 | 7.043 | 7.050 | 7.057 | 7.064 |
| 50 | 7.071 | 7.078 | 7.085 | 7.092 | 7.099 | 7.106 | 7.113 | 7.120 | 7.127 | 7.134 |
| 1 | 7.141 | 7.148 | 7.155 | 7.162 | 7.169 | 7.176 | 7.183 | 7.190 | 7.197 | 7.204 |
| 2 | 7.211 | 7.218 | 7.225 | 7.232 | 7.239 | 7.246 | 7.253 | 7.259 | 7.266 | 7.273 |
| 3 | 7.280 | 7.287 | 7.294 | 7.301 | 7.308 | 7.314 | 7.321 | 7.328 | 7.335 | 7.342 |
| 4 | 7.348 | 7.355 | 7.362 | 7.369 | 7.376 | 7.382 | 7.389 | 7.396 | 7.403 | 7.409 |
| 55 | 7.416 | 7.423 | 7.430 | 7.436 | 7.443 | 7.450 | 7.457 | 7.463 | 7.470 | 7.477 |
| 6 | 7.483 | 7.490 | 7.497 | 7.503 | 7.510 | 7.517 | 7.523 | 7.530 | 7.537 | 7.543 |
| 7 | 7.550 | 7.556 | 7.563 | 7.570 | 7.576 | 7.583 | 7.589 | 7.596 | 7.603 | 7.609 |
| 8 | 7.616 | 7.622 | 7.629 | 7.635 | 7.642 | 7.649 | 7.655 | 7.662 | 7.668 | 7.675 |
| 9 | 7.681 | 7.688 | 7.694 | 7.701 | 7.707 | 7.714 | 7.720 | 7.727 | 7.733 | 7.740 |
| 60 | 7.746 | 7.752 | 7.759 | 7.765 | 7.772 | 7.778 | 7.785 | 7.791 | 7.797 | 7.804 |
| 1 | 7.810 | 7.817 | 7.823 | 7.829 | 7.836 | 7.842 | 7.849 | 7.855 | 7.861 | 7.868 |
| 2 | 7.874 | 7.880 | 7.887 | 7.893 | 7.899 | 7.906 | 7.912 | 7.918 | 7.925 | 7.931 |
| 3 | 7.937 | 7.944 | 7.950 | 7.956 | 7.962 | 7.969 | 7.975 | 7.981 | 7.987 | 7.994 |
| 4 | 8.000 | 8.006 | 8.012 | 8.019 | 8.025 | 8.031 | 8.037 | 8.044 | 8.050 | 8.056 |
| 65 | 8.062 | 8.068 | 8.075 | 8.081 | 8.087 | 8.093 | 8.099 | 8.106 | 8.112 | 8.118 |
| 6 | 8.124 | 8.130 | 8.136 | 8.142 | 8.149 | 8.155 | 8.161 | 8.167 | 8.173 | 8.179 |
| 7 | 8.185 | 8.191 | 8.198 | 8.204 | 8.210 | 8.216 | 8.222 | 8.228 | 8.234 | 8.240 |
| 8 | 8.246 | 8.252 | 8.258 | 8.264 | 8.270 | 8.276 | 8.283 | 8.289 | 8.295 | 8.301 |
| 9 | 8.307 | 8.313 | 8.319 | 8.325 | 8.331 | 8.337 | 8.343 | 8.349 | 8.355 | 8.361 |
| 70 | 8.367 | 8.373 | 8.379 | 8.385 | 8.390 | 8.396 | 8.402 | 8.408 | 8.414 | 8.420 |
| 1 | 8.426 | 8.432 | 8.438 | 8.444 | 8.450 | 8.456 | 8.462 | 8.468 | 8.473 | 8.479 |
| 2 | 8.485 | 8.491 | 8.497 | 8.503 | 8.509 | 8.515 | 8.521 | 8.526 | 8.532 | 8.538 |
| 3 | 8.544 | 8.550 | 8.556 | 8.562 | 8.567 | 8.573 | 8.579 | 8.585 | 8.591 | 8.597 |
| 4 | 8.602 | 8.608 | 8.614 | 8.620 | 8.626 | 8.631 | 8.637 | 8.643 | 8.649 | 8.654 |
| 75 | 8.660 | 8.666 | 8.672 | 8.678 | 8.683 | 8.689 | 8.695 | 8.701 | 8.706 | 8.712 |
| 6 | 8.718 | 8.724 | 8.729 | 8.735 | 8.741 | 8.746 | 8.752 | 8.758 | 8.764 | 8.769 |
| 7 | 8.775 | 8.781 | 8.786 | 8.792 | 8.798 | 8.808 | 8.809 | 8.815 | 8.820 | 8.826 |
| 8 | 8.832 | 8.837 | 8.843 | 8.849 | 8.854 | 8.860 | 8.866 | 8.871 | 8.877 | 8.883 |
| 9 | 8.888 | 8.894 | 8.899 | 8.905 | 8.911 | 8.916 | 8.922 | 8.927 | 8.933 | 8.939 |
| 80 | 8.944 | 8.950 | 8.955 | 8.961 | 8.967 | 8.972 | 8.978 | 8.983 | 8.989 | 8.994 |
| 1 | 9.000 | 9.006 | 9.001 | 9.017 | 9.022 | 9.028 | 9.033 | 9.039 | 9.044 | 9.050 |
| 2 | 9.055 | 9.061 | 9.066 | 9.072 | 9.077 | 9.083 | 9.088 | 9.094 | 9.099 | 9.105 |
| 3 | 9.110 | 9.116 | 9.121 | 9.127 | 9.132 | 9.138 | 9.143 | 9.149 | 9.154 | 9.160 |
| 4 | 9.165 | 9.171 | 9.176 | 9.182 | 9.187 | 9.192 | 9.189 | 9.203 | 9.209 | 9.214 |
| 85 | 9.220 | 9.225 | 9.230 | 9.236 | 9.241 | 9.247 | 9.252 | 9.257 | 9.263 | 9.268 |
| 6 | 9.274 | 9.279 | 9.284 | 9.290 | 9.295 | 9.301 | 9.306 | 9.311 | 9.317 | 9.322 |
| 7 | 9.327 | 9.333 | 9.338 | 9.343 | 9.349 | 9.354 | 9.359 | 9.365 | 9.370 | 9.375 |
| 8 | 9.381 | 9.386 | 9.391 | 9.397 | 9.402 | 9.407 | 9.413 | 9.418 | 9.423 | 9.429 |
| 9 | 9.434 | 9.439 | 9.445 | 9.450 | 9.455 | 9.460 | 9.466 | 9.471 | 9.476 | 9.482 |
| 90 | 9.487 | 9.492 | 9.497 | 9.503 | 9.508 | 9.513 | 9.518 | 9.524 | 9.529 | 9.534 |
| 1 | 9.539 | 9.545 | 9.550 | 9.555 | 9.560 | 9.566 | 9.571 | 9.576 | 9.581 | 9.586 |
| 2 | 9.592 | 9.597 | 9.602 | 9.607 | 9.612 | 9.618 | 9.623 | 9.628 | 9.633 | 9.638 |
| 3 | 9.644 | 9.649 | 9.654 | 9.659 | 9.664 | 9.670 | 9.675 | 9.680 | 9.685 | 9.690 |
| 4 | 9.695 | 9.701 | 9.706 | 9.711 | 9.716 | 9.721 | 9.726 | 9.731 | 9.737 | 9.742 |
| 95 | 9.747 | 9.752 | 9.757 | 9.762 | 9.767 | 9.772 | 9.778 | 9.783 | 9.788 | 9.793 |
| 6 | 9.798 | 9.803 | 9.808 | 9.813 | 9.818 | 9.823 | 9.829 | 9.834 | 9.839 | 9.844 |
| 7 | 9.849 | 9.854 | 9.859 | 9.864 | 9.869 | 9.874 | 9.879 | 9.884 | 9.889 | 9.894 |
| 8 | 9.899 | 9.905 | 9.910 | 9.915 | 9.920 | 9.925 | 9.930 | 9.935 | 9.940 | 9.945 |
| 9 | 9.950 | 9.955 | 9.960 | 9.965 | 9.970 | 9.975 | 9.980 | 9.985 | 9.990 | 9.995 |